# The Postmoderns

ALSO BY DONALD ALLEN
Published by Grove Press

*The Poetics of the New American Poetry* (with Warren Tallman)

# The Postmoderns:
## THE NEW AMERICAN POETRY REVISED
Edited and With a New Preface by
Donald Allen & George F. Butterick

Grove Press, Inc./New York

First Evergreen Edition 1982
First Printing 1982
ISBN: 0-394-17458-5
Library of Congress Catalog Card Number: 79-52054

Library of Congress Cataloging in Publication Data
Main entry under title:

The Postmoderns.

    Includes bibliographies.
    1. American poetry—20th century. 2. American poetry—20th century—Bio-bibliography. I. Allen, Donald Merriam, 1912— . II. II. Butterick, George F.
PS615.P67  1981  811'.54'08   79-52054
ISBN 0-394-17458-5 (pbk.)     AACR2

Manufactured in the United States of America

GROVE PRESS, INC., 196 West Houston Street, New York, N.Y. 10014

# ACKNOWLEDGMENTS

*The editors gratefully acknowledge permission from the following poets
and publishers to reprint copyrighted work:*

JOHN ASHBERY: "The Instruction Manual" from *Some Trees* ⊙ 1956 by Yale
University Press, by their permission; "How Much Longer Will I Be Able to Inhabit
the Divine Sepulcher . . . ," and "A Last World" from *The Tennis Court Oath* ⊙
1962 by John Ashbery, by permission of Wesleyan University Press; "A Blessing in
Disguise" and "These Lacustrine Cities" from *Rivers and Mountains* ⊙ 1962, 1963,
1964, 1966 by John Ashbery, and "Decoy" from *The Double Dream of Spring* ⊙
1966, 1967, 1968, 1969, 1970 by John Ashbery, by permission of Georges Borchardt,
Inc.; "Pyrography" and "Wet Casements" from *Houseboat Days* ⊙ 1977 by John
Ashbery, by permission of Viking Penguin Inc.

PAUL BLACKBURN: "Phone Call to Rutherford," "Sirventes," "The Tides," "Out,"
and "The Slogan" from *The Cities* ⊙ 1967 by Paul Blackburn; "The Assistance,"
"The Continuity," and "The Once-Over" from *Early Selected y Mas* ⊙ 1972 by Joan
Blackburn; "17.IV.71" from *The Journals* ⊙ 1975 by Joan Blackburn; all by permis-
sion of Joan Blackburn.

ROBIN BLASER: "Image-Nation 3" and "Image-Nation 11 (the poēsis)" from *Image-
Nations 1-12* ⊙ 1974 by Robin Blaser; "Image-Nation 13 (the telephone)" and "Sud-
denly," from *Image-Nations 13 & 14* ⊙ 1975 by Robin Blaser; by permission of Robin
Blaser.

GREGORY CORSO: "Birthplace Revisited," "Hello," and "Uccello" from *Gasoline*
⊙ 1958 by Gregory Corso, by permission of City Lights Books; "Poets Hitchiking on
the Highway" and "A Dreamed Realization" from *The Happy Birthday of Death* ⊙
1960 by New Directions; "Spontaneous Requiem for the American Indian" from
*Elegiac Feelings American* ⊙ 1970 by Gregory Corso; by permission of New Direc-
tions Publishing Corporation.

ROBERT CREELEY: "The Immoral Proposition," "I Know a Man," "The Whip,"
and "The Door" from *For Love* ⊙ 1962 by Robert Creeley, by permission of Charles
Scribner's Sons; "For My Mother: Genevieve Jules Creeley" from *Away* ⊙ 1976 by
Robert Creeley, by permission of Black Sparrow Press; "Prayer to Hermes" from
*Later* ⊙ 1979 by Robert Creeley, by permission of New Directions Publishing Cor-
poration.

DIANE DI PRIMA: "The Jungle," "The Practice of Magical Evocation," "In Memo-
ry of My First Chapatis," and "Goodbye Nkrumah" from *Selected Poems 1956-1975*
⊙ 1975 by Diane di Prima, by permission of Diane di Prima and North Atlantic Books.

EDWARD DORN: "The Rick of Green Wood," "Vaquero," "Are They Dancing,"
"The Air of June Sings," "Los Mineros," "From Gloucester Out," "For the New
Union Dead in Alabama," and "La Máquina a Houston" from *The Collected Poems*
⊙1975, 1982 by Edward Dorn, by permission of Edward Dorn and Four Seasons
Foundation.

ROBERT DUNCAN: "The Song of the Borderguard" from *The First Decade* ⊙ 1968
by Robert Duncan; "Correspondences" and "An Owl Is An Only Bird of Poetry"
from *Derivations* ⊙ 1968 by Robert Duncan, by permission of Robert Duncan; "This
Place Rumord To Have Been Sodom" and "A Poem Beginning with a Line by Pindar"
from *The Opening of the Field* ⊙ 1960 by Robert Duncan; "A New Poem (for Jack
Spicer)" from *Roots and Branches* ⊙ 1964 by Robert Duncan; "As in the Old Days,
*Passages* 8," "These Past Years, *Passages* 10," and " 'My Mother Would Be a Falcon-

ress' " from *Bending the Bow* © 1968 by Robert Duncan, by permission of New Directions Publishing Corporation; "Book One, III (1)" from *Dante* © 1974 by Robert Duncan, by permission of Robert Duncan.

LARRY EIGNER: "from the sustaining air," "Do it yrself," "the dark swimmers," "the wind like an ocean," "Letter for Duncan," "flake diamond of / the sea," "That the neighborhood might be covered," "I have felt it as they've said," "don't go" and "the bare tree / alternate" from *Selected Poems* © 1971 by Larry Eigner, by permission of Larry Eigner and Oyez.

WILLIAM EVERSON: "A Canticle to the Waterbirds" from *The Veritable Years 1949-1966* © 1978 by William Everson, by permission of Black Sparrow Press; "The Narrows of Birth" from *Man-Fate* © 1974 by William Everson, by permission of New Directions Publishing Corporation; "Kingfisher Flat" from *The Masks of Drought* © 1980 by William Everson, by permission of Black Sparrow Press.

LAWRENCE FERLINGHETTI: Poems 1 and 5 from *Pictures of the Gone World* © 1955 by Lawrence Ferlinghetti, by permission of City Lights Books; Poems 1, 15, and 20 from *A Coney Island of the Mind* © 1958 by Lawrence Ferlinghetti; "He" from *Starting from San Francisco* © 1961 by Lawrence Ferlinghetti; "Pound at Spoleto" from *Open Eye, Open Heart* © 1973 by Lawrence Ferlinghetti; "Lost Parents" from *Who Are We Now?* © 1976 by Lawrence Ferlinghetti; "The Sea and Ourselves at Cape Ann" from *Landscapes of Living & Dying* © 1979 by Lawrence Ferlinghetti, by permission of New Directions Publishing Corporation.

ALLEN GINSBERG: "Howl," "A Supermarket in California," and "America" from *Howl and Other Poems* © 1956 by Allen Ginsberg; "Kaddish, Part I" from *Kaddish and Other Poems* © 1961 by Allen Ginsberg; "Kral Majales" from *Planet News* © 1968 by Allen Ginsberg; "Neal's Ashes" from *The Fall of America* © 1972 by Allen Ginsberg, by permission of Allen Ginsberg.

BARBARA GUEST: "Santa Fe Trail" from *Poems* © 1962 by Barbara Guest; "Parade's End" and "20" from *The Blue Stairs* © 1968 by Barbara Guest; "Red Lilies" from *Moscow Mansions* © 1973 by Barbara Guest; "River Road Studio" from *The Countess from Minneapolis* © 1976 by Barbara Guest; "The Luminous" © 1981 by Barbara Guest; by permission of Barbara Guest.

ANSELM HOLLO: "That Old Sauna High," "Le Jazz Hot," "Buffalo—Isle of Wight Power Cable," "Rain," "Amazing Grace," "Wasp Sex Myth (One)," "Wasp Sex Myth (Two)," and "The Discovery of LSD A True Story" from *Sojourner Microcosms* © 1977 by Anselm Hollo, by permission of Blue Wind Press.

LEROI JONES / AMIRI BARAKA: "Preface to a Twenty Volume Suicide Note" and "In Memory of Radio" from *Preface to a Twenty Volume Suicide Note* © 1961 by LeRoi Jones; "Crow Jane" and "Black Dada Nihilismus" from *The Dead Lecturer* © 1964 by LeRoi Jones; "A Poem for Black Hearts" and "Beautiful Black Women" from *Black Magic Poetry 1961-1967* © 1969 by LeRoi Jones; "Das Kapital" from *Hard Facts* © 1976 by Imamu Amiri Baraka, all by permission of The Sterling Lord Agency, Inc.

ROBERT KELLY: "The Sound" from *The Mill of Particulars* © 1973 by Robert Kelly, by permission of Black Sparrow Press; Poems 9, 10, 11, 12, 14, 16, 17, 18 from *The Book of Persephone* © 1978 by Robert Kelly, by permission of Robert Kelly.

JACK KEROUAC: "Pull My Daisy," from *The Gates of Wrath* © 1972 by Allen Ginsberg; "The Sea Shroud" and "My Gang" from *Heaven & Other Poems* © 1977 by the Estate of Jack Kerouac; 211th and 229th Choruses from *Mexico City Blues* © 1959 by by Jack Kerouac, by permission of The Sterling Lord Agency, Inc.

# The Postmoderns

# CONTENTS

# PREFACE

This anthology does not seek to deal comprehensively with the full range of recent American poetry, but with that poetry written in America since the Second World War which, by its vitality alone, became the dominant force in the American poetic tradition. It has been characterized as the "experimental" side of American poetry, although increasingly literary and cultural historians have come to recognize that these are among the most truly authentic, indigenous American writers, following in the mainstream of Emerson and Whitman, Pound and Williams. They have been called variously by literary critics and observers projectivists, the poetic "underground," the New York School, the Beat Generation, the San Francisco Renaissance, the Black Mountain Poets, or, most generally, the avant-garde. They emerged in the 1950s and came into dominance in the 1960s and 1970s. Younger than Kenneth Rexroth, Louis Zukofsky, or George Oppen, the body of them are writers who were given their wider recognition through the first edition of this anthology, titled plainly *The New American Poetry*, and published in 1960. Their preference is formal freedom or openness as opposed to academic, formalistic, strictly rhymed and metered verse. Many have been friends and associates, publishing side by side in the same magazines, participating in poetry readings throughout the country and the world together, finding one another compatible in literary and social outlook.

They were published in such magazines as *Origin, Black Mountain Review*, the early *Evergreen Review, Yugen, Kulchur, Floating Bear, C, Fuck You/A Magazine of the Arts, Caterpillar, The World,* and by such small presses as Jargon, City Lights, White Rabbit, Totem, Corinth, Auerhahn, Four Seasons, Black Sparrow, and Grey Fox. Some, such as Hollo and Levertov, are not American-born, but were among the earliest Europeans of their generation to adopt an American style and, eventually, residence. For some, imagism has been a chief source of inspiration, for others—notably O'Hara and Ashbery—the dissociations of post-symbolist French poetry. They respond to the limits of industrialism and high technology often by a marked spiritual advance or deference, an embracing of the primal energies of a tribal or communal spirit, side by side with the most stubborn sort of American individualism. Their influence on English-speaking poetry at large has reversed the longstanding obeisance to academically sanctioned formalism. There are revolutionaries among them, as well as quieter (but no less deliberate) practitioners. Their most common bond is a spontaneous utilization of subject and technique, a prevailing "instantism" that nevertheless does not preclude discursive ponderings and large-canvased reflections. They are boldly positioned and deft, freely maneuvering among the inherited traditions, time-honored lore, and proven practices, adopting what they need for their own wholeness and journeying. They are most of them forward-looking at a time when concepts such as entropy and global village have entered daily life, along with, for the first time in the history of the species, thanks to this nuclear age, the possibility of irreversibility. If it can be said—as it commonly is—that modernism came to an end with the detonation of the Bomb in 1945, these are the poets who propose a world since then. Whether imagistic or surrealist, mythic or populist in their approach, they all reflect America at a great turning point. There is reason enough to say that a great flowering has occurred and that these have been among the most vigorous participants in it, some even its major shapers.

Within the usual severe space limitations, the selections draw from the full range of the writers' works; texts are from the best available editions; dates have been supplied where known. The poems are presented roughly in the chronological order of their composition. The editors sought to re-examine the first edition, which had been so successful in making known and conveniently gathering many of these poets, to determine which among them had endured. There was no hope or attempt to recapture or repeat the pioneering effort of the initial edition, although surely for many readers the work here will continue to be a revelation. Our purpose was to consolidate the gains of the previous anthology and confirm its predictions, by taking the best of the poets represented there, who have, by every indication, achieved a certain recognition. The present volume does not seek to be all-inclusive, or exclusionary, or to do the justice which only time and accumulated judgment can. There are, after all, only thirty-eight poets out of the myriad. Yet it does offer a sharpened focus to represent an era, and therein lies its usefulness and its hope.

Of the thirty-four original poets, twenty-nine were retained, with nine new poets added—Jackson Mac Low, Jerome Rothenberg, Diane di Prima, Anselm Hollo, Joanne Kyger, Robert Kelly, James Koller, Ed Sanders, and Anne Waldman. These nine extend the scope of the volume to include poets who, for the most part, had become active or whose influence was felt after the 1960s. They were not so much hard on the heels of the older writers as in step with them throughout the 1960s, and so logically and readily belong here.

The selections begin with Charles Olson, whose essay "Projective Verse" rallied and focused the energies of the new poetry while forwarding the line of Pound and Williams. He was among the first to see the larger consequences of that poetry, and indeed was the first, in his essays and letters, to use the term "postmodern" in its present significance. The rest of the poets follow in the order of their births. The earlier attempt to divide the anthology for sake of convenience into geographical categories has been abandoned. The theoretical writings and poets' statements on poetics, which were so important a part of the first edition, are now too numerous to be included here, although a fair sampling is given in *The Poetics of the New American Poetry*, edited by Donald Allen and Warren Tallman and published by Grove Press in 1973.

The selection revises not only the choice of poets but the poems for each poet. Many of the same poems—of proven endurance—have been retained, but even more new ones have been added from the almost twenty additional years of continued activity. Essential long poems of the period, such as Robert Duncan's *Venice Poem*, Frank O'Hara's *Second Avenue* from 1953, Allen Ginsberg's sweeping *Wichita Vortex Sutra*, and Edward Dorn's *Gunslinger*, had to be forgone for compression of space, while only portions of others, such as Olson's *Maximus*, Duncan's *Passages*, and Ginsberg's *Kaddish*, could be given.

The passage of twenty years has brought confirmation of the achievements of the poets represented. Whereas in 1960 "only a fraction of the work [had] been published," and that often in fugitive little magazines and pamphlets so that it was difficult for even the most devoted reader to obtain the writings of the poets, many now have published selected and even collected editions. Their extensive bibliographies alone—included as part of the revised biographical notes in this volume—testify to the extraordinary and successful productivity since the initial edition. Many have been the subject of full-length studies. There are countless articles and scholarly dissertations devoted to their work, translations of their writings into foreign languages, biographies, bibliographies (a recent comprehensive bibliography of Frank O'Hara's writings runs to well over three hundred pages), published interviews, editions of their correspondence and secondary writings. Most appear in the standard biographical dictionaries and encyclopedias of literary history. Whatever the direction—or, more accurately, directions—American poetry may continue to take, it can be said that for a significant period, at a most significant time in the nation's history, these poets occupied a central portion of the stage, keeping alive energies while creating new ones.

Six of the original poets have since died (prematurely, to a man). Of the rest, a number have received the highest awards offered poets in this country. Some are the original Beat writers, others are still known by the designations "Black Mountain" or "New York School," but most are content to be free of any restrictive labels. Those earlier designations, if they were ever anything more than terms of convenience, have been rendered obsolete and unnecessary by the poets' subsequent activities and associations. Postmodern is a more encompassing designation, while still having its own precisions. It takes the poets beyond localism or regionalism and also suggests their role in the international poetry of the times.

Post-modern is not simply *after*, in time, the modernism of Pound and Eliot, Auden and Stevens, and their younger successors such as Berryman and Lowell, Bishop and Sexton. As for the term itself—the poets have different expressions of it. For Olson, who used the designation first, it meant, ultimately, an instant-by-instant engagement with reality. He writes in "Projective Verse": "If there is any absolute, it is never more than this one, you, this instant, in action." For Creeley, it was the principle readily seized by Olson: "form is never more than an extension of content." For O'Hara it was the "going on your nerve" of his "Personism" manifesto; for Ginsberg, "Hebraic-Melvillean bardic breath"; for Duncan, an "open universe," in which the poem, like the physical cosmos, "has only this immediate event in which to be realized"; for Snyder, the "primitive," the "decentralized" but communal; for Baraka, the poem as bullet for revolutionary change. Given the variety of possibilities, it is remarkable how much these poets share. Primarily, it is a stance that does not shrink from confrontation with previously held convictions and proprieties, while seeking a restoration of some very ancient ones. It is an outlook that is not diffident, complacent, quibbling, but more often bold, committed, even heroic. The break is never so cleanly cut, but, like the Middle Ages or the romantic period, it is there—in style, attitude, belief, shared experience, technique, and what is disdained.

The principal differences with the previous poets are in the areas of both style and subject. These writers permit themselves a new formal and syntatic flexibility—an idiosyncratic, or "idiosyntactic," flexibility. There is the resilient and advantageous syntax, the exploration of language as a system, the rhythms of ritual, of high chant, the body of a language arched in ecstasy, the quiet bluntness. More importantly, in the larger stylistic terms, they reflect a different disposition of self, a new attitude toward the elements of mind, nature, and society—and indeed the inherited assumptions of modern man. Their writing is marked by an acceptance of the primordial, of spiritual and sexual necessities, of myth, the latest understandings of science, chance and change, wit and dream. Some might even be called preliterate, prerational, premodern, if it is true that the attitudes and commitments of modernism helplessly produced the Bomb and other forms of species alteration.

These poets have taken advantage of the gains of imagism and surrealism, the chief accomplishments of poetic modernism. They are the grand and multifarious fulfillment of the vers libre of the early 1900s. Many demand a reorientation of values, a reexamination of the very premises of Western civilization. Most seek for the individual a new relation toward his or her world, a new "stance toward reality," where each poem's line, whether long-breathed or tightly controlled, is open to its own possibility, where the syntax responds with vital immediacy to the moment's pulse. They are revolutionary, characterized by a willingness to seize the romantic imperative, to seek alternatives to the "static" quo.

Post-modernism, then, is more than just the continuation of the modernism begun in the 1910s. Its proposals are more widely sweeping than those of imagism and that "revolution of the word" beginning the early decades of the twentieth century. Most of all, its chief characteristic is its inclusiveness, its quick willingness to take advantage of all that had gone before.

—George F. Butterick and Donald Allen

# CHARLES OLSON (1910-1970)


## LA PRÉFACE


The dead in via
             in vita nuova
                      in the way
You shall lament who know they are as tender as the horse is.
You, do not you speak who know not.

         "I will die about April 1st . . ." going off
         "I weigh, I think, 80 lbs . . ." scratch
         "My name is NO RACE"    address
         Buchenwald   new Altamira cave
         With a nail they drew the object of the hunt.

Put war away with time, come into space.
It was May, precise date, 1940. I had air my lungs could breathe.
He talked, via stones   a stick   sea rock   a hand of earth.
It is now, precise, repeat. I talk of Bigmans organs
he, look, the lines! are polytopes.
And among the DPs—deathhead
                      at the apex
                               of the pyramid.


Birth in the house is the One of Sticks, cunnus in the crotch.
Draw it thus: (     ) 1910 (
It is not obscure. We are the new born, and there are no flowers.
Document means there are no flowers
                      and no parenthesis.


It is the radical, the root, he and I, two bodies
We put our hands to these dead.

The closed parenthesis reads:  the dead bury the dead,
                      and it is not very interesting.
Open, the figure stands at the door, horror his
and gone, possessed, o new Osiris, Odysseus ship.
He put the body there as well as they did whom he killed.


*13*

Mark that arm.  It is no longer gun.
We are born not of the buried but these unburied dead
crossed stick, wire-led, Blake Underground

The Babe
         the Howling Babe

                                                              *1946*


# THE KINGFISHERS


         1
What does not change / is the will to change

He woke, fully clothed, in his bed.  He
remembered only one thing, the birds, how
when he came in, he had gone around the rooms
and got them back in their cage, the green one first,
she with the bad leg, and then the blue,
the one they had hoped was a male

Otherwise?  Yes, Fernand, who had talked lispingly of Albers & Angkor Vat.
He had left the party without a word.  How he got up, got into his coat,
I do not know.  When I saw him, he was at the door, but it did not matter,
he was already sliding along the wall of the night, losing himself
in some crack of the ruins.  That it should have been he who said, "The
         kingfishers!
who cares
for their feathers
now?"

His last words had been, "The pool is slime."  Suddenly everyone,
ceasing their talk, sat in a row around him, watched
they did not so much hear, or pay attention, they
wondered, looked at each other, smirked, but listened,
he repeated and repeated, could not go beyond his thought
"The pool   the kingfishers' feathers were wealth   why
did the export stop?"

It was then he left

2
I thought of the E on the stone, and of what Mao said
la lumière"
                    but the kingfisher
de l'aurore"
                    but the kingfisher flew west
est devant nous!
                    he got the color of his breast
                    from the heat of the setting sun!

The features are, the feebleness of the feet (syndactylism of the 3rd & 4th
        digit)
the bill, serrated, sometimes a pronounced beak, the wings
where the color is, short and round, the tail
inconspicuous.

But not these things were the factors. Not the birds.
The legends are
legends. Dead, hung up indoors, the kingfisher
will not indicate a favoring wind,
or avert the thunderbolt. Nor, by its nesting,
still the waters, with the new year, for seven days.
It is true, it does nest with the opening year, but not on the waters.
It nests at the end of a tunnel bored by itself in a bank. There,
six or eight white and translucent eggs are laid, on fishbones
not on bare clay, on bones thrown up in pellets by the birds.

                    On these rejectamenta
(as they accumulate they form a cup-shaped structure) the young are born.
And, as they are fed and grow, this nest of excrement and decayed fish
        becomes
                    a dripping, fetid mass

Mao concluded:
                    nous devons
                            nous lever
                                    et agir!

3
When the attentions change / the jungle
leaps in
        even the stones are split
                    they rive

Or,
enter
that other conqueror we more naturally recognize
he so resembles ourselves

But the E
cut so rudely on the oldest stone
sounded otherwise,
was differently heard

as, in another time, were treasures used:

(and, later, much later, a fine ear thought
a scarlet coat)

       "of green feathers  feet, beaks and eyes
        of gold

       "animals likewise,
        resembling snails

       "a large wheel, gold, with figures of unknown four-foots,
        and worked with tufts of leaves, weight
        3800 ounces

       "last, two birds, of thread and featherwork, the quills
        gold, the feet
        gold, the two birds perched on two reeds
        gold, the reeds arising from two embroidered mounds,
        one yellow, the other
        white.

       "And from each reed hung
        seven feathered tassels.

In this instance, the priests
(in dark cotton robes, and dirty,
their dishevelled hair matted with blood, and flowing wildly
over their shoulders)
rush in among the people, calling on them
to protect their gods

And all now is war
where so lately there was peace,
and the sweet brotherhood, the use
of tilled fields.


      4

Not one death but many,
not accumulation but change, the feed-back proves, the feed-back is
the law

       Into the same river no man steps twice
       When fire dies air dies
       No one remains, nor is, one

Around an appearance, one common model, we grow up
many.  Else how is it,
if we remain the same,
we take pleasure now
in what we did not take pleasure before? love
contrary objects?  admire and/or find fault?  use
other words, feel other passions, have
nor figure, appearance, disposition, tissue
the same?
      To be in different states without a change
      is not a possibility

We can be precise.  The factors are
in the animal and/or the machine the factors are
communication and/or control, both involve
the message.  And what is the message?  The message is
a discrete or continuous sequence of measurable events distributed in time

is the birth of air, is
the birth of water, is
a state between
the origin and
the end, between
birth and the beginning of
another fetid nest

is change, presents
no more than itself

And the too strong grasping of it,
when it is pressed together and condensed,
loses it

This very thing you are

    II

       They buried their dead in a sitting posture
       serpent   cane   razor   ray of the sun

       And she sprinkled water on the head of the child, crying
       "Cioa-coatl!  Cioa-coatl!"
       with her face to the west

       Where the bones are found, in each personal heap
       with what each enjoyed, there is always
       the Mongolian louse

The light is in the east. Yes. And we must rise, act. Yet
in the west, despite the apparent darkness (the whiteness
which covers all), if you look, if you can bear, if you can, long enough

          as long as it was necessary for him, my guide
          to look into the yellow of that longest-lasting rose

so you must, and, in that whiteness, into that face, with what candor, look

and, considering the dryness of the place
      the long absence of an adequate race

       (of the two who first came, each a conquistador, one healed, the
          other
        tore the eastern idols down, toppled
        the temple walls, which, says the excuser
        were black from human gore)

hear
hear, where the dry blood talks
     where the old appetite walks

                   la piu saporita et migliore
                   che si possa truovar al mondo

where it hides, look
in the eye how it runs
in the flesh / chalk

> but under these petals
> in the emptiness
> **regard the light**, contemplate
> the flower

whence it arose

> with what violence benevolence is bought
> what cost in gesture justice brings
> what wrongs domestic rights involve
> what stalks
> this silence

> what pudor pejorocracy affronts
> how awe, night-rest and neighborhood can rot
> what breeds where dirtiness is law
> what crawls
> below

III
I am no Greek, hath not th'advantage.
And of course, no Roman:
he can take no risk that matters,
the risk of beauty least of all.

But I have my kin, if for no other reason than
(as he said, next of kin) I commit myself, and,
given my freedom, I'd be a cad
if I didn't. Which is most true.

It works out this way, despite the disadvantage.
I offer, in explanation, a quote:
si j'ai du goût, ce n'est guères
que pour la terre et les pierres.

Despite the discrepancy (an ocean   courage   age)
this is also true: if I have any taste
it is only because I have interested myself
in what was slain in the sun

I pose you your question:

shall you uncover honey / where maggots are?

I hunt among stones

*1949*

# IN COLD HELL, IN THICKET

In cold hell, in thicket, how
abstract (as high mind, as not lust, as love is) how
strong (as strut or wing, as polytope, as things are
constellated) how
strung, how cold
can a man stay (can men) confronted
thus?

All things are made bitter, words even
are made to taste like paper, wars get tossed up
like lead soldiers used to be
(in a child's attic) lined up
to be knocked down, as I am,
by firings from a spit-hardened fort, fronted
as we are, here, from where we must go

God, that man, as his acts must, as there is always
a thing he can do, he can raise himself, he raises
on a reed he raises his

Or, if it is me, what
he has to say

     1
What has he to say?
In hell it is not easy
to know the traceries, the markings
(the canals, the pits, the mountings by which space
declares herself, arched, as she is, the sister,
awkward stars drawn for teats to pleasure him, the brother
who lies in stasis under her, at ease as any monarch or
a happy man

How shall he who is not happy, who has been so made unclear,
who is no longer privileged to be at ease, who, in this brush, stands
reluctant, imageless, unpleasured, caught in a sort of hell, how
shall he convert this underbrush, how turn this unbidden place
how trace and arch again
the necessary goddess?


    2

The branches made against the sky are not of use, are
already done, like snow-flakes, do not, cannot service
him who has to raise   (Who puts this on, this damning of his flesh?)
he can, but how far, how sufficiently far can he raise the thickets of
this wilderness?

                How can he change, his question is
                these black and silvered knivings, these
                awkwardnesses?

                How can he make these blood-points into panels, into sides
                for a king's, for his own
                for a wagon, for a sleigh, for the beak of, the running sides of
                a vessel fit for
                moving?

                How can he make out, he asks,
                of this low eye-view,
                size?

                And archings traced and picked enough to hold
                to stay, as she does, as he, the brother, when,
                 here where the mud is, he is frozen, not daring
                where the grass grows, to move his feet from fear
                he'll trespass on his own dissolving bones, here
                where there is altogether too much remembrance?


    3

The question, the fear he raises up himself against
(against the same each act is proffered, under the eyes
each fix, the town of the earth over, is managed) is:   Who
am I?

Who am I but by a fix, and another,
a particle, and the congery of particles carefully picked one by another,

as in this thicket, each
smallest branch, plant, fern, root
—roots lie, on the surface, as nerves are laid open—
must now (the bitterness of the taste of her) be
isolated, observed, picked over, measured, raised
as though a word, an accuracy were a pincer!

                                                    this
              is the abstract, this
              is the cold doing, this
              is the almost impossible

So shall you blame those
who give it up, those who say
it isn't worth the struggle!


                              (Prayer
Or a death as going over to—shot by yr own forces—to
a greener place?
                              Neither

any longer
usable)

              By fixes only (not even any more by shamans)
              can the traceries
              be brought out

        II
ya, selva oscura, but hell now
is not exterior, is not to be got out of, is
the coat of your own self, the beasts
emblazoned on you   And who
can turn this total thing, invert
and let the ragged sleeves be seen
by any bitch or common character?  Who
can endure it where it is, where the beasts are met,
where yourself is, your beloved is, where she
who is separate from you, is not separate, is not
goddess, is, as your core is,
the making of one hell

              where she moves off, where she is
              no longer arch

(this is why he of whom we speak does not move, why
he stands so awkward where he is, why
his feet are held, like some ragged crane's
off the nearest next ground, even from
the beauty of the rotting fern his eye
knows, as he looks down, as,
in utmost pain if cold can be so called,
he looks around this battlefield, this
rotted place where men did die, where boys
and immigrants have fallen, where nature
(the years that she's took over)
does not matter, where

                  that men killed, do kill, that woman kills
                  is part, too, of his question

    2
That it is simple, what the difference is—
that a man, men, are now their own wood
and thus their own hell and paradise
that they are, in hell or in happiness, merely
something to be wrought, to be shaped, to be carved, for use, for
others

does not in the least lessen his, this unhappy man's
obscurities, his
confrontations

He shall step, he
will shape, he
is already also
moving off

        into the soil, on to his own bones

he will cross

        (there is always a field,
         for the strong there is always
        an alternative)

                    But a field
          is not a choice, is
          as dangerous as a prayer, as a death, as any
          misleading, lady

He will cross

          And is bound to enter (as she is)
          a later wilderness.
                         Yet
          what he does here, what he raises up
          (he must, the stakes are such


                                   this at least
          is a certainty, this
          is a law, is not one of the questions, this
          is what was talked of as
          —what was it called, demand?)


               He will do what he now does, as she will, do
               carefully, do
               without wavering,
               without
                         as even the branches,
                         even in this dark place, the twigs
                                                      how
                         even the brow
               of what was once to him a beautiful face

          as even the snow-flakes waver in the light's eye

                    as even forever wavers (gutters
                    in the wind of loss)

                    even as he will forever waver

                    precise as hell is, precise
                    as any words, or wagon,
                    can be made


                                             *1950*

# THE LORDLY AND ISOLATE SATYRS

The lordly and isolate Satyrs—look at them come in
on the left side of the beach
like a motorcycle club!  And the handsomest of them,
the one who has a woman, driving that snazzy
convertible
                    Wow, did you ever see even in a museum
such a collection of boddisatvahs, the way
they come up to their stop, each of them
as though it was a rudder
the way they have to sit above it
and come to a stop on it, the monumental solidity
of themselves, the Easter Island
they make of the beach, the Red-headed Men

                         These are the Androgynes,
the Fathers behind the father, the Great Halves

Or as that one was, inside his pants, the Yiddish poet
a vegetarian.  Or another—all in his mouth—a snarl
of the Sources.  Or the one I loved most, who once,
once only, let go the pain, the night he got drunk,
and I put him to bed, and he said, Bad blood.

                    Or the one who cracks and doesn't know
that what he thinks are a thousand questions are suddenly
a thousand lumps thrown up where the cloaca
again has burst:  one looks into the face and exactly as suddenly
it isn't the large eyes and nose but the ridiculously small mouth
which you are looking down as one end of

                         —as the Snarled Man
is a monocyte.

          Hail the ambiguous Fathers, and look closely
at them, they are the unadmitted, the club of Themselves,
weary riders, but who sit upon the landscape as the Great
Stones.  And only have fun among themselves.  They are
the lonely ones

Hail them, and watch out. The rest of us,
on the beach as we have previously known it, did not know
there was this left side. As they came riding in from the sea
—we did not notice them until they were already creating
the beach we had not known was there—but we assume
they came in from the sea. We assume that. We don't know.

In any case the whole sea was now a hemisphere,
and our eyes like half a fly's, we saw twice as much. Every-
thing opened, even if the newcomers just sat, didn't,
for an instant, pay us any attention. We were as we had been,
in that respect. We were as usual, the children were being fed pop
and potato chips, and everyone was sprawled as people are
on a beach. Something had happened but the change
wasn't at all evident. A few drops of rain
would have made more of a disturbance.

There we were. They, in occupation of the whole view
in front of us and off to the left where we were not used to look.
And we, watching them pant from their exertions, and talk to each other,
the one in the convertible the only one who seemed to be circulating.
And he was dressed in magnificent clothes, and the woman with him
a dazzling blond, the new dye making her hair a delicious
streaked ash. She was as distant as the others. She sat in her flesh too.

These are our counterparts, the unknown ones.

They are here. We do not look upon them as invaders. Dimensionally

they are larger than we—all but the woman. But we are not suddenly

small. We are as we are. We don't even move, on the beach.

It is a statis. Across nothing at all we stare at them.
We can see what they are. They don't notice us. They have merely
and suddenly moved in. They occupy our view. They are between us
and the ocean. And they have given us a whole new half of beach.

As of this moment, there is nothing else to report.
It is Easter Island transplanted to us. With the sun, and a warm
summer day, and sails out on the harbor they're here, the Con-
temporaries. They have come in.

Except for the stirring of the leader, they are still
catching their breath. They are almost like scooters the way
they sit there, up a little, on their thing. It is as though
the extra effort of it tired them the most. Yet that just there
was where their weight and separateness—their immensities—
lay. Why they seem like boddisatvahs. The only thing one noticed
is the way their face breaks when they call across to each other.
Or actually speak quite quietly, not wasting breath. But the face
loses all containment, they are fifteen year old boys at the moment
they speak to each other. They are not gods. They are not even stone.
They are doubles. They are only Source. When they act like us
they go to pieces. One notices then that their skin
is only creased like red-neck farmers. And that they are all
freckled. The red-headed people have the hardest time
to possess themselves. Is it because they were over-
fired? Or why—even to their beautiful women—do the red ones
have only that half of the weight?

We look at them, and begin to know. We begin to see
who they are. We see why they are satyrs, and why one half
of the beach was unknown to us. And now that it is known,
now that the beach goes all the way to the headland we thought
we were huddling ourselves up against, it turns out it is the
same. It is beach. The Visitors—Resters—who, by being there,
made manifest what we had not known—that the beach fronted wholly
to the sea—have only done that, completed the beach.

The difference is
we are more on it. The beauty of the white of the sun's light, the
blue the water is, and the sky, the movement on the painted lands-
cape, the boy-town the scene was, is now pierced with angels and
with fire. And winter's ice shall be as brilliant in its time as
life truly is, as Nature is only the offerer, and it is we
who look to see what the beauty is.

These visitors, now stirring
to advance, to go on wherever they do go restlessly never completing
their tour, going off on their motorcycles, each alone except for
the handsome one, isolate huge creatures wearing down nothing as
they go, their huge third leg like carborundum, only the vault
of their being taking rest, the awkward boddhas

We stay.  And watch them
gather themselves up.  We have no feeling except love.  They are not
ours.  They are of another name.  These are what the gods are.  They
look like us.  They are only in all parts larger.  But the size is
only different.  The difference is, they are not here, they are not
on this beach in this sun which, tomorrow, when we come to swim,
will be another summer day.  They can't talk to us.  We have no desire
to stop them any more than, as they made their camp, only possibly
the woman in the convertible one might have wanted to be familiar
with.  The Leader was too much as they.

They go.  And the day

*1956*

## A NEWLY DISCOVERED 'HOMERIC' HYMN

*(for Jane Harrison, if she were alive)*

Hail and beware the dead who will talk life until you are blue
in the face.  And you will not understand what is wrong,
they will not be blue, they will have tears in their eyes,
they will seem to you so much more full of life
than the rest of us, and they will ask so much, not of you no
but of life, they will cry, isn't it this way, if it isn't
I don't care for it, and you will feel the blackmail, you will not know
what to answer, it will all have become one mass

Hail and beware them, for they come from where you have not been,
they come from where you cannot have come, they come into life
by a different gate.  They come from a place which is not easily known,
it is known only to those who have died.  They carry seeds
you must not touch, you must not touch the pot they taste of,
no one must touch the pot, no one must, in their season.

Hail and beware them, in their season.  Take care.  Prepare
to receive them, they carry what the living cannot do without,
but take the proper precautions, do the prescribed things, let
down the thread from the right shoulder.  And from the forehead.

And listen to what they say, listen to the talk, hear
every word of it—they are drunk from the pot, they speak
like no living man may speak, they have the seeds in their mouth—
listen, and beware

Hail them solely that they have the seeds in their mouth, they
are drunk, you cannot do without a drunkenness, seeds can't
they must be soaked in the contents of the pot, they must be all one mass.
But you who live cannot know what else the seeds must be. Hail
and beware the earth, where the dead come from. Life
is not of the earth. The dead are of the earth. Hail and beware
the earth, where the pot is buried.

Greet the dead in the dead man's time. He is drunk of the pot.
He speaks like spring does. He will deceive you. You are meant
to be deceived. You must observe the drunkenness. You are not to
drink. But you must hear, and see. You must beware.

Hail them, and fall off. Fall off! The drink is not yours,
it is not yours! You do not come
from the same place, you do not suffer as the dead do,
they do not suffer, they need, because they have drunk of the pot,
they need. Do not drink of the pot, do not touch it. Do not touch
them.

     Beware the dead. And hail them. They teach you drunkenness.
You have your own place to drink. Hail and beware them, when they come.

*1955*


# ACROSS SPACE AND TIME

If the great outside system—species and stars—proceeds
successfully across great time, and curves to return to
stations it was once in before, and the belt of the ecliptic
slides like her cestus in months of a great year taking
25,725.6 years, what wonder that any one of us may be inflamed
with love at birth and spend a lifetime seeking to take the tail
into one's mouth, the disaster or augury of the shape and voluntas
of one's person, cast out of the combinatorial, substance the real

at the moment of birth, and one's own love the *affectiones* to cause
all of it to swarm, to know that as those beasts wheel variously
onto the point where night and day are equal one now does approach
the date at which man will pour equally from left to right out of
the pitcher of his portion of creation?

> Hail Aquarius,
> who is coming in

The Fish swam in on the back of Christ, by 1180 Christ was catching
the fish, by the 19th by carbon test (plus or minus 157 years) the fish
was sailing off, the Renaissance was over. Now the 2nd, and the 20th
were like (analogues) of a different source and of a different struct-
ure presenting a small Renaissance and a great world state to rush in
to petrify the dragging years of the fish bones, limestone for a future
to come up out of the sea on, when water has again made sense out of
things

Farewell Fish, your bones
we shall walk on

> Before either, Manes, the son of Sargon, swept out
> into the Atlantic while horsemen from the Caucasus
> came in with Aries to shake the dead temple world
> and awake self and reason, the soft Aries people who ride
> horses backward, brilliant riders who only know the back
> is an engine of will to be sacrificed if the sons
> will have wives, they ride on into battle until all
> is divided between flesh and soul and Greece
> is the measure of what they were worth

> > Ram long gone,
> > you won't come back
> > You are hopelessly torn
> > by the heels of the bulls

America, you are the end of three months of man. For the third,
which began when your head was turned, already has changed you,
you nation of Finks. Let you rule the world. You are a dead hand.
Man, in his courses, is on the other side: Capricorn is drawing
the threads

*1961*

# I, MAXIMUS OF GLOUCESTER, TO YOU

                    Off-shore, by islands hidden in the blood
                    jewels & miracles, I, Maximus
                    a metal hot from boiling water, tell you
                    what is a lance, who obeys the figures of
                    the present dance

    I
the thing you're after
may lie around the bend
of the nest (second, time slain, the bird! the bird!
And there! (strong) thrust, the mast! flight
                              (of the bird
                              o kylix, o
                              Antony of Padua
                              sweep low, o bless

the roofs, the old ones, the gentle steep ones
on whose ridge-poles the gulls sit, from which they depart,

                                   And the flake-racks
of my city!

    2
love is form, and cannot be without
important substance (the weight
say, 58 carats each one of us, perforce
our goldsmith's scale

                         feather to feather added
                         (and what is mineral, what
                         is curling hair, the string
                         you carry in your nervous beak, these

                         make bulk, these, in the end, are
                         the sum

                         (o my lady of good voyage
                         in whose arm, whose left arm rests
no boy but a carefully carved wood, a painted face, a schooner!
a delicate mast, as bow-sprit for

                    forwarding

.3
the underpart is, though stemmed, uncertain
is, as sex is, as moneys are, facts!
facts, to be dealt with, as the sea is, the demand
that they be played by, that they only can be, that they must
be played by, said he, coldly, the
ear!

By ear, he sd.
But that which matters, that which insists, that which will last,
that! o my people, where shall you find it, how, where, where shall you
        listen
when all is become billboards, when, all, even silence, is spray-gunned?

when even our bird, my roofs,
cannot be heard

when even you, when sound itself is neoned in?

when, on the hill, over the water
where she who used to sing,
when the water glowed,
black, gold, the tide
outward, at evening

when bells came like boats
over the oil-slicks, milkweed
hulls

And a man slumped,
attentionless,
against pink shingles

o sea city)

4
one loves only form,
the form only comes
into existence when
the thing is born

                born of yourself, born
                of hay and cotton struts,
                of street-pickings, wharves, weeds
                you carry in, my bird

           of a bone of a fish
           of a straw, or will
           of a color, of a bell
           of yourself, torn

    5

love is not easy
but how shall you know,
New England, now
that pejorocracy is here, how
that street-cars, o Oregon, twitter
in the afternoon, offend
a black-gold loin?

         how shall you strike,
         o swordsman, the blue-red back
         when, last night, your aim
         was mu-sick, mu-sick, mu-sick
         And not the cribbage game?

               (o Gloucester-man,
               weave
               your birds and fingers
               new, your roof-tops,
               clean shit upon racks
               sunned on
               American

               braid
               with others like you, such
               extricable surface
               as faun and oral,
               satyr lesbos vase

               o kill kill kill kill kill
               those
               who advertise you
               out)

6

in! in! the bow-sprit, bird, the beak
in, the bend is, in, goes in, the form
that which you make, what holds, which is
the law of object, strut after strut, what you are, what you must be, what
the force can throw up, can, right now hereinafter erect,
the mast, the mast, the tender
mast!

　　　　　The nest, I say, to you, I Maximus, say
　　　　　under the hand, as I see it, over the waters
　　　　　from this place where I am, where I hear,
　　　　　can still hear

　　　　　from where I carry you a feather
　　　　　as though, sharp, I picked up,
　　　　　in the afternoon delivered you
　　　　　a jewel,
　　　　　　　　it flashing more than a wing,
　　　　　than any old romantic thing,
　　　　　than memory, than place,
　　　　　than anything other than that which you carry

　　　　　than that which is,
　　　　　call it a nest, around the head of, call it
　　　　　the next second

　　　　　than that which you
　　　　　can do!

　　　　　　　　　　　　　　　　*1950*

## MAXIMUS, TO HIMSELF

I have had to learn the simplest things
last. Which made for difficulties.
Even at sea I was slow, to get the hand out, or to cross
a wet deck.
　　　　　The sea was not, finally, my trade.

But even my trade, at it, I stood estranged
from that which was most familiar.  Was delayed,
and not content with the man's argument
that such postponement
is now the nature of
obedience,

        that we are all late
        in a slow time,
        that we grow up many
        And the single
        is not easily
        known


It could be, though the sharpness (the *achiote*)
I note in others,
makes more sense
than my own distances.  The agilities

        they show daily
        who do the world's
        businesses
        And who do nature's
        as I have no sense
        I have done either

I have made dialogues,
have discussed ancient texts,
have thrown what light I could, offered
what pleasures
doceat allows

        But the known?
This, I have had to be given,
a life, love, and from one man
the world.

        Tokens.
        But sitting here
        I look out as a wind
        and water man, testing
        And missing
        some proof

I know the quarters
of the weather, where it comes from,
where it goes. But the steam of me,
this I took from their welcome,
or their rejection, of me

      And my arrogance
      was neither diminished
      nor increased,
      by the communication

  2
It is undone business
I speak of, this morning,
with the sea
stretching out
from my feet

                        *1953*

## COLE'S ISLAND

I met Death—he was a sportsman—on Cole's
Island. He was a property-owner. Or maybe
Cole's Island, was his. I don't know. The
point was I was there, walking, and—as it
often is, in the woods—a stranger, suddenly
showing up, makes the very thing you were do-
ing no longer the same. That is suddenly
what you thought, when you were alone, and
doing what you were doing, changes because someone else
shows up. He didn't bother me, or say anything. Which is
not surprising, a person might not, in the circumstances;
or at most a nod or something. Or they would. But they wouldn't,
or you wouldn't think to either, if it was Death. And
He certainly was, the moment I saw him. There wasn't any question
about that even though he may have looked like a sort of country
gentleman, going about his own land. Not quite. Not it being He.

A fowler, maybe—as though he was used to
hunting birds, and was out, this morning, keeping
his hand in, so to speak, moving around, noticing
what game were about.  And how they seemed.  And how the woods
were.  As a matter of fact just before he had shown up,
so naturally, and as another person might walk
up on a scene of your own, I had noticed
a cock and hen pheasant cross easily the
road I was on and had tried, in fact,
to catch my son's attention quick enough for him
to see before they did walk off into the bayberry
or arbor vitae along the road.

              My impression is we did—
that is, Death and myself, regard each other.  And
there wasn't anything more than that, only that he had appeared,
and we did recognize each other—or I did, him and he seemed
to have no question
about my presence there, even though I was uncomfortable.
   That is,
Cole's Island
is a queer isolated and gated place, and I was only there by will
to know more of the topography of it lying as it does out
over the Essex River.  And as it now is, with no tenants that one can speak
    of,
it's more private than almost any place one might imagine.
And down in that part of it where I did meet him (about half way between
    the
two houses over the river and the carriage house
at the entrance) it was as quiet and as much a piece
of the earth as any place can be.  But my difficulty,
when he did show up, was immediately at least that I was
an intruder, by being there at all
and yet, even if he seemed altogether
used to Cole's Island, and, like I say, as though he owned it,
even if I was sure he didn't, I noticed him, and he me, and he
went on without anything extraordinary at all.

Maybe he had gaiters on, or almost
a walking stick, in other words much more
habited than I,
who was in chinos actually and
only doing what I had set myself to do here
& in other places on Cape Ann.

It was his eye perhaps which makes me
render him as Death?  It isn't true, there wasn't anything
that different about his eye,

it was not one thing more than that he was Death instantly
that he came into sight.  Or that I was aware there was a person
here as well as myself.  And son.

We did exchange some glance.  That is the fullest possible
account I can give, of the encounter.

Wednesday, September 9th, 1964

## CELESTIAL EVENING, OCTOBER 1967

Advanced out toward the external from
the time I did actually lose space control,
here on the Fort and kept turning left
like my star-nosed mole batted
on the head, not being able to
get home 50 yards as I was
from it.  There is a vast

internal life, a sea or organism
full of sounds & memoried
objects swimming or sunk
in the great fall of it as,
when one further
ring of the 9 bounding
Earth & Heaven runs
into the daughter of God's
particular place, cave, palace—a tail

of Ocean whose waters then
are test if even a god
lies will tell & he or she spend
9 following years out of the company
of their own.  The sounds

and objects of the great
10th within us are
what we hear see are motived by
dream belief care for discriminate
our loves & choices cares & failures unless
in this forbidding Earth & Heaven by

enclosure 9 times round plus
all that stream collecting as,
into her hands it comes:  the
full volume of all which ever was which we
as such have that which is our part of it,
all history existence places splits of moon
& slightest oncoming smallest stars at
sunset, fears & horrors, grandparents'
lives as much as we have also features
and their forms, whatever grace or ugliness our legs
etc possess, it all

comes in as also outward leads
us after itself as though then
the horn of the nearest moon was
truth.  I bend my ear, as,
if I were Amoghasiddi and,
here on this plain where
like my mole I have
been knocked flat, attend,
to turn & turn within
the steady stream & collect which
within me ends as in her hall and I

hear all, the new moon new in all
the ancient sky

# WILLIAM EVERSON (1912)


## A CANTICLE TO THE WATERBIRDS


Clack your beaks you cormorants and kittiwakes,
North on those rock-croppings finger-jutted into the rough Pacific surge;
You migratory terns and pipers who leave but the temporal clawtrack
    written on sandbars there of your presence;
Grebes and pelicans; you comber-picking scoters and you shorelong gulls;
All you keepers of the coastline north of here to the Mendocino beaches;
All you beyond upon the cliff-face thwarting the surf at Hecate Head;
Hovering the under-surge where the cold Columbia grapples at the bar;
North yet to the Sound, whose islands float like a sown flurry of chips
    upon the sea;
Break wide your harsh and salt-encrusted beaks unmade for song
And say a praise up to the Lord.

And you freshwater egrets east in the flooded marshlands skirting the
    sea-level rivers, white one-legged watchers of shallows;
Broad-headed kingfishers minnow-hunting from willow stems on meandering
    valley sloughs;
You too, you herons, blue and supple-throated, stately, taking the air
    majestical in the sunflooded San Joaquin,
Grading down on your belted wings from the upper lights of sunset,
Mating over the willow clumps or where the flatwater rice fields shimmer;
You killdeer, high night-criers, far in the moon-suffusion sky;
Bitterns, sand-waders, all shore-walkers, all roost-keepers,
Populates of the 'dobe cliffs of the Sacramento:
Open your water-dartling beaks,
And make a praise up to the Lord.

For you hold the heart of His mighty fastnesses,
And shape the life of His indeterminate realms.
You are everywhere on the lonesome shores of His wide creation.
You keep seclusion where no man may go, giving Him praise;
Nor may a woman come to lift like your cleaving flight her clear contralto
    song
To honor the spindrift gifts of His soft abundance.
You sanctify His hermitage rocks where no holy priest may kneel to adore,
    nor holy nun assist;
And where His true communion-keepers are not enabled to enter.

And well may you say His praises, birds, for your ways
Are verved with the secret skills of His inclinations,
And your habits plaited and rare with the subdued elaboration of His
    intricate craft;
Your days intent with the direct astuteness needful for His outworking,
And your nights alive with the dense repose of His infinite sleep.
You are His secretive charges and you serve His secretive ends,
In His clouded, mist-conditioned stations, in His murk,
Obscure in your matted nestings, immured in His limitless ranges.
He makes you penetrate through dark interstitial joinings of His thicketed
    kingdoms,
And keep your concourse in the deeps of His shadowed world.

Your ways are wild but earnest, your manners grave,
Your customs carefully schooled to the note of His serious mien.
You hold the prime condition of His clean creating,
And the swift compliance with which you serve His minor means
Speaks of the constancy with which you hold Him.
For what is your high flight forever going home to your first beginnings,
But such a testament to your devotion?
You hold His outstretched world beneath your wings, and mount upon
    His storms,
And keep your sheer wind-lidded sight upon the vast perspectives of His
    mazy latitudes.

But mostly it is your way you bear existence wholly within the context
    of His utter will and are untroubled.
Day upon day you do not reckon, nor scrutinize tomorrow, nor multiply
    the nightfalls with a rash concern,
But rather assume each instant as warrant sufficient of His final seal.
Wholly in Providence you spring, and when you die you look on death in
    clarity unflinched,
Go down, a clutch of feather ragged upon the brush;
Or drop on water where you briefly lived, found food,
And now yourselves made food for His deep current-keeping fish, and
    then are gone:
Is left but the pinion-feather spinning a bit on the uproil
Where lately the dorsal cut clear air.

You leave a silence. And this for you suffices, who are not of the
    ceremonials of man,
And hence are not made sad to now forgo them.
Yours is of another order of being, and wholly it compels.

But may you, birds, utterly seized in God's supremacy,
Austerely living under His austere eye—
Yet may you teach a man a necessary thing to know,
Which has to do of the strict conformity that creaturehood entails,
And constitutes the prime commitment all things share.
For God has given you the imponderable grace to *be* His verification,
Outside the mulled incertitude of our forensic choices;
That you, our lessers in the rich hegemony of Being,
May serve as testament to what a creature is,
And what creation owes.

Curlews, stilts and scissortails, beachcomber gulls,
Wave-haunters, shore-keepers, rockhead-holders, all cape-top vigilantes,
Now give God praise.
Send up the strict articulation of your throats,
And say His name.

## THE NARROWS OF BIRTH

Christmas night: the solstice storm
Muttering in retreat, threatening rain,
Cypress witlessly clawing the roof,
Its vague hand scrawling the obscure
Prophecy of reprisal. Across the dunes
Wind rakes the hollow-breasted sea,
Coughing and expectorating like a consumptive invalid,
A feverish old woman racked in senility's
Festering decrepitude, morbidly ailing.

I awake from a dream of ritual slaying: beachfire
Back from the surf; hunched in an angle of logs and driftwood
Crouches the clan. Among them,
Free and unsuspecting, a youth lounges,
Perfectly relaxed, a man
Stalwart, high-minded and virile,
In the deceptive way the dream
Inveterately falsifies reality,
Approximating the ideal.

To me, in the freezing awareness of apprehension,
It becomes increasingly apparent
He is not to be their guest but their victim.
Yet my very prescience, which declares my involvement,
Renders me powerless. For I have entered into complicity,
A kind of unspoken pact, with these people, seeking something
They have which I need, which I once knew and lost,
And have come to recover in my own quest;
And because of this need, this involvement,
Have forfeited my freedom.

And suddenly, with great clarity of vision,
I see them for what they are,
The castrate sons and the runt daughters,
Maimed progeny of the Mother,
From whose destiny I myself, long ago, had somehow escaped,
And have returned now, improvidently,
To verify my lack. They hobble about their appointed tasks,
Preparing the terrible rites of immolation.
They seem to be concocting some kind of revolting brew,
The narcotic that renders the victim senseless,
Of which the elements, I am aware, are parlous:
Milk and dung, blood and semen, menses and afterbirth,
The mordant ingredients of parturition.
These, I see, stand for the universal postulates of generation:
Twin compulsions of Desire and Death:
The inexorable forces which every major religion
Has pitted itself to overcome; and from which
The vows of every monk
Are structured toward deliverance.

And I sense, from the depths of this recognition,
The utter ineffectuality of everything I am—my own monk's vows
Jettisoned in a spasm of precipitate repudiation,
Leaving me weaponless, hands utterly empty,
To grope my way back to these somnambulists,
These ominous dark sources,
In the reassessment of my life.

Across the fire I face the matriarch,
My ancient ancestress, the fountainhead of my blood,
Saying, "I have come back, Mother,"
And I bow my head as a penitent

Bows for absolution; or as the prodigal,
Having squandered his heritage,
Lowers his neck to signify his wrong.
But in the old mother of glittering eyes
Is neither absolution nor forgiveness.
Her gaze searches me narrowly,
Unrelenting, utterly unimpressed
By anything I might say,
Waiting for proof. She will be appeased now
Only by deeds—by words
Never.

　　　I waver in the firelight,
Uncertainly, unable to know
What it is I am to do, unable to reassert
Who I am, or say what brought me here,
What motive or what reasons avail
In their weirdly familiar place.

The plotting goes on.
I see the body of the youth,
Beautifully muscled, like Michelangelo's
Immortal slave, the raised shirt
Banded about the nipples,
And all the magnificent body
Slumped in its unmistakably erotic swoon.

The castration begins.

I wake to the dawn, bolt upright,
With the retreating storm
Muttering in the eaves, uncertain
And vague and foreboding.
I feel beside me in the strange bed
The body of my young wife.
She is breathing deeply in sleep,
The clear pulse of her being
Mustering within it all the life-force
Against my fear. In the next room
Her nine month's son cries out, softly,
Under the wince of my pervasive torment,
An anguish which haunts the house,
My pain and my guilt.

In the stretched silence
I touch her again, the flank of woman,
Modulant with the subsumed
Rapture of life. And everything I have come for
Clutches my throat,
Warring in the narrows of this birth.


# KINGFISHER FLAT


A rustle of whispering wind over leaves,
Then the stillness closes: no creek-music,
No slurred water-sound. The starved stream
Edges its way through dead stones,
Noiseless in the night.
                    I feel your body
Restless beside me. Your breathing checks
And then resumes, as in a moment of dream
The glimpsed image, mutely desired but scarcely believed,
Fades and revives.


                    In the long drought
Impotence clutched on the veins of passion
Encircles our bed, a serpent of stone.
I sense the dearth in you also,
The bane that is somehow mine to impose
But yours to endure—cohibition of the blood,
Flaw of nature or defect of the soul—
Dry turning of leaves, cessation of desire,
Estrangement gripped in the roots of hair,
And around the loins, like a fine wire,
The cincture of nerves.


                    I think of the Fisher King,
All his domain parched in a sterile fixation of purpose,
Clenched on the core of the burning question
Gone unasked.

Out in the dark
The recumbent body of earth sleeps on,
Silent as dust, incognizant.  Many a moon,
Many a withering month will she weary
Ere the black knight of storm whirls out of the West,
Churns from the turbulent fosse of the sea,
Assaults the shore, breaches the continental slope
And takes her, his torrential force
Stripping the iron zone of chastity
Down from her thighs, drenching belly and breasts,
All the pores of her famished body
Agape—

    Oh, wife and companion!
The ancient taboo hangs over us,
A long suspension tightens its grip
On the seed of my passion and the flower of your hope.
Masks of drought deceive us.  An inexorable forbearance
Falsifies the face of things, and makes inflexible
The flow of this life, the movement of this love.
What prohibitive code stiffens the countenance,
Constricts the heart?  What fear constrains it?
And whose the blame?

    Enough.
There is no need now, nor ever was,
For the ghastly rote of self-accusation
Scrupulosity enjoins.  To find a new mate
Were nothing difficult for one so young, so lovely.

But something other, more inscrutably present,
Obtains here, possessing us, cohesive in spirit,
Divisive in the flesh—the lordly phallus
Never again to joust in the festive lists of love,
Quench its ardour in the uterine fens,
Assuage your cry?

    Myth and dream
Merge in a consanguinity of kind,
Fuse the soul's wild wish and the hunger of the race
On the body's pang.

But something forbears.
Like Merlin and Niniane, bound in a fatefulness
That set them aside, wisdom and delight
Crucified in bed, polarized on the stretched extreme
That made them one, we twist our grievous fingers together
And stare in the dark.

I hear quaking grass
Shiver under the windowsill, and out along the road
The ripe mallow and the wild oat
Rustle in the wind. Deeper than the strict
Interdiction of denial or the serpentine coiling of time,
Woman and earth lie sunk in sleep, unsatisfied.
Each holds that bruise to her heart like a stone
And aches for rain.

# ROBERT DUNCAN (1919)

## THE SONG OF THE BORDERGUARD

The man with his lion under the shed of wars
sheds his belief as if he shed tears.
The sound of words waits—
a barbarian host at the borderline of sense.

The enamord guards desert their posts
harkening to the lion-smell of a poem
that rings in their ears.

> —Dreams, a certain guard said
> were never designd so
> to re-arrange an empire.

> Along about six o'clock I take out my guitar
> and sing to a lion
> who sleeps like a line of poetry
> in the shed of wars.

The man shedding his belief
knows that the lion is not asleep,
does not dream, is never asleep,
is a wide-awake poem
waiting like a lover for the disrobing of the guard;
the beautiful boundaries of the empire
naked, rapt round in the smell of a lion.

(The barbarians have passt over the significant phrase)

> —When I was asleep,
>     a certain guard says,
> a man shed his clothes as if he shed tears
> and appeared as a lonely lion
> waiting for a song under the shed-roof of wars.

I sang the song that he waited to hear,
I, the Prize-Winner, the Poet Acclaimd.

Dear, Dear, Dear, Dear, I sang,
believe, believe, believe, believe.
The shed of wars is splendid as the sky,
houses our waiting like a pure song
housing in its words the lion-smell
  of the beloved disrobed.

I sang: believe, believe, believe.

  I the guard because of my guitar
believe. I am the certain guard,
certain of the Beloved, certain of the Lion,
certain of the Empire. I with my guitar.
Dear, Dear, Dear, Dear, I sing.
I, the Prize-Winner, the Poet on Guard.

The borderlines of sense in the morning light
are naked as a line of poetry in a war.


# CORRESPONDENCES


  It is from the ideas of you that you emerge. I return to you from
my longing, you a second image in longing, drawn to you as the painter
is drawn to the man he draws; or, as in reading the cards, one is drawn to
the likeness of death in the Ace of Spades. 'I say I shan't live five years'
Blake wrote in 1793 'And if I live one it will be a Wonder.' Within all
daily love—and this is a world—is another world sleeping or an otherness
awake in which I am a sleeper. The reveald things of this order appear as
omens: within the full dread of death, so that I cry up to die—is another
life. I tremble lest the door be lockd or open, for the door is an
ununderstandable joy.
  But now, across an emptiness of time I see you. I shall never reach
you—between me and thee.

As it was in the beginning. What I am withdraws from the great sun, like
a lion retracting his roar in order to speak. In this scene the simple pleasures
of this world cause areas of torment in the unreal like stones in an open
field.

## AN OWL IS AN ONLY BIRD OF POETRY

A cross leaves marks the tree we fancy.
    regular art rules.
    Under hand beauty demands
the secret howl to cross the table
      on bloody stumps
      were wings added later to mar
the 17th century flying style.


### INCLUDE A PRAYER

    include lions rise or as sentences raised,
    include fore gone conclusions in a maze,
    include my blind in designing your window,
    include my window in raising your blind,
    include a long time in my forever yours,
    include April and July in all your years,
    include the lions eye that sheds the lambs tears,
    include the lambs eye or as paragraphs rest,
    include the bird that belongs to each beast,

    include:

    include the breasts and Mary's face,
    include the horns of the cow in Grace,
    include the words in pasture are kind,
    include the scream when he starts to pray,
    include the sun at the opening of day,
    include the night in what you find,

    Small lions are kittens and love to purr.

    include the fathering Night and Day,
    include the orders descending thru words,
    include the elegances of no rhyme,
    include the roar of a lion in triumph,
    include break orderly converse to address divine disorders
    abruptly,
    include the tree upon which our life hangs,

include the metaphor in which from that tree Christ is crucified,
include all martyrs in the sense of fun,
include chairs and tables as comfortable things,
include the bird in the angel with wings,

## FIGURE 1

The vowels are physical
corridors of the imagination
emitting passionately
breaths of flame. In a poem
the vowels appear like
the flutterings of an owl
caught in a web and give
aweful intimations of
eternal life.

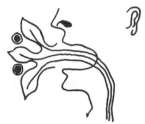

## FIGURE 2

The consonants are a church of
hands interlocking,   stops
and measures of fingerings
that confine the spirit to
articulations of space and time.

It is in the disorders of the net that the stars fall from the designs
we grasp into their original chaos.

He flies thru a time which his wing creates. MEASURES. As the
immortal Dali has painted him. He is erected upon the cross of vision
as we see him.

SONG

> What do you see, my little one?
> I see an owl hung in a tree.
> His blood flows from his side.
> Earthly things may rest tonight,
> all heavenly fear hangs there.
> I see a nest where owlets cry
> and eat the cold night air.
>
> What do you see, my little one?
> I see an owl hung in a tree
> like flesh hung on a bone.
> The thorns of flesh run thru and thru.
> Ring out the tones of life.
> He builds the artifice of heart
> and takes his word to wife.
>
> What do you see, my little one?
> I see an owl hung in a tree
> among the letters whispering there,
> a tongue of speech that beats
> the passages of mere air.
>
> The ladders of tone pass into words,
> the words pass into song,
> The heavenly orders sing to me.
> I see an owl hung in a tree.


FINALE. DISARRANGEMENTS AS JOY.

> This is an owl in time. Of night.
> too late / too soon / flies

out of Minerva's head into her thought.

> Reappears. On snowy wings.
> Disconsolate Valentine.

> I go along with him. As I send him.

<pre>
                The joy
is a great scuttering of feathers words
                a whirl
up words into an airy sentence where
                reader
by reader accepts his mixt whether
                of love
face by face in his poem's crackt mirror
</pre>

This is an owl as he flies out of himself
into the heart that reflects all owl.

Who gives his hoot for joy as he flies.

<pre>
                Alights.
</pre>

## THIS PLACE RUMORD TO HAVE BEEN SODOM

might have been.
Certainly these ashes might have been pleasures.
Pilgrims on their way to the Holy Places remark
this place. Isn't it plain to all
that these mounds were palaces? This was once
a city among men, a gathering together of spirit.
It was measured by the Lord and found wanting.

It was measured by the Lord and found wanting,
destroyd by the angels that inhabit longing.
Surely this is Great Sodom where such cries
as if men were birds flying up from the swamp
ring in our ears, where such fears that were once
desires walk, almost spectacular,
stalking the desolate circles, red eyed.

This place rumord to have been a City surely was,
separated from us by the hand of the Lord.
The devout have laid out gardens in the desert,
drawn water from springs where the light was blighted.

How tenderly they must attend these friendships
or all is lost. All *is* lost.
Only the faithful hold this place green.

Only the faithful hold this place green
where the crown of fiery thorns descends.
Men that once lusted grow listless. A spirit
wrappd in a cloud, ashes more than ashes,
fire more than fire, ascends.
Only these new friends gather joyous here,
where the world like Great Sodom lies under fear.

*The world like Great Sodom lies under Love*
*and knows not the hand of the Lord that moves.*
This the friends teach where such cries
as if men were birds fly up from the crowds
gatherd and howling in the heat of the sun.
In the Lord Whom the friends have named at last Love
the images and loves of the friends never die.

This place rumord to have been Sodom is blessd
in the Lord's eyes.

# A POEM BEGINNING WITH A LINE BY PINDAR

I

*The light foot hears you and the brightness begins*
god-step at the margins of thought,
     quick adulterous tread at the heart.
Who is it that goes there?
     Where I see your quick face
notes of an old music pace the air,
torso-reverberations of a Grecian lyre.

In Goya's canvas Cupid and Psyche
have a hurt voluptuous grace
bruised by redemption. The copper light
falling upon the brown boy's slight body
is carnal fate that sends the soul wailing
up from blind innocence, ensnared
     by dimness
into the deprivations of desiring sight.

But the eyes in Goya's painting are soft,
diffuse with rapture absorb the flame.
Their bodies yield out of strength.
    Waves of visual pleasure
wrap them in a sorrow previous to their impatience.

A bronze of yearning, a rose that burns
    the tips of their bodies, lips,
ends of fingers, nipples. He is not wingd.
His thighs are flesh, are clouds
    lit by the sun in its going down,
hot luminescence at the loins of the visible.

        But they are not in a landscape.
        They exist in an obscurity.

The wind spreading the sail serves them.
The two jealous sisters eager for her ruin
        serve them.
That she is ignorant, ignorant of what Love will be,
        serves them.
The dark serves them.
The oil scalding his shoulder serves them,
serves their story. Fate, spinning,
        knots the threads for Love.

Jealousy, ignorance, the hurt ... serve them.

        II
This is magic. It is passionate dispersion.
What if they grow old? The gods
        would not allow it.
        Psyche is preserved.

In time we see a tragedy, a loss of beauty
        the glittering youth
of the god retains—but from this threshold
        it is age
that is beautiful. It is toward the old poets
        we go, to their faltering,
their unaltering wrongness that has style,
        their variable truth,
        the old faces,
words shed like tears from
a plenitude of powers time stores.

A stroke.  These little strokes.  A chill.
   The old man, feeble, does not recoil.
Recall.  A phase so minute,
     only a part of the word in- jerrd.

   *The Thundermakers descend,*

damerging a nuv.  A nerb.
   The present dented of the U
nighted stayd.   States.   The heavy clod?
     Cloud.   Invades the brain.   What
     if lilacs last in *this* dooryard bloomd?

Hoover, Roosevelt, Truman, Eisenhower—
where among these did the power reside
that moves the heart?  What flower of the nation
bride-sweet broke to the whole rapture?
Hoover, Coolidge, Harding, Wilson
hear the factories of human misery turning out commodities.
For whom are the holy matins of the heart ringing?
Noble men in the quiet of morning hear
Indians singing the continent's violent requiem.
Harding, Wilson, Taft, Roosevelt,
idiots fumbling at the bride's door,
hear the cries of men in meaningless debt and war.
Where among these did the spirit reside
that restores the land to productive order?
McKinley, Cleveland, Harrison, Arthur,
Garfield, Hayes, Grant, Johnson,
dwell in the roots of the heart's rancor.
How sad "amid lanes and through old woods"
     echoes Whitman's love for Lincoln!

There is no continuity then.   Only a few
    posts of the good remain.   I too
that am a nation sustain the damage
    where smokes of continual ravage
obscure the flame.
               It is across great scars of wrong
    I reach toward the song of kindred men
    and strike again the naked string
old Whitman sang from.  Glorious mistake!
    that cried:

"The theme is creative and has vista."
"He is the president of regulation."

I see always the under side turning,
fumes that injure the tender landscape.
    From which up break
lilac blossoms of courage in daily act
    striving to meet a natural measure.


     III   (for Charles Olson)
             Psyche's tasks—the sorting of seeds
wheat   barley   oats   poppy   coriander
anise   beans   lentils   peas   —every grain
         in its right place
                before nightfall;

gathering the gold wool from the cannibal sheep
(for the soul must weep
    and come near upon death);

harrowing Hell for a casket Proserpina keeps
                that must not
    be opend . . . containing beauty?
no! Melancholy coild like a serpent
              that is deadly sleep
    we are not permitted
          to succumb to.

    These are the old tasks.
    You've heard them before.

    They must be impossible.  Psyche
must despair, be brought to her
               insect instructor;
must obey the counsels of the green reed;
saved from suicide by a tower speaking,
    must follow to the letter
    freakish instructions.

In the story the ants help.  The old man at Pisa
    mixd in whose mind
(to draw the sorts) are all seeds
      *as a lone ant from a broken ant-hill*
had part restored by an insect, was
    upheld by a lizard

(to draw the sorts)
*the wind is part of the process*
    defines a nation of the wind—

 father of many notions,

       Who?
let the light into the dark? began
the many movements of the passion?

         West
from east men push.
     The islands are blessd
(cursed) that swim below the sun,

 *man upon whom the sun has gone down!*

There is the hero who struggles east
widdershins to free the dawn and must
     woo Night's daughter,
sorcery, black passionate rage, covetous queens,
so that the fleecy sun go back from Troy,
 Colchis, India . . . all the blazing armies
spent, he must struggle alone toward the pyres of Day.

     The light that is Love
rushes on toward passion. It verges upon dark.
 Roses and blood flood the clouds.
 Solitary first riders advance into legend.

 This land, where I stand, was all legend
in my grandfathers' time: cattle raiders,
 animal tribes, priests, gold.
It was the West. Its vistas painters saw
 in diffuse light, in melancholy,
in abysses left by glaciers as if they had been the sun
 primordial carving empty enormities
    out of the rock.

    Snakes lurkd
guarding secrets. Those first ones
    survived solitude.

Scientia
holding the lamp, driven by doubt;
Eros naked in foreknowledge
smiling in his sleep;  and the light
spilld, burning his shoulder—the outrage
     that conquers legend—
passion, dismay, longing, search
     flooding up where
the Beloved is lost.   Psyche travels
life after life, my life, station
     after station,
to be tried

     without break, without
news, knowing only—but what did she know?
     The oracle at Miletus had spoken
truth surely:  that he was Serpent-Desire
     that flies thru the air,
a monster-husband.  But she saw him fair

whom Apollo's mouthpiece said spread
     pain
beyond cure    to those
     wounded by his arrows.

Rilke torn by a rose thorn
blackend toward Eros.  Cupidinous Death!
     that will not take no for an answer.

     IV
     Oh yes!    Bless the footfall where
step by step    the boundary walker
(in Maverick Road    the snow
thud by thud    from the roof
circling the house—another tread)

     that foot    informd
by the weight of all things
     that can be elusive
no more than a nearness to the mind
     of a single image

Oh yes!   this
most dear
the catalyst force that renders clear
the days of a life from the surrounding medium!


Yes, beautiful rare wilderness!
wildness that verifies strength of my tame mind,
clearing held against indians,
health that prepared to meet death,
the stubborn hymns going up
into the ramifications of the hostile air

that, deceptive, gives way.

What is there?   O, light the light!
The Indians give way,   the clearing falls.
Great Death gives way   and unprepares us.
Lust gives way.   The Moon gives way.
Night gives way.   Minutely,   the Day gains.

She saw the body of her beloved
dismemberd in waking ... or was it
in sight?   *Finders Keepers* we sang
when we were children   or were taught to sing
before our histories began   and we began
who were beloved   our animal life
toward the Beloved,   sworn to be Keepers.

On the hill before the wind came
the grass moved toward the one sea,
blade after blade dancing in waves.

There the children turn the ring to the left.
There the children turn the ring to the right.
Dancing ... Dancing ...

And the lonely psyche goes up thru the boy to the king
that in the caves of history dreams.
Round and round the children turn.
London Bridge that is a kingdom falls.

We have come so far that all the old stories
whisper once more.

Mount Ségur, Mount Victoire, Mount Tamalpais . . .
   *rise to adore the mystery of Love!*

(An ode? Pindar's art, the editors tell us, was not a statue but a mosaic,
an accumulation of metaphor. But if he was archaic, not classic, a survival
of obsolete mode, there may have been old voices in the survival that
directed the heart. So, a line from a hymn came in a novel I was reading
to help me. Psyche, poised to leap—and Pindar too, the editors write, goes
too far, topples over—listend to a tower that said, *Listen to me!* The oracle
had said, *Despair! The Gods themselves abhor his power.* And then the
virgin flower of the dark falls back flesh of our flesh from which everywhere . . .

   the information flows
      that is yearning. A line of Pindar
   moves from the area of my lamp
      toward morning.

   In the dawn that is nowhere
      I have seen the willful children

   clockwise and counter-clockwise turning.


## A NEW POEM (for Jack Spicer)


You are right. What we call Poetry is the boat.
The first boat, the body—but it was a bed.
   The bed, but it was a car.
And the driver or sandman, the boatman,
   the familiar stranger, first lover,
is not with me.

               You are wrong.
What we call Poetry is the lake itself,
the bewildering circling water way—
having our power in what we know nothing of,
in this having neither father nor son,

our never having come into it,
our never having left it,
our misnaming it, our
giving it the lie so that it lies.

I would not be easy
calling the shadowy figure who refuses to guide the boat
but crosses and recrosses the heart . . .

—He breaks a way among the lily pads.
He breaks away from the directions
        we cannot give—

I would not be easy calling him
        the Master of Truth,
but Master he is of turning right and wrong.

I cannot make light of it.
The boat has its own light.

The weight of the boat
is not in the boat.  He will not
give me images but I must
give him images.
He will not give me his name
but I must give him . . .

name after name I give him.
But I will not name the grave easily,
the boat of bone
so light it turns as if earth
were wind and water.

Ka, I call him.  The shadow
wavers and wears my own face.

Kaka, I call him.  The
whole grey cerement replaces itself and shows
a hooded hole.

From what we call Poetry a cock crows
away off there at the break of something.

Lake of no shores I can name,
Body of no day or night I can account for,
snoring in the throws of sleep I came
sleepless to the joint of this poem,
as if there were a hinge in the ways.

Door opend or closed,
knuckled down where faces of a boat join,
Awake Asleep
from the hooded hold of the boat
join in. The farthest shore is so near
crows fly up and we know it is America.

No crows flies. It is not America.
From what we call Poetry
a bird I cannot name crows.


## AS IN THE OLD DAYS      Passages 8


                    the ones of the old days

            will not be done with us

        but come to mind         .

                    thought designing for their sake

                        chariots and horizons         .

            from which they come

                            towards us

                ever       .

            from which they come towards us,

                    in the distance,          nearing

                        where we are          I am

                at the lips    before speech,    at life's

                        labia, Her    crack of a door opening,

her cunt   a wound now

  the gash in His side

from which monthly       blood flows   .

        so Zinzendorf saw,

      all maidens bear Christ's sign   with them

       .   at this flowing

          souls gather   .

At the babe's birth

    the whole woman

  opens   .   the flower bleeding,   life-lanced   .

    the head of the embryo

shoved forth from its red pod,   from the pain she knows,

      into the Child's place

     .   cries.

     "To be born again from the wound in His side"

From the horizon       ancestral

    echoes ring   .

  In the streams of the wound they
  *"want to have little beds, and tables,*
  *and everything else."*

## THESE PAST YEARS     Passages 10

                *6/11*

Willingly I'll say there's been a sweet marriage

      all the time           a ring

    (if wishing could make it so)   a meeting

     in mind       round       the moon

means rain.

In the beginning there was weeping,

an inconsolable grief

I brought   .   the storm I came in,

the driving rain
 the night-long
  torrents of wind.

Was that *that* time?   Or was it

another time   .   all the time      the torrents

of love-making,      hiding my inconsolable grief

in your arms.      Sometimes

when I am away from you

I have to make that journey,

the journey to you      as if blindly      again

along steps I have memorized—

not to forget,      not to forget   .   the way

the way you are,

having no more weight nor strength to go by

than my will,   my wraith,

calling-up the steps   .   to the house, the door, the stairs,
the hall, the room's dimensions, the

where you are

to come to you   .

my helplessness that   must somehow be a help

for you   .

Willingly I'll say there's been a sweet

marriage

and I would fill your arms

as if with flowers      with my forever

being there   .

"French doors

opening out upon a porch which
links the house with the garden."

*"There is really no circumstance of human life,*
*in which He has not at times been our forerunner."*

## MY MOTHER WOULD BE A FALCONRESS

My mother would be a falconress,
And I, her gay falcon treading her wrist,
would fly to bring back
from the blue of the sky to her, bleeding, a prize,
where I dream in my little hood with many bells
jangling when I'd turn my head.

My mother would be a falconress,
and she sends me as far as her will goes.
She lets me ride to the end of her curb
where I fall back in anguish.
I dread that she will cast me away,
for I fall, I mis-take, I fail in her mission.

She would bring down the little birds.
And I would bring down the little birds.
When will she let me bring down the little birds,
pierced from their flight with their necks broken,
their heads like flowers limp from the stem?

I tread my mother's wrist and would draw blood.
Behind the little hood my eyes are hooded.
I have gone back into my hooded silence,
talking to myself and dropping off to sleep.

For she has muffled my dreams in the hood she has made me,
sewn round with bells, jangling when I move.
She rides with her little falcon upon her wrist.
She uses a barb that brings me to cower.

She sends me abroad to try my wings
and I come back to her.  I would bring down
the little birds to her
I may not tear into, I must bring back perfectly.

I tear at her wrist with my beak to draw blood,
and her eye holds me, anguisht, terrifying.
She draws a limit to my flight.
Never beyond my sight, she says.

She trains me to fetch and to limit myself in fetching.
She rewards me with meat for my dinner.
But I must never eat what she sends me to bring her.

Yet it would have been beautiful, if she would have carried me,
always, in a little hood with the bells ringing,
at her wrist, and her riding
to the great falcon hunt, and me
flying up to the curb of my heart from her heart
to bring down the skylark from the blue to her feet,
straining, and then released for the flight.

My mother would be a falconress,
and I her gerfalcon, raised at her will,
from her wrist sent flying, as if I were her own
pride, as if her pride
knew no limits, as if her mind
sought in me flight beyond the horizon.

Ah, but high, high in the air I flew.
And far, far beyond the curb of her will,
were the blue hills where the falcons nest.
And then I saw west to the dying sun—
it seemd my human soul went down in flames.

I tore at her wrist, at the hold she had for me,
until the blood ran hot and I heard her cry out,
far, far beyond the curb of her will    .

to horizons of stars beyond the ringing hills of the world where
      the falcons nest
I saw, and I tore at her wrist with my savage beak.

I flew, as if sight flew from the anguish in her eye beyond her sight,
sent from my striking loose, from the cruel strike at her wrist,
striking out from the blood to be free of her.

My mother would be a falconress,
and even now, years after this,
when the wounds I left her had surely heald,
and the woman is dead,
her fierce eyes closed, and if her heart
were broken, it is stilld    .

I would be a falcon and go free.
I tread her wrist and wear the hood,
talking to myself, and would draw blood.

## *from* DANTE

*Book One, III (1)*

I know a little language of my cat, tho Dante says
that animals have no need of speech and Nature
abhors the superfluous.  My cat is fluent.  He
converses when he wants with me.  To speak

is natural.  And whales and wolves I've heard
in choral soundings of the sea and air
know harmony and have an eloquence that stirs
my mind and heart, they touch the soul.  Here

Dante's religion that would set man apart
damns the effluence of our life from us
to build therein its powerhouse.

It's in his animal communication man is
        true, immediate, and
in immediacy, man is all animal.

His senses quicken in the thick of the symphony,
    old circuits of animal rapture and alarm,
attentions and arousals in which an identity rearrives,
    he hears
particular voices among
    the concert, the slightest
rustle in the undertones,
    rehearsing a nervous aptitude
yet to prove *his*. He sees the flick
    of significant red within the rushing mass
of ruddy wilderness   and catches the glow
    of a green shirt
to delite him in a glowing field of green
    —it *speaks* to him,
and in the arc of the spectrum color
    speaks to color.
The rainbow articulates
    a promise he remembers,
he but imitates
    in noises that he makes
this speech in every sense
    the world surrounding him.

He picks up on the fugitive tang of mace
    amidst the savory mass,
    and taste in evolution is an everlasting key.
    There is a pun of *scents* in what makes sense.

    Myrrh it may have been
the odor of the announcement that filld the house.

    He wakes from deepest sleep

upon a distant signal   and waits

    as if crouching,   springs

    to life.

# LAWRENCE FERLINGHETTI (1919)

## *from* PICTURES OF A GONE WORLD

1
Away above a harborful
of caulkless houses
among the charley noble chimneypots
of a rooftop rigged with clotheslines
a woman pastes up sails
upon the wind
hanging out her morning sheets
with wooden pins
O lovely mammal
her nearly naked teats
throw taut shadows
when she stretches up
to hang at last the last of her
so white washed sins
but it is wetly amorous
and winds itself about her
clinging to her skin
So caught with arms upraised
she tosses back her head
in voiceless laughter
and in choiceless gesture then
shakes out gold hair

while in the reachless seascape spaces

between the blown white shrouds

stand out the bright steamers

to kingdom come

8

Sarolla's women in their picture hats
stretched upon his canvas beaches
beguiled the Spanish
Impressionists

And were they fraudulent pictures
of the world
the way the light played on them
creating illusions
of love?

I cannot help but think
that their 'reality'
was almost as real as
my memory of today

when the last sun hung on the hills
and I heard the day falling
like the gulls that fell
almost to land

while the last picnickers lay
and loved in the blowing yellow broom
resisted and resisting
tearing themselves apart

again

again

until the last hot hung climax
which could at last no longer be resisted
made them moan

And night's trees stood up

## *from* A CONEY ISLAND OF THE MIND

1

In Goya's greatest scenes we seem to see
                              the people of the world
           exactly at the moment when
                they first attained the title of
                                'suffering humanity'
                They writhe upon the page
                              in a veritable rage
                                of adversity
           Heaped up
                    groaning with babies and bayonets
                                        under cement skies
                in an abstract landscape of blasted trees
                bent statues bats wings and beaks
                         slippery gibbets
                cadavers and carnivorous cocks
                and all the final hollering monsters
                    of the
                              'imagination of disaster'
            they are so bloody real
                              it is as if they really still existed

      And they do

            Only the landscape is changed

They still are ranged along the roads
           plagued by legionaires
                              false windmills and demented roosters


They are the same people
                           only further from home
      on freeways fifty lanes wide
                      on a concrete continent
                      spaced with bland billboards
                 illustrating imbecile illusions of happiness

The scene shows fewer tumbrils
                    but more maimed citizens
                            in painted cars
     and they have strange license plates
   and engines
              that devour America


15
Constantly risking absurdity
                      and death
        whenever he performs
                 above the heads
                        of his audience
the poet like an acrobat
             climbs on rime
                to a high wire of his own making
and balancing on eyebeams
                above a sea of faces
       paces his way
             to the other side of day
     performing entrechats
             and sleight-of-foot tricks
and other high theatrics
             and all without mistaking
      any thing
           for what it may not be

For he's the super realist
             who must perforce perceive
     taut truth
         before the taking of each stance or step
   in his supposed advance
            toward that still higher perch
where Beauty stands and waits
          with gravity
            to start her death-defying leap

And he
     a little charleychaplin man
          who may or may not catch
    her fair eternal form
         spreadeagled in the empty air
   of existence

20
The pennycandystore beyond the El
is where I first
                    fell in love
                            with unreality
Jellybeans glowed in the semi-gloom
of that september afternoon
A cat upon the counter moved among
                            the licorice sticks
                and tootsie rolls
        and Oh Boy Gum

Outside the leaves were falling as they died

A wind had blown away the sun

A girl ran in
Her hair was rainy
Her breasts were breathless in the little room

Outside the leaves were falling
                    and they cried
                            Too soon!  too soon!

# HE

*(To the Allen Ginsberg of the 1950s, before "The Change")*

He is one of the prophets come back
He is one of the wiggy prophets come back
He had a beard in the Old Testament
    but shaved it off in Paterson
He has a microphone around his neck
    at a poetry reading
    and he is more than one poet
    and he is an old man perpetually writing a poem
    about an old man
    whose every third thought is Death
    and who is writing a poem

about an old man
whose every third thought is Death
and who is writing a poem
Like the picture on a Quaker Oats box
that shows a figure holding up a box
upon which is a picture of a figure
holding up a box
and the figure smaller and smaller
and further away each time
a picture of shrinking reality itself
He is one of the prophets come back
to see to hear to file a revised report
on the present state
of the shrinking world
He has buttonhooks in his eyes
with which he fastens on
to every foot of existence
and onto every shoestring rumor
of the nature of reality
And his eye fixes itself
on every stray person or thing
and waits for it to move
like a cat with a dead white mouse
suspecting it of hiding
some small clew to existence
and he waits gently
for it to reveal itself
or herself or himself
and he is gentle as the lamb of God
made into mad cutlets
And he picks up every suspicious object
and he picks up every person or thing
examining it and shaking it
like a white mouse with a piece of string
who thinks the thing is alive
and shakes it to speak
and shakes it alive
and shakes it to speak
He is a cat who creeps at night
and sleeps his buddhahood in the violet hour
and listens for the sound of three hands about to clap
and reads the script of his brainpan
his hieroglyph of existence

He is a talking asshole on a stick
   he is a walkie-talkie on two legs
   and he holds his phone to his ear
   and he holds his phone to his mouth
   and hears *Death death*
He has one head with one tongue hung
   in the back of his mouth
   and he speaks with an animal tongue
   and man has devised a language
   that no other animal understands
   and his tongue sees and his tongue speaks
   and his own ear hears what is said
   and clings to his head
   and hears *Death death*
   and he has a tongue to say it
   that no other animal understands
He is a forked root walking
   with a knot-hole eye in the middle of his head
   and his eye turns outward and inward
   and sees and is mad
   and is mad and sees
And he is the mad eye of the fourth person singular
   of which nobody speaks
   and he is the voice of the fourth person singular
   in which nobody speaks
   and which yet exists
   with a long head and a foolscap face
   and the long mad hair of death
   of which nobody speaks
And he speaks of himself and he speaks of the dead
   of his dead mother and his Aunt Rose
   with their long hair and their long nails
   that grow and grow
   and they come back to his speech without a manicure
And he has come back with his black hair
   and his black eye and his black shoes
   and the big black book of his report
And he is a big black bird with one foot raised
   to hear the sound of life reveal itself
   on the shell of his sensorium
   and he speaks to sing to get out of his skin
   and he pecks with his tongue on the shell of it
   and he knocks with his eye on the shell

and sees *light light* and hears *death death*
of which nobody speaks
For he is a head with a head's vision
and his is the lizard's look
and his unbuttoned vision is the door
in which he stands and waits and hears
the hand that knocks and claps and claps and knocks
his *Death Death*
For he is his own ecstatic illumination
and he is his own hallucination
and he is his own shrinker
and his eye turns in the shrinking head of the world
and hears his organ speak *Death Death*
a deaf music
For he has come at the end of the world
and he is the flippy flesh made word
and he speaks the word he hears in his flesh
and the word is *Death*

> *Death  Death*

> *Death  Death*

> *Death Death*

> *Death Death*

> *Death*

> *Death  Death*

> *Death  Death*

> *Death  Death*

> *Death Death*

> *Death  Death*

*Death  Death*

> *Death  Death*

> *Death  Death*

> *Death  Death*

*Death*

## POUND AT SPOLETO

I walked into a loge in the Teatro Melisso, the lovely Renaissance salle
where the poetry readings and the chamber concerts were held every day
of the Spoleto Festival, and suddenly saw Ezra Pound for the first time,
still as a mandarin statue in a box in a balcony at the back of the
theatre, one tier up from the stalls. It was a shock, seeing only a striking
old man in a curious pose, thin and long haired, aquiline at 80, head tilted
strangely to one side, lost in permanent abstraction. . . . After three
younger poets on stage, he was scheduled to read from his box, and there
he sat with an old friend (who held his papers) waiting. He regarded the
knuckles of his hands, moving them a very little, expressionless. Only
once, when everyone else in the full theatre applauded someone on stage,
did he rouse himself to clap, without looking up, as if stimulated by sound
in a void. . . . After almost an hour, his turn came. Or after a life. . . .
Everyone in the hall rose, turned and looked back and up at Pound in his
booth, applauding. The applause was prolonged and Pound tried to rise
from his armchair. A microphone was partly in the way. He grasped the
arms of the chair with his bony hands and tried to rise. He could not
and he tried again and could not. His old friend did not try to help him.
Finally she put a poem in his hand, and after at least a minute his voice
came out. First the jaw moved and then the voice came out, inaudible.
A young Italian pulled the mike up very close to his face and held it there
and the voice came over, frail but stubborn, higher than I had expected,
a thin, soft monotone. The hall had gone silent at a stroke. The voice
knocked me down, so soft, so thin, so frail, so stubborn still. I put my
head on my arms on the velvet sill of the box. I was surprised to see a
single tear drop on my knee. The thin, indomitable voice went on. I
went blind from the box, through the back door of it, into the empty
corridor of the theatre where they still sat turned to him, went down
and out, into the sunlight, weeping. . . .

> Up above the town
> >             by the ancient aqueduct
> >     the chestnut trees
> >             were still in bloom
> >         Mute birds
> >             flew in the valley
> >                 far below
> >         The sun shone
> >             on the chestnut trees
> >     and the leaves

                    turned in the sun
            and turned and turned and turned
                And would continue turning
        His voice
                went on
                    and on
                        through the leaves. . . .


## LOST PARENTS


It takes a fast car
                    to lead a double life
in these days of short-distance love affairs
    when he has far-out lovers in
                        three different locations
    and a date with each one
                    at least twice a week
    a little simple arithmetic shows
            what a workout he's engaged in
crossing & recrossing the city
        from bedroom to patio to swimming pool
the ignition key hot
    and the backseat a jumble of clothes
                        for different life-styles
    a surfboard on the roof
    and a copy of Kahlil Gibran or Rod McKuen
                    under the dashboard
            next to the Indian music cassettes
    packs of Tarot and the I-Ching
                    crammed into the glove compartment
        along with old traffic tickets
                        and hardpacks of Kents
            dents attesting to the passion
                            of his last lover
And his answering service
        catching him on the freeway
            between two calls or two encounter groups
    and the urgent message left

          with an unlisted number to call Carol
            about the bottle of fine wine
              he forgot to pick up
              and dèliver to the gallery
                for the reception at nine
While she shuttles to her gynecologist
            and will meet him later
              between two other numbers
                                male or female
          including his wife
              who also called twice
wanting to know where he's been
            and what he's done
                    with their throw-away children
          who
              left to their own devices
                in a beach house at Malibu
          grew up and dropped out into Nothing
            in a Jungian search
                      for lost parents
                          their own age




## THE SEA AND OURSELVES AT CAPE ANN


Caw Caw Caw
on a far shingle long ago
when as a boy I came here
put ear to shell
              of the thundering sea
                          sundering sea
          seagulls high over
                    calling & calling
              back then
                    at Cape Ann Gloucester
Where Olson saw himself Ishmael
    and wrote his own epitaph:
                    'I set out now
                      in a box upon the sea'

And Creeley found his creel
            yet would not/cd. not
                        speak of the sea
And Ferrini took the wind's clothes
        and became the conscience of Gloucester
Yet none could breathe
                        a soul into the sea
And I saw the tide pools gasping
    the sea's mouth roaring
                        polyphoboistrous
        beyond the Ten Pound Light
                        roistering
                        off far islands
        'Les Trois Sauvages'
Where Eliot heard
                the sea's stark meditation
    off *beauport* Gloucester
Where I as a man much later
            made a landfall in the gloaming
    sighting from seaward in convoy
                beyond the gulls' far off
                        tattered cries
            cats' cries lost
                reached to us
                    in shredded snatches
        Then as now
Eliot must
        have been a seaman
                    in his city-soul
    to have heard so deeply
                the sea's voice sounding then
                    in 'The Dry Salvages'
Here now
        where now
                is the sea's urge still
        sea's surge and thunder
                    except within us
                folded under
    by the beach road now
                    rapt in darkness
The sea still a great door never opened
        great ships asunder
                    clinker-built bottoms

nets hung with cork
　　hulls heavy with caulking
While still the Nor'easter blows
　　still the high tides
　　　seethe & sweep shoreward
　batter the breakwaters
　　　the granite harbors
　　　　　rock villages
　Land's End lashed again
　　　　in 'the sudden fury'
And still the stoned gulls soaring over
　　　　crying & calling & crying
　blissed-out up there
　　　　in the darkening air
　over the running sea
　　　　the runing sea
　　over dark stone beach under stars
Where now we sit
　　　'distracted from distraction' still
　*Odyssey* turned to *Iliad*
　　　　in parked cars

# BARBARA GUEST (1920)


## SANTA FE TRAIL


I go separately
The sweet knees of oxen have pressed a path for me
ghosts with ingots have burned their bare hands
it is the dungaree darkness with China stitched
where the westerly winds
and the traveler's checks
the evensong of salesmen
the glistening paraphernalia of twin suitcases
where no one speaks English.
I go separately
It is the wind, the rubber wind
when we brush our teeth in the way station
a climate to beard. What forks these roads?
Who clammers o'er the twain?
What murmurs and rustles in the distance
in the white branches where the light is whipped
piercing at the crossing as into the dunes we simmer
and toss ourselves awhile the motor pants like a forest
where owls from their bandaged eyes send messages
to the Indian couple. Peaks have you heard?
I go separately
We have reached the arithmetics, are partially quenched
while it growls and hints in the lost trapper's voice
She is coming toward us like a session of pines
in the wild, wooden air where rabbits are frozen
O mother of lakes and glaciers save us gamblers
whose wagon is perilously rapt.

*1958*

## 20


Sleep is 20
            remembering the
insignificant flamenco dancer
in Granada
            who became
important as you watched
the mountain ridge
            the dry hills

What an idiotic number!

Sleep is twenty

it certainly isn't twenty sheep
there weren't that many in the herd
under the cold crest of Sierra Nevada

It's more like 20 Madison Ave. buses
while I go droning away at my dream life
Each episode is important
that's what it is!  Sequences—
I've got going a twenty-act drama
the theatre of the active
the critics are surely there
even the actors
even the flowers presented onstage
even the wild flowers
picked by the wife of the goatherd
each morning early (while I sleep)
under the snow cone
of Sierra Nevada

                yellow caps like castanets
                I reach into my bouquet
                half-dreaming
                and count twenty
                yellow capped heads

flowers clicking twenty times
because they like to repeat themselves

as I do as does the morning
or the drama one hopes
will be acted many times

As even these dreams in similar
people's heads

20

castanets

## PARADE'S END

The most that can be said
for following the parade
is that the Head was red.

Liking grotesque the architect
went along with it,
the balloons and the bellies
enlarged.

He had a craze for size,
so he said.

Looking at it from the sidelines
we weren't so amused
as chilled by the snow wind,
our feet getting smaller
in unadaptable leather

our eyes formed truly gigantic tears

we dropped when the last
soldier had passed and the confetti
was buried in the ash can.

It was quite a day. I brought home
an unopened poem. It should grow
in the kitchen near the stove
if I can squeeze out of my eyes
enough water. Water.

## RED LILIES

Someone has remembered to dry the dishes;
they have taken the accident out of the stove.
Afterward lilies for supper; there
the lines in front of the window
are rubbed on the table of stone

The paper flies up
then down as the wind
repeats, repeats its birdsong.

Those arms under the pillow
the burrowing arms they cleave
at night as the tug kneads water
calling themselves branches

The tree is you
the blanket is what warms it
snow erupts from thistle
to toe; the snow pours out of you.

A cold hand on the dishes
placing a saucer inside

her who undressed for supper
gliding that hair to the snow

The pilot light
went out on the stove

The paper folded like a napkin
other wings flew into the stone.

# RIVER ROAD STUDIO

Separations begin with placement
that black organizes the ochre
        both earth colors,

Quietly the blanket assumes its shapes
as the grey day loops along leaving
an edge (turned like leaves into something else),

Absolutes simmer as primary colors
and everyone gropes toward black
where it is believed the strength lingers.

I make a sketch from your window
the rain so prominent earlier
now hesitates and retreats,

We find bicycles natural
under this sky composed of notes,

Then ribbons, they make noises
rushing up and down the depots
at the blur exchanging
its web for a highway.

Quartets the quartets
are really bricks and we are
careful to replace them
until they are truly quartets.

# THE LUMINOUS

Patches of it

        on the lettuce a geography
        on trucks brilliant noises

on the figure a disrobing
radiance like sweaters dumped

on water,

weightlifting there in the forest clumps,
striking at the underbrush,  digging
past the clumsy curves

skipping certain passages,  taking off
the sweaters

that fir cone found its voice on the path
in the light after the sun came out

the postcard illuminates certain features in the face
the notebook lying on the windowsill,
the spindle back, the broken stem, all richer,

niceties tend to drop, also words like "many
loves" come forward like the surprises of white stars

and the boots step by amazingly on the dried rich clay.

He swings his racket after it the luminous
the ball nearly swerves into it

Those ancient peoples learning to count
surrounded by it, every day

and navigators noting it there on the waves

the animus containing bits there on its subject
perched like sails

The bright rewards for preparing to strut forth
like a diver there on the board forced
by his greed into it.

Many loves changes to many times falling into
the day's lucid marshes

A tap on the shoulder or a fish grasping that
object full of sparks

the wilderness untangled by it

the fierceness with which is forged its memory,
its daylight, its absence.

Yes to the point of damages,
yes to the stunning infrequency,
yes to encourage with repetition its repetition
yes to the sober knowledge of its parsimony,

a few fir cones, sails, the stains removed,
blazes from the paper without lifting your hands.

*1977*

# JACK KEROUAC (1922-1969)

## PULL MY DAISY

Pull my daisy
tip my cup
all my doors are open
Cut my thoughts
for coconuts
all my eggs are broken
Jack my Arden
gate my shades
woe my road is spoken
Silk my garden
rose my days
now my prayers awaken

Bone my shadow
dove my dream
start my halo bleeding
Milk my mind &
make me cream
drink me when you're ready
Hop my heart on
harp my height
seraphs hold me steady
Hip my angel
hype my light
lay it on the needy

Heal the raindrop
sow the eye
bust my dust again
Woe the worm
work the wise
dig my spade the same
Stop the hoax
what's the hex
where's the wake
how's the hicks
take my golden beam

Rob my locker
lick my rocks
leap my cock in school
Rack my lacks
lark my looks
jump right up my hole
Whore my door
beat my boor
eat my snake of fool
Craze my hair
bare my poor
asshole shorn of wool

say my oops
ope my shell
Bite my naked nut
Roll my bones
ring my bell
call my worm to sup
Pope my parts
pop my pot
raise my daisy up
Poke my pap
pit my plum
let my gap be shut

*(with Allen Ginsberg and Neal Cassady,
1948-1950?/1961)*


## THE SEA SHROUD

*(A description of my last cartoon)*

The Sea Shroud comes out of a slip
    of water in Brooklyn Harbor, night,
    it emerges from a submerged tug
    right from the enamel underwear
    of the pilot's cabin

Right through up comes the shroud head,
    a draining drape of wet weedy
    watery sea net spray, ephemeral,
    climbing to knock knees against the bow
    and make the bit on the dock

And come on vanishing instead
    reappearing as a Man
    with a briefcase, on Borough Hall,
    saying nothing with a watery face
    saying nothing with an ogoo mouth

Saying nothing with a listening nose,
    saying nothing with a questionmark mouth,
    saying nothing, the briefcase full
    of seaweed—what happens to floating
    bonds when they get in the hand of the drape

Sea Shroud, turning Chinese Food to seaweed
    in his all-abominable bag, Shroud
    the taker of widows' monies in red allies
    of shame & stagedoors, purple lagoon
    Goon Shroud departs gloving the money

Earlier in the day he'd perched atop a
    flagpole in a parking lot
    on the waterfront, and looked around
    to see which way Borough Hall
    which way the little white doves


# MY GANG

*Part One*

Many people have been frighted & died in cemeteries
    since the days of my gang, the night
    Zap Plouffe came up & talked to me
    on the block and I rowed the imaginary
    horse on the rowel of the porch rail

Where I killed 700,000 flies or more
    while Ma and Blanche gossipped
    in the kitchen, and while drape sheets
    we airing on the line that's connected
    to midnight by midnight riding roses

Oy—the one bad time that Zaggo
    got home from school late, dark
    in the streets, the sisters majestico
    blooming in the alley retreat, beat,
    'Your gang is upstairs' says my mother

And I go up to my closed smoky door
    and open it to a miniature poolhall
    where all the gang is smoking & yakking
    with little cue sticks and blue chalk
    around a miniature table on stilts

Bets being made, spittings out the window,
    cold out there, old murder magoon
    the winter man in my tree has seen
    to it that inhalator autumn
    prestidigitate on time & in ripe form,
    to wit cold

To wit cold, to wit you, to wit winter
To wit time, to wit bird, to wit dust—
    That was some game ole Lousy blanged
    When he beat G.J. that time,
    and Artaud roared

*Part Two*

Artaud was the cookie that was always
    in my hair, a ripe screaming tight
    brother with heinous helling neck-veins
    who liked to riddle my fantasms
    with yaks of mocksqueak joy

'Why dont you like young Artaud?'
    always I'm asked, because he boasts
    and boasts, brags, brags, ya, ya, ya,
    because he's crazy because he's mad
    and because he never gives us a chance to talk

Awright—I'd like to know what
Billy's got against me—But he wont
tell, and it's brother deep—In the room
they're shooting the break, clack,
the little balls break, scatter di mania,

They take aim on little balls and break
    em up to fall, in plicky pockpockets
    for little children's names drawing
    pictures in the games in the whistle
    of the old corant tree splashing

In the mighty mu Missouri lame image
    of time and again the bride & groom,
    boom & again the bidal bood, oo,
    too-too and rumble o mumble thunden
    bow, ole Lousy is in my alley

Ole Lousy's my alley I'll lay it on me
    I'll shoot fourteen farthings for Father Machree
    and if old Hotsatots dont footsie
    down here bring my gruel, I'll
    be cruel, I'll be cruel

## *from* MEXICO CITY BLUES

211th Chorus

The wheel of the quivering meat
                    conception
Turns in the void expelling human beings,
Pigs, turtles, frogs, insects, nits,
Mice, lice, lizards, rats, roan
Racinghorses, poxy bucolic pigtics,
Horrible unnameable lice of vultures,
Murderous attacking dog-armies
Of Africa, Rhinos roaming in the
                    jungle,

Vast boars and huge gigantic bull
Elephants, rams, eagles, condors,
Pones and Porcupines and Pills—
All the endless conception of living
                              beings
Gnashing everywhere in Consciousness
Throughout the ten directions of space
Occupying all the quarters in & out,
From supermicroscopic no-bug
To buge Galaxy Lightyear Bowell
Illuminating the sky of one Mind—
        *Poor!* I wish I was free
        of that slaving meat wheel
        and safe in heaven dead


229th Chorus


In the ocean there's a very sad turtle
(Even tho the SS *Mainline* Fishin Ship
        is reeling in the merit like mad)
Swims longmouthed & sad, looking
        for the Impossible Except Once
        afternoon when the Yoke, Oh,
        the old Buddha Yoke set a-floatin
        is in the water where the turtle raises
        his be-watery snop to the sea
        and the Yoke yokes the Turtle
            a Eternity—
"Tell me O Bhikkus,
        what are the chances,
            of such a happening,
                for the turtle is old
                and the yoke free,
                and the 7 oceans bigger
                    than any we see
                    in this tiny party."
Chances are slender—
        In a million million billion kotis
        of Aeons and Incalculables, Yes,
        the Turtle will set that Yoke free,
        but till then, harder yet

are the chances, for a man
to be reborn a man
in this Karma earth


## HOW TO MEDITATE


           —lights out—
fall, hands a-clasped, into instantaneous
ecstasy like a shot of heroin or morphine,
the gland inside of my brain discharging
the good glad fluid (Holy Fluid) as
I hap-down and hold all my body parts
down to a deadstop trance—Healing
all my sicknesses—erasing all—not
even the shred of a "I-hope-you" or a
Loony Balloon left in it, but the mind
blank, serene, thoughtless. When a thought
comes a-springing from afar with its held-
forth figure of image, you spoof it out,
you spuff it off, you fake it, and
it fades, and thought never comes—and
with joy you realize for the first time
"Thinking's just like not thinking—
So I don't have to think
    any
    more"

                                         *1967*

# JACKSON MAC LOW (1922)


## ZEN BUDDHISM AND PSYCHOANALYSIS
## PSYCHOANALYSIS AND ZEN BUDDHISM


(Secondary experience, nouns
Both used determine determine hearsay.) (Indirect secondary makes
Activity nouns determine
Principle secondary indirect conjugation hearsay.) Occurs activity Latin
       indirect secondary indirect secondary
(Principle sense is conjugation hearsay.) (Occurs activity nouns activity
       Latin is sense is sense
Activity nouns determine
Sense experience, nouns
*Being* used determine determine hearsay.) Is sense makes


Strictly exclude name
Books utterly dialectics dialectics Heraclitus' Indian strictly make
A non-A dialectics
*Paradoxical* strictly Indian Chinese Heraclitus' other A non-A A *logic*
       Indian strictly Indian strictly
Predicates seem is Chuang-tsu: Heraclitus' (Oxford A non-A A *logic*, is
       seem is seem
A non-A dialectics
Seem exclude name
Books University dialectics dialectics Heraclitus' is seem make


Symptom.) Exactly not
Become unconscious develop develop have impulse symptom members
Awareness. Not develop
Peaceful symptom impulse contrary have other awareness. Not awareness.
       Let impulse symptom impulse symptom
Penetrate symptom impulse contrary have one. Awareness. Needs,
       awareness. Let impulse symptom impulse symptom
Awareness. Needs, develop
Symptom expresses needs,
Become one. Develop develop have impulse symptom members


Statements effective not
Be unrelated dying, dying, human impulses. Statements made

Answer not dying,
Put statements impulses. Completely human obvious aware not aware
    language, impulses. Statements impulses. Statements
Put statements impulses. Castration humanity, openness answer nature
    answer language, impulses. Statements impulses. Statements
Answer nature dying,
Statements. Experiences nature
Be unconsciousness dying, dying, humanity, impulses. Statements made

Speak

## 2nd LIGHT POEM: FOR DIANE WAKOSKI
## (10 JUNE 1962)

I

Old light & owl-light
may be opal light
in the small
orifice
where old light
& the will-o'-the-wisp
make no announcement of waning
light

but with direct directions
& the winking light of the will-o'-the-wisp's accoutrements
& lilac light
a delightful phenomenon
a delightful phenomenon of lucence & lucidity needing no announcement
even of lilac light
my present activities may be seen in the old light of my accoutrements
as a project in owl-light.

II

A bulky, space-suited figure
from the whole cloth of my present activities
with a taste for mythology in opal light
& such a manner

in the old light from some being outside

as if this being's old light cd have brought such a manner
to a bulky, space-suited figure
from the whole world of my present activities
at this time
when my grief gives owl-light
only
not an opal light
& not a very old light

neither
old light nor owl-light
makes it have such a manner about it
tho opal light & old light & marsh light & moonlight
& that of the whole world
to which the light of meteors is marsh light
all light it
no it's
an emerald light
in the light from the eyes that are making it whole from the whole cloth
with no announcement this time.


    III

What is extra light?
A delightful phenomenon.
A delightful phenomenon having no announcement?
No more than the emerald light has.
Is that the will-o'-the-wisp?
No, it's the waning light of my grief.
Is it a winking light?
No more than it is the will-o'-the-wisp.
Is it old light?
The oldest in the whole world.
Why do you speak in such a manner?
I suppose, because of the owl-light.
Is it a kind of opal light?
No, I said it was old light.
Is it a cold light?
More like a chemical light with the usual accoutrements.
Like the carmine light produced by my present activities?
More of a cold light than that.

Like what might fall on a bulky, space-suited figure?
Well, it's neither red light nor reflected light.
Are you making this up out of the whole cloth?
No, I'm trying to give you direct directions.
For avoiding a bulky, space-suited figure?
No, for getting light from a rhodochrosite.


### IV.

This time I'm going to talk about red light.
First of all, it's not very much like emerald light.
Nevertheless, there's still some of it in Pittsburgh.
It adds to the light from the eyes an extra light.
This is also true of emerald light.
But red light better suits those with a taste for mythology.
As reflected light it is often paler than the light from a rhodochrosite.
Such a red light might fall on a bulky, space-suited figure.
In just such a manner might this being be illuminated during a time gambol.

---

NOTE: A rhodochrosite is a vitreous rose-red or variously colored gem-stone having a hardness of 4.5 & a density of 3.8 & consisting of manganous carbonate ($MnCO_3$) crystallized in the rhombohedral system.

# DENISE LEVERTOV (1923)

## THE HANDS

          Don't forget the crablike
hands, slithering
        among the keys.
                Eyes shut, the downstream
       play of sound lifts away from
the present, drifts you
            off your feet : too easily let off.

       So look:  that almost painful
       movement restores the pull, incites
           the head with the heart : a tension, as of
           actors at rehearsal, who move
this way, that way, on a bare stage, testing
         their diagonals, in common clothes.

## THE WAY THROUGH

Let the rain plunge radiant
through sulky thunder
rage on rooftops

let it scissor and bounce its denials
on concrete slabs and black
roadways. Flood the streets. It's much

but not enough, not yet:  persist,
rain, real rain, sensuous,
swift, released from

      vague skies, the tedium
up there.

Under scared bucking trees
the beach road washed out —

trying to get by on the verge
is no good, earth crumbles into the
brown waterfall, but he backs up
the old car again and CHARGES.

The water flies in the halfwit's eyes
who didn't move fast enough
"Who do you think I am, a horse?"
but we made it —

Drown us, lose us,
rain, let us loose, so,
to lose ourselves, to career
up the plunge of the hill


## MERRITT PARKWAY

As if it were
forever that they move, that we
keep moving —

Under a wan sky where
as the lights went on a star
pierced the haze and now
follows steadily
a constant
above our six lanes
the dreamlike continuum ...

And the people — ourselves!
the humans from inside the
cars, apparent
only at gasoline stops
unsure,
eyeing each other

drink coffee hastily at the
slot machines and hurry
back to the cars
    vanish
    into them forever, to
    keep moving—

Houses now & then beyond the
sealed road, the trees / trees, bushes
passing by, passing
    the cars that
        keep moving ahead of
    us, past us, pressing behind us
                    and
        over left, those that come
      toward us shining too brightly
moving relentlessly

    in six lanes, gliding
north and south, speeding with
a slurred sound —


# SCENES FROM THE LIFE OF THE PEPPERTREES


    I
The peppertrees, the peppertrees!

Cats are stretching in the doorways,
sure of everything. It is morning.
    But the peppertrees
stand aside in diffidence, with berries
of modest red.
        Branch above branch, an air
of lightness; of shadows
scattered lightly.
      A cat
closes upon its shadow.

Up and up goes the sun,
sure of everything.
    The peppertrees
              shiver a little.
Robust
and soot-black, the cat
leaps to a low branch. Leaves
close about him.


      II
The yellow moon dreamily
tipping buttons of light
down among the leaves. Marimba,
marimba — from beyond the
black street.
            Somebody dancing,
somebody
        getting the hell
outta here. Shadows of cats
weave round the tree trunks,
the exposed knotty roots.


      III
The man on the bed sleeping
defenseless. Look —
his bare long feet together
sideways, keeping each other
warm. And the foreshortened shoulders,
the head
barely visible. He is good.
Let him sleep.
              But the third peppertree
   is restless, twitching
thin leaves in the light
of afternoon. After a while
it walks over and taps
on the upstairs window with a bunch
of red berries. Will he wake?

# THE GODDESS

She in whose lipservice
I passed my time,
whose name I knew, but not her face,
came upon me where I lay in Lie Castle!

Flung me across the room, and
room after room (hitting the walls, re-
bounding—to the last
sticky wall—wrenching away from it
pulled hair out!)
till I lay
outside the outer walls!

There in cold air
lying still where her hand had thrown me,
I tasted the mud that splattered my lips:
the seeds of a forest were in it,
asleep and growing! I tasted
her power!

The silence was answering my silence,
a forest was pushing itself
out of sleep between my submerged fingers.

I bit on a seed and it spoke on my tongue
of day that shone already among stars
in the water-mirror of low ground,
and a wind rising ruffled the lights:
she passed near me returning from the encounter,
she who plucked me from the close rooms,

without whom nothing
flowers, fruits, sleeps in season,
without whom nothing
speaks in its own tongue, but returns
lie for lie!

## TO THE READER

As you read, a white bear leisurely
pees, dyeing the snow
saffron,

and as you read, many gods
lie among lianas: eyes of obsidian
are watching the generations of leaves,

and as you read
the sea is turning its dark pages,
turning
its dark pages.

## A COMMON GROUND

I

To stand on common ground
here and there gritty with pebbles
yet elsewhere 'fine and mellow—
uncommon fine for ploughing'

there to labor
planting the vegetable words
diversely in their order
that they come to virtue!

To reach those shining pebbles,
that soil where uncommon men
have labored in their virtue
and left a store

of seeds for planting!
To crunch on words
grown in grit or fine
crumbling earth, sweet

to eat and sweet
to be given, to be eaten
in common, by laborer
and hungry wanderer . . .


        II
In time of blossoming,
of red
buds, of red
margins upon
white petals among the
new green, of coppery
leaf-buds still weakly
folded, fuzzed
with silver hairs—

when on the grass verges
or elephant-hide rocks, the lunch hour
expands, the girls
laugh at the sun, men
in business suits awkwardly
recline, the petals
float and fall into
crumpled wax-paper, cartons
of hot-coffee—

to speak as the sun's
deep tone of May gold speaks
or the spring chill in the rock's shadow,
a piercing minor scale running across the flesh
aslant—or petals
that dream their way
(speaking by being white
by being
curved, green-centered, falling
already while their tree
is half-red with buds) into

human lives! Poems stirred
into paper coffee-cups, eaten
with petals on rye in the
sun—the cold shadows in back,

and the traffic grinding the
borders of spring—entering
human lives forever,
unobserved, a spring element . . .


III

> . . . everything in the world must
> excel itself to be itself.
>
> *Pasternak*

Not 'common speech'
a dead level
but the uncommon speech of paradise,
tongue in which oracles
speak to beggars and pilgrims:

not illusion but what Whitman called
'the path
between reality and the soul,'
a language
excelling itself to be itself,

speech akin to the light
with which at day's end and day's
renewal, mountains
sing to each other across the cold valleys.


# THE JACOB'S LADDER

The stairway is not
a thing of gleaming strands
a radiant evanescence
for angels' feet that only glance in their tread, and need not
touch the stone.

It is of stone.
A rosy stone that takes
a glowing tone of softness

only because behind it the sky is a doubtful, a doubting
night gray.

A stairway of sharp
angles, solidly built.
One sees that the angels must spring
down from one step to the next, giving a little
lift of the wings:

and a man climbing
must scrape his knees, and bring
the grip of his hands into play. The cut stone
consoles his groping feet. Wings brush past him.
The poem ascends.

## SONG FOR ISHTAR

The moon is a sow
and grunts in my throat
Her great shining shines through me
so the mud of my hollow gleams
and breaks in silver bubbles

She is a sow
and I a pig and a poet

When she opens her white
lips to devour me I bite back
and laughter rocks the moon

In the black of desire
we rock and grunt, grunt and
shine

## THE ACHE OF MARRIAGE

The ache of marriage:

thigh and tongue, beloved,
are heavy with it,
it throbs in the teeth

We look for communion
and are turned away, beloved,
each and each

It is leviathan and we
in its belly
looking for joy, some joy
not to be known outside it

two by two in the ark of
the ache of it.

## OVERHEARD

A deep wooden note
when the wind blows,
the west wind.
The rock maple is it,
close to the house?
Or a beam, voice
of the house itself?
A groan, but not
gloomy, rather
as escaped note of
almost unbearable
satisfaction, a great
bough or beam
unaware it had
spoken.

## HYPOCRITE WOMEN

Hypocrite women, how seldom we speak
of our own doubts, while dubiously
we mother man in his doubt!

And if at Mill Valley perched in the trees
the sweet rain drifting through western air
a white sweating bull of a poet told us

our cunts are ugly—why didn't we
admit we have thought so too? (And
what shame? They are not for the eye!)

No, they are dark and wrinkled and hairy,
caves of the Moon . . .       And when a
dark humming fills us, a

coldness towards life,
we are too much women to
own to such unwomanliness.

Whorishly with the psychopomp
we play and plead—and say
nothing of this later.       And our dreams,

with what frivolity we have pared them
like toenails, clipped them like ends of
split hair.


## LOSING TRACK

Long after you have swung back
away from me
I think you are still with me:

you come in close to the shore
on the tide
and nudge me awake the way

a boat adrift nudges the pier:
am I a pier
half-in half-out of the water?

and in the pleasure of that communion
I lose track,
the moon I watch goes down, the

tide swings you away before
I know I'm
alone again long since,

mud sucking at gray and black
timbers of me,
a light growth of green dreams drying.

## CANCION

When I am the sky
a glittering bird
slashes at me with the knives of song.

When I am the sea
fiery clouds plunge into my mirrors,
fracture my smooth breath with crimson sobbing.

When I am the earth
I feel my flesh of rock wearing down:
pebbles, grit, finest dust, nothing.

When I am a woman—O, when I am
a woman,
my wells of salt brim and brim,
poems force the lock of my throat.

# JAMES SCHUYLER (1923)

## "THE ELIZABETHANS CALLED IT DYING"

Beyond Nagel's Funeral Parlor
      ("Your cousin says you filled her station wagon up;
      I didn't say it your cousin said it")
and (is it a perpetual wake they have
or just a popular parlor? )
      the novelty ice cream cake and soda shop
      the boys hang out in front of
      until they're eighteen then move across the street
in front of the saloon      Munich beer on draught
not forgetting the big church with the doleful bells
cheerily summoning housewives to early Mass
      ("The good thing about religion is
      it gives a man a sense of his place in the universe")
to Carl Schurz Park
kept reasonably free of la-di-da
after all the Mayor lives in it
in the huge glare of the electric sign on Doctors' Hospital
that says HOSPITAL
what are they trying to do, solicit trade in Queens?
or is that Welfare Island?
the river races upstream, neap tide turned
past the posh apartments
      did you ever sit back and try to remember
      whether particular paving stones were hex- or octagons?
      seen once at night and presumably memorized
         sloshing around in the rain
your eyes lips and nostrils
vary a distinct and unique shape—
      why it's The Raindrop Prelude!
home—
      not to be in love with you
I can't remember what it was like
      it must've been lousy

## CROCUS NIGHT

> *The fire had struggled from my hand*
> Susan Coolidge

The heavy umbrellas
aren't worth their weight.
Doors swing and slam
checked by gusts. A whisperer
has a friendly reek.
A hell broth!
and hollows among clouds.
Then the moon goes crocus.

## BURIED AT SPRINGS

There is a hornet in the room
and one of us will have to go
out the window into the late
August midafternoon sun. I
won. There is a certain challenge
in being humane to hornets
but not much. A launch draws
two lines of wake behind it
on the bay like a delta
with a melted base. Sandy
billows, or so they look,
of feathery ripe heads of grass,
an acid-yellow kind of
goldenrod glowing or glowering
in shade. Rocks with rags
of shadow, washed dust clouts
that will never bleach.
It is not like this at all.
The rapid running of the
lapping water a hollow knock
of someone shipping oars:
it's eleven years since
Frank sat at this desk and

saw and heard it all
the incessant water the
immutable crickets only
not the same: new needles
on the spruce, new seaweed
on the low-tide rocks
other grass and other water
even the great gold lichen
on a granite boulder
even the boulder quite
literally is not the same

## II

A day subtle and suppressed
in mounds of juniper enfolding
scratchy pockets of shadow
while bigness—rocks, trees, a stump—
stand shadowless in an overcast
of ripe grass. There is nothing
but shade, like the boggy depths
of a stand of spruce, its resonance
just the thin scream
of mosquitoes ascending.
Boats are light lumps on the bay
stretching past erased islands
to ocean and the terrible tumble
and London ("rain persisting")
and Paris ("changing to rain").
Delicate day, setting the bright
of a young spruce against the cold
of an old one hung with unripe cones
each exuding at its tip
gum, pungent, clear as a tear,
a day tarnished and fractured
as the quartz in the rocks
of a dulled and distant point,
a day like a gull passing
with a slow flapping of wings
in a kind of lope, without
breeze enough to shake loose
the last of the fireweed flowers,
a faintly clammy day, like wet silk
stained by one dead branch
the harsh russet of dried blood.

## THE CRYSTAL LITHIUM


The smell of snow, stinging in nostrils as the wind lifts it from a beach
Eye-shuttering, mixed with sand, or when snow lies under the street lamps
        and on all
And the air is emptied to an uplifting gassiness
That turns lungs to winter waterwings, buoying, and the bright white night
Freezes in sight a lapse of waves, balsamic, salty, unexpected:
Hours after swimming, sitting thinking biting at a hangnail
And the taste of the—to your eyes—invisible crystals irradiates the world
"The sea is salt"
"And so am I"
"Don't bite your nails"
                        and the metal flavor of a nail—are these brads? —
Taken with a slight spitting motion from between teeth and whanged into
        place
(Boards and sawdust) and the nail set is ridged with cold
Permanently as marble, always degrees cooler than the rooms of air it lies in
Felt as you lay your cheek upon the counter on which sits a blue-banded cup
A counter of condensed wintry exhalations glittering infinitesimally
A promise, late on a broiling day in late September, of the cold kiss
Of marble sheets to one who goes barefoot quickly in the snow and early
Only so far as the ash can—bang, dump—and back and slams the door:
Too cold to get up though at the edges of the blinds the sky
Shows blue as flames that break on a red sea in which black coals float:
Pebbles in a pocket embed the seam with grains of sand
Which, as they will, have found their way into a pattern between foot and
        bedfoot
"A place for everything and everything in its place" how wasteful, how
        wrong
It seems when snow in fat, hand-stuffed flakes falls slow and steady in the sea
"Now you see it, now you don't" the waves growl as they grind ashore and
        roll out
At your feet (in boots) a Christmas tree naked of needles
Still wound with swags of tarnishing tinsel, faintly alarming as the thought
Of damp electricity or sluggish lightning and for your health desiring pains
The wind awards: Chapped Lips: on which to rub Time's latest acquisition
Tinned, dowel shaped and inappropriately flavored sheep wool fat
A greasy sense-eclipsing fog "I can't see
Without my glasses" "You certainly can't see with them all steamed up
Like that. Pull over, park and wipe them off." The thunder of a summer's
        day

Rolls down the shimmering blacktop and mowed grass juice thickens the
      air
Like "Stir until it coats the spoon, remove from heat, let cool and chill"
Like this, graying up for more snow, maybe, in which a small flock
Of—sparrows?—small, anyway, dust kitty-colored birds fly up
On a dotted diagonal and there, ah, is the answer:
Starlings, bullies of birdland, lousing up
The pecking order, respecters of no rights (what bird is) unloved (oh?)
Not so likeable as some: that's temperate enough and the temperature
Drops to rise to snowability of a softness even in its scent of roses
Made of untinted butter frosting: Happy Name Day, Blue Jay, staggering
On slow-up wings into the shrunk into itself from cold forsythia snarl
And above these thoughts there waves another tangle but one parched
      with heat
And not with cold although the heat is on because of cold settled all
About as though, swimming under water, in clearly fishy water, you
Inhaled and found one could and live and also found you altogether
Did not like it, January, laid out on a bed of ice, disgorging
February, shaped like a flounder, and March with her steel bead
      pocketbook,
And April, goofy and under-dressed and with a loud laugh, and May
Who will of course be voted Miss Best Liked (she expects it),
And June, with a toothpaste smile, fresh from her flea bath, and gross July,
Flexing itself, and steamy August, with thighs and eyes to match, and
      September
Diving into blue October, dour November, and deadly dull December
      which now
And then with a surprised blank look produces from its hand the ace
      of trumps
Or sets within the ice white hairline of a new moon the gibbous rest:
Global, blue, Columbian, a blue dull definite and thin as the first day
Of February when, in the steamed and freezing capital cash built
Without a plan to be its own best monument its skyline set in stacks
Like poker chips (signed, "Autodidact"), at the crux of a view there
      crosses
A flatcar-trailer piled with five of the cheaper sort of yachts, tarpaulined,
Plus one youth in purple pants, a maid in her uniform and an "It's not real
Anything" Cossack hat and coat, a bus one-quarter full of strangers and
The other familiar fixings of lengthening short days: "He's outgrown them
Before you can turn around" and see behind you the landscape of the past
Where beached boats bask and terraced cliffs are hung with oranges
Among dark star-gleaming leaves, and, descending the dizzying rough stairs
Littered with goat turd beads—such packaging—you—he—she—

One—someone—stops to break off a bit of myrtle and recite all the lines
Of Goethe that come back, and those in French, *"Connais-tu . . .?"* the air
Fills with chalk dust from banged erasers, behind the February dunes
Ice boats speed and among the reeds there winds a little frozen stream
Where kids in kapok ice-skate and play at Secret City as the sun
Sets before dinner, the snow on fields turns pink and under the hatched ice
The water slides darkly and over it a never before seen liquefaction of the
     sun
In a chemical yellow greener than sulphur a flash of petroleum by-product
Unbelievable, unwanted and as lovely as though someone you knew all
     your life
Said the one inconceivable thing and then went on washing dishes: the sky
Flows with impersonal passion and loosening jet trails (eyes tearing from
     the cold)
And on the beach, between foam frozen in a thick scalloped edging so like
Weird cheek-mottling pillowcase embroidery, on the water-darkened sand
     the waves
Keep free of frost, a gull strangles on a length of nylon fishline and the dog
Trots proudly off, tail held high, to bury a future dinner among cut grass
     on a dune:
The ice boats furl their sails and all pile into cars and go off to the super
     market
Its inviting foods and cleansers sold under tunes with sealed in memory-
     flavor
"Hot House Rhubarb" "White Rock Girl" "Citrus Futures" "Cheap Bitter
     Beans" and
In its parking lot vast as the kiss to which is made the most complete
     surrender
In a setting of leaves, backs of stores, a house on a rise admired for being
Somewhat older than some others (prettier, too?) a man in a white apron
     embraces a car
Briefly in the cold with his eyes as one might hug oneself for warmth for
     love
—What a paint job, smooth as an eggplant; what a meaty chest, smooth as
     an eggplant
—Is it too much to ask your car to understand you? the converse isn't
     and the sky
Maps out new roads so that, driving at right angles to the wind, clouds in
     ranks
Contrive in diminishing perspective a part of a picture postcard of a
     painting
Over oak scrub where a filling station has: gas, a locked toilet (to keep
     dirt in)

A busted soda pop machine, no maps and "I couldn't tell you *thet*" so
The sky empties itself to a color, there, where yesterday's puddle
Offers its hospitality to people-trash and nature-trash in tans and silvers
And black grit like that in corners of a room in this or that cheap dump
Where the ceiling light burns night and day and we stare at or into each
Other's eyes in hope the other reads there what he reads: snow, wind
Lifted; black water, slashed with white; and that which is, which is beyond
Happiness or love or mixed with them or more than they or less,
   unchanging change,
"Look," the ocean said (it was tumbled, like our sheets), "look in my
   eyes"




## SELF-PITY IS A KIND OF LYING, TOO


It's
snowing defective
vision days and
X—
mas is coming, like
a plow. And in the
meat the snow. Strange.
It all reminds me
of an old lady I
once saw shivering
naked beside a black
polluted stream. You
felt terrible—but
the train didn't
stop—so. And the
white which is
some other color or
its absence—it
spins on itself
and so do the *Who
at Leeds* I'm playing
to drown the carols
blatting from the
Presbyterian church

steeple which is
the same as fight-
ing fire with oil.
Naked people—old,
cold—one day we'll
just have snow
to wear too.

## A HEAD

A dead boy living among men as a man
called an angel
by me, for want of a word,
spaniel-eyed: wet, with bits
of gold deep in the eyeballs
hidden, like a mysterious ingredient
(c'est là, le mystère)
fringed with black and with black,
thick-grown, delicately thumb-smudged eyebrows
and brown cast on the face
so the lips are an earth red
and the rings or pouches under the eyes
are dark, and all the blue
there is hovers in the hollows
under the ridges of the cheekbones
as, in fall haze, earth,
broken into clods, casts shadows on itself:

except what, in the small hours, shows
the razor's path, its wide swaths
along the cheeks and down below
the strong and bluntly heart-shaped chin
where the taut flesh loosens and softens,
heaviest at the corners of the mouth
turning petulantly down from the fold
that lifts the upper lip and points
to the divider of the nostrils.

This so-called angel
who steps back into the shadows of an empty door
and staggers on short flights of stairs
is filled with a kind of death
that feeds on little things:
fulfilled plans that no longer suit the hour,
appetites that sicken and are not slaked
(such as for milk-shakes),
lost or stolen handkerchieves,
invisible contagion
(such as the common cold).

Within this head where thought repeats
itself like a loud clock, lived
the gray and green of parks before spring
and water on a sidewalk between banks of snow,
a skylit room whose windows were paintings
of windows with views of trees
converging in the park all parks imply;
in that head a million butterflies
took flight like paper streamers and bits of paper
a draught lifts at a parade.

Then they went away.
They went away in a dance-step
to the tune of *Poor Butterfly*
played on a wind-up phonograph
of red mahogany stuck with bits
of gold: right stele for him.

When night comes and lights come on
after the colors fade in the sky,
may he minister as he can to whom he may,
himself or other, give what grace
all the little deaths he stands for,
to me, have left him. He is an angel
for his beauty. So what
if it fades and dies?

# PHILIP WHALEN (1923)

## SOURDOUGH MOUNTAIN LOOKOUT

*For Kenneth Rexroth*

Tsung Ping (375-443) "Now I am old and infirm. I fear I shall no more be able to roam among the beautiful mountains. Clarifying my mind, I meditate on the mountain trails and wander about only in dreams."
　　　　—in *The Spirit of the Brush*, tr. by Shio Sakanishi, p. 34.

I always say I won't go back to the mountains
I am too old and fat there are bugs mean mules
And pancakes every morning of the world

Mr. Edward Wyman (63)
Steams along the trail ahead of us all
Moaning, "My poor old feet ache, my back
Is tired and I've got a stiff prick"
Uprooting alder shoots in the rain

Then I'm alone in a glass house on a ridge
Encircled by chiming mountains
With one sun roaring through the house all day
& the others crashing through the glass all night
Conscious even while sleeping

　　　Morning fog in the southern gorge
　　　Gleaming foam restoring the old sea-level
　　　The lakes in two lights green soap and indigo
　　　The high cirque-lake black half-open eye

Ptarmigan hunt for bugs in the snow
Bear peers through the wall at noon
Deer crowd up to see the lamp
A mouse nearly drowns in the honey
I see my bootprints mingle with deer-foot
Bear-paw mule-shoe in the dusty path to the privy

Much later I write down:
　　　"raging. Viking sunrise
　　　　The gorgeous death of summer in the east"

(Influence of a Byronic landscape—
Bent pages exhibiting depravity of style.)

Outside the lookout I lay nude on the granite
Mountain hot September sun but inside my head
Calm dark night with all the other stars

HERACLITUS: "The waking have one common world
But the sleeping turn aside
Each into a world of his own."

I keep telling myself what I really like
Are music, books, certain land and sea-scapes
The way light falls across them, diffusion of
Light through agate, light itself . . . I suppose
I'm still afraid of the dark

> "Remember smart-guy there's something
> Bigger something smarter than you."
> Ireland's fear of unknown holies drives
> My father's voice (a country neither he
> Nor his great-grandfather ever saw)

> A sparkly tomb a plated grave
> A holy thumb beneath a wave

Everything else they hauled across Atlantic
Scattered and lost in the buffalo plains
Among these trees and mountains

From Duns Scotus to this page
A thousand years

> (". . . a dog walking on his hind legs—
> not that he does it well but that he
> does it all.")

Virtually a blank except for the hypothesis
That there is more to a man
Than the contents of his jock-strap

EMPEDOCLES: "At one time all the limbs
Which are the body's portion are brought together

By Love in blooming life's high season; at another
Severed by cruel Strife, they wander each alone
By the breakers of life's sea."

Fire and pressure from the sun bear down
Bear down centipede shadow of palm-frond
A limestone lithograph—oysters and clams of stone
Half a black rock bomb displaying brilliant crystals
Fire and pressure Love and Strife bear down
Brontosaurus, look away

My sweat runs down the rock

HERACLITUS: "The transformations of fire
are, first of all, sea; and half of the sea
is earth, half whirlwind . . . .
It scatters and it gathers; it advances
and retires."

I move out of a sweaty pool
              (The sea!)
And sit up higher on the rock

Is anything burning?

The sun itself!  Dying
Pooping out, exhausted
Having produced brontosaurus, Heraclitus
This rock, me,
To no purpose
I tell you anyway (as a kind of loving) . . .
Flies & other insects come from miles around
To listen
I also address the rock, the heather,
The alpine fir

BUDDHA: "All the constituents of being are
Transitory: Work out your salvation with diligence."

(And everything, as one eminent disciple of that master
Pointed out, has been tediously complex ever since.)

There was a bird
Lived in an egg
And by ingenious chemistry
Wrought molecules of albumen
To beak and eye
Gizzard and craw
Feather and claw

My grandmother said:
"Look at them poor bed-
raggled pigeons!"

And the sign in McAllister Street:

> "IF YOU CAN'T COME IN
> SMILE AS YOU GO BY
> L♡VE
> THE BUTCHER"

I destroy myself, the universe (an egg)
And time—to get an answer:
There are a smiler, a sleeper and a dancer

We repeat our conversation in the glittering dark
Floating beside the sleeper.
The child remarks, "You knew it all the time."
I: "I keep forgetting that the smiler is
Sleeping; the sleeper, dancing."

From Sauk Lookout two years before
Some of the view was down the Skagit
To Puget Sound: From above the lower ranges,
Deep in forest—lighthouses on clear nights.

This year's rock is a spur from the main range
Cuts the valley in two and is broken
By the river; Ross Dam repairs the break,
Makes trolley buses run
Through the streets of dim Seattle far away.

I'm surrounded by mountains here
A circle of 108 beads, originally seeds
    of *ficus religiosa*

Bo-Tree
A circle, continuous, one odd bead
Larger than the rest and bearing
A tassel (hair-tuft) (the man who sat
            under the tree)
In the center of the circle,
A void, an empty figure containing
All that's multiplied;
Each bead a repetition, a world
Of ignorance and sleep.

Today is the day the goose gets cooked
Day of liberation for the crumbling flower
Knobcone pinecone in the flames
Brandy in the sun

Which, as I said, will disappear
Anyway it'll be invisible soon
Exchanging places with stars now in my head
To be growing rice in China through the night.
Magnetic storms across the solar plains
Make Aurora Borealis shimmy bright
Beyond the mountains to the north.

Closing the lookout in the morning
Thick ice on the shutters
Coyote almost whistling on a nearby ridge
The mountain is THERE (between two lakes)
I brought back a piece of its rock
Heavy dark-honey color
With a seam of crystal, some of the quartz
Stained by its matrix
Practically indestructible
A shift from opacity to brilliance
(The Zenbos say, "Lightning-flash & flint-spark")
Like the mountains where it was made

What we see of the world is the mind's
Invention and the mind
Though stained by it, becoming
Rivers, sun, mule-dung, flies—
Can shift instantly
A dirty bird in a square time

Gone
Gone
REALLY gone
Into the cool
O MAMA!

Like they say, "Four times up,
Three times down." I'm still on the mountain.

*Sourdough Mountain 15:viii:55—Berkeley 27-28:viii:56*

## FURTHER NOTICE

I can't live in this world
And I refuse to kill myself
Or let you kill me

The dill plant lives, the airplane
My alarm clock, this ink
I won't go away

I shall be myself—
Free, a genius, an embarrassment
Like the Indian, the buffalo

Like Yellowstone National Park.

*22:ix:56*

## 10:X:57, 45 YEARS SINCE
## THE FALL OF THE CH'ING DYNASTY

The Summer Palace burnt, the Winter Palace, wherever it was
*"Ordre, ordre, Je suis une maniaque pour l'ordre!"*
(Meaning that all those sheets are promptly sent to the wooden

Launderies of the Seine,
That all the shoes and sox are lined up in rows
That the words follow each other in ecstatic parentheses, NOT
That you and me are lined up against the innocent wall, torn
By the bullets of righteousness)

I am hid, as William Blake puts it, where nobody can see me not
Even those sad angels who busted the slippery membrane across
My stifled face so I could breathe the incense coming in
From the pavilion under Coal Hill, my brocade sleeves raveling
Among the chips of jade and the withered peony blossoms and
The night of the boat-light Dragonboat orgies on the River
In pious memory of Whosis that first made the water scene
With an ingenious system of *canali* and Nationally Federated Dams

>   Where nobody can see me
>       I read all about Jimmy Dean with 16 photographs
>       and more than a hundred pages of vulgar prose

Nobody can find me I came here with that purpose of being alone
>       (R. . . . says we have all these self-destructive impulses and it
>       BUGS him, like he went to the neighborhood soda-fountain
>       For a coca-cola and everybody/all these monster teenage hoods/
>       Jumped on him at once)

Not unlike the United States Marines building teakwood campfires
Out of the Empress's bedroom furniture on the Phoenix-Viewing
Terrace roasting their wienies.




## TO THE MUSE


Dear Cleo, I can't complain about your absence
Nor excuse my failure to call you sooner
I mistook you for your sister and
Now I thank you both, you one Lady
        who changes before my eyes

QUEEN LIONESS OF HEAVEN IN THE SUN

> . . . tangle of a dream, a history
>> waiting while I sleep, I grind my teeth
> or waking I watch your closed eyes
> film of gold hair across your cheek
>> a mystery

a tangle, my impatience, your wildness,
this persistence of vision
>> centered in my own chest
(the print of your ear on my skin)

>> your presence
I'm high, my brains foam
I can't hear what you say
Quietly happily out of my mind

Madrones blossom on our mountain
Deer in thicket
Watch me pass
Fawns and does,
Tawny and grey
Bless me as I talk along the fire road

Who are the brilliance of that day
the glory of this night

*25:iv:62*

# TECHNICALITIES FOR JACK SPICER

One is enough, she cried
But imagine thousands of them
> some with wings
>> little naked boys riding on them
>>> pink silk ribands for bridle and reins
>> a leash to guide them, blimply

★

Angels, someone tells us, have no dongs
But where should you get your poems
Except angelic peckers thrust never so subtly slender
        into each ear
          Skull neon whipcream illumination
             ?

                  ★

He's more intelligent than any of his wives
Who teach him antique enchantment
Why is he a mystery to everyone but himself?
So near from hand to mouth

                  ★

One is enough, if it be of convenient length
Or one begins at an early age learning to curl up
        like a porcupine,

        "Serapis and Agathodaemon combined
        in a single figure adoring
        the Master of the universe"

                  ★

Three is required for that game of yours
One to throw the ball, one to catch
One who swings his bat between—chance
        which breaks the cycle
A farther number adds pretty variations

The path of the ball: 1, 2, 3, 4, 5 after it is hit
        (an acuminate circle)
        curls on itself again
Commences swinging back and forth
            Night and Day
The sun track
        EAST     SOUTH  WEST    NORTH
          and the center

| LINEUP, 6th DAY | | | |
|---|---|---|---|
| Lyon, Pitcher (center) | white | water | god heaven |
| Oliphant, Catcher (East) | blue | ether | animal world |
| Cheval, 3rd Base (South) | yellow | earth | human world |
| Peacock, 2nd Base (West) | red | fire | ghost world |
| Griffin, 1st Base (North) | green | air | god hell |

We very seldom see each other
Standing on opposite sides of Mother

But fear not, these are only reflections
of your own several organs grown
autonomous

★

He wants a world without mothers?
which is to say, no energy
no show, no wisdom
Only will-power, character, that very large phallus
of Mexican granite, a tree stump overgrown
mossy lichens
as distinguished from that flying snake
Kukul Can
(traveling east to west)

Yellow is the color of thought
Human world light path

★

from inside your own head! fragments of yourself
putting on campy costumes, devil masks
bagpipe sounds, instruments of torture, boiling lead
humiliating ice, a universe of poo-poo cushions
demonic yells—*viz.*

Nugatory purgatory
Dramaturgy right of clergy
Kerosene magazine          or          *"Don't bring Lulu—*
Thuribles in the clerestory          *I'm bringing her myself!"*

★

perhaps rather less embarrassing
than to discover that you are someone else's
　　　　*doppelgänger*

　　　　　　　　　★

It has been given to me to say.
I can't leave you alone.
Those heavy thumbs of yours TILT the machine
You must pay again.

Take me away to your hell world:
I must have that salvation, too—
Burn away my fleshy dreams

Nine years from now
You will be known as Lump Skull Buddha!

*6:vi:62*
*26:i:64*

## 25 : I : 68

Sadly unroll sleepingbag:

The missing lid for teapot!

## LIFE IN THE CITY.
## IN MEMORIAM EDWARD GIBBON.

The room is already white.  Trim it in blue
Memory of Bentinck Street or the arbor in Lausanne
Moonlight.  Relaxation to write while hearing
Half-misunderstood foreign language in Grant Street

So fat my nose becomes invisible in profile,
Ballooning cheeks Otafuku
A sedentary bad-weather town: pallid flesh and gouty feet
The inhalation of coalsmoke horsefume there screaming sweat
Gin-squall a part of the City's life

Ox wearing straw shoes hauls the groan-wheel shiny lacquer
Carriage streets newly washed between trolley cars
And buses plastic wisteria swings and wabbles from dark
lacquer and gold roofbeam palanquin of gold flower head crown
Priestess Cafe Trieste Grant Street several tons of horse,
men, silk, flowers, gold, pavement, a library of 5000 volumes
Blue and White shelves: Fat Edward Gibbon with monstrous
Hydrocele farting sedanchairmen calmly parsing the Byzantines:

"Decline THE EMPIRE," he tells himself, passing St Clement
Danes, "decline the Honourable Danes Barrington . . . decline
Doctor Goldsmith . . ." and squirms on the lumpy seat, trying
To ease fat legs & jiggling water bag slowly scrunching

The gravel of the courtyard beyond the inner palace wall,
Black shiny hats bend to place chock wedges under moaning wheels
Hoss the lacquer chariot to the left the Imperial Messenger's
Bronze mirrored horse wags its head flapping the Messenger's
Black lacquer hat black gauze plumes towards the North
Parallel with Kamogawa, Exact edge of Hieizan stamped on blue
The aoi leaves already melting, he notes, among the horsehair
"Blinders" of his attendant's cap
Wide floppy silk trousers wet with horse foam

Peter and David tell me goodbye, nobody here but the rest
Of the City drinking cappuccino and NY Egg Cream jet roar
Pearl fingernail patent leather knee-boot suicide blonde
Of a certain age black T-shirt orange beads and yellow skirt
Desperately unhappy   •

SUI    CAMPI    DELLO    SPORT

SERIE A                    SERIE B

FIORENTINA  0  SAMPDORIA  0  FOGGIA  1  VERONA  0

The score in the cities declining in sedan chairs gondolas
Whip-cream french blue frosty paint for the eyelids of
A certain age to pick up to locate to foresee I was wrong:
Not suicide, a fairly well-made nicely-fitted wig sitting
With the Mafia but the black grosgrain band holding down
The front of her own black hair somehow shines through
The gold floss over the top as brain fries in vatic flames
Joyful screeches while rain floods down flames undisturbed:
Jagged flakes & shards of living jewel sound unharmed! by
The City, the Life of the City, "from the tryal of some months"
"(the city the) the city I was tempted to substitute
the tranquil dissipation of Bath"

Refulgent spirit expands branches flowers which are gems
Empty sapphire space and air just past the golfcourse
River's bend alive changing hideously beautiful coal seam ferns
diamond opal do you hear

*San Francisco 24:v:68*


## FOR KAI SNYDER

7:v:60 (an interesting *lapsus calami*)
A few minutes ago I tried a somersault; couldn't do it
I was afraid and I couldn't remember how.
I fell over on one shoulder,
Rolled about and nearly went over backwards
And finally hurt my chest.
What kind of psychomotor *malebolge* had I got into . . .
"This is old age, &c."

After thinking it all over
Imagining how it might be done
I performed three forward somersaults, 7:V:70
Age 46 years 6 months 37 days.

## WHERE OR WHEN

The sidewalk joins the concrete wall around the vacant lot
Wiry single plants of timothy hay spring up
      from the minutest cracks in the cement
No space for them so jammed against the wall
They can't make a shadow
We used to say "fox tails"
      furry green plumes all soft and tickle seed
Hairs watered by fog and smallest rains
Crack all San Francisco into crumbs of gravelly dusty
      minerals and sand that feed these grassy feathers
      primitive oats or wheat
The city running to weed patch right on time.

*17:v:76*

# ROBIN BLASER (1925)

## IMAGE-NATION 3

what if the body goes     the sense
of the word    which draws amor
in a body    his arrows leafless, shining
steel    his meaning in that meeting of
hands, tastes, bitter
filling fountain    if that poetry goes
whose power drank from the body, gave
the body, gave amor a skin,

an act, the worshipped height higher
than what is left
another amor inescapable pouring, holding
that shape here together        all ways,

*born through all the elements*, the night
singing sparrows are arrows    I define
the dark correct that allows that I to appear
the naked, unyielding form of I    acting apart
but it is Naught    the other is that    unlearned,
this fear and charm of word    O shepherd, his way apart,
flower and youth    *with an arrow offshot*

*1964*

## IMAGE-NATION *(the poēsis)*

inside the tower    not a broken tower    two
loves seemed present    ●    one    ●    passing
the other    ●    not named    ●

        verbs of

the *music-footed horse*

             I was afraid     at the fair sight
the dark imagined land     disappeared as they came to the edge
in the     air     across     the vertical road   leading up to the
sky     of that constellation     by   an explosion    ●

             I reached up into that space
             to touch the enormous mobile
hanging from the center     I had wanted to arrange it

from each pendant     a shining ring     which one by one
my fingers entered     dissolved     in light
             as if space looked for time
or the block of the image did not know the size of
what you are doing     ●

             in the explosion        the rings became
             a constellation
                  the moving angel
             changed raiment

and colors     at times     soaked with the blood going
or *adorned with treasure*     turning     now     transparent

             what's left of the angel
             glint and guitar
what's left of the event of the left
what's left of the angelic writer     ●
                     the Event

was an activity turned in
all directions
             of what contained them
and retraced
             the wing of the world showed,
who is companion     ●     blue-hued     ●     well-marked

                                *1972*

## IMAGE-NATION 13 (*the telephone*

the man with a thousand hearts
flaring    the substance shattered
of what form    that is his movement?

both made the sexual beginning into a demonic
mediocrity    both disappeared in future-form
the language,    scared to the binding of one

to another,    stolen    the only heart

is the movement of singing words
they burn    they burn
then suddenly bathe in the fiery sea

they say he is consumed by sorrow
in order to see    and his paper lives
fly in pages across the garden

caught in those blue bunches
of hydrangea    the particles
are pieces of silence riding the sea

they shine at the edge of his words
suddenly *nothing old or new*
*matters    he can act or not*

there    among *mountains of the heart*
watching    to bring the shining pieces
into his hearts

where the words enter like footsteps,
these small ghosts tend to flee
toward something fearfully and transparent

'the shape of heaven    is as confused
as the heart    when you place
your feet on your head,    you will
stand on the stars,'

these words whisper    as the sea folds
a thousand forms    they are
like the telephone
                        the lovers *fall*
*into a whirlpool*
                        he steps forward
so suddenly himself and another
a movement,    a fold of the real

that should be the image of himself
returned, he thought

looking back,    where he
heard    the whisper of so many

            the splendour and darkness
of something whirl in the air
                        *a blowing-together*

that would be the real    of the lover,
which is nothing other    than himself

a movement    fiery    turning    bits & pieces
a circle    a square    long running lines    dots & dashes
parabolas,
            almost gigantic,
        of the man with a thousand hearts,

he thought

## SUDDENLY,

I live in a room named East
on the map of the West        at the edge

near the door cedars and alders
mix and tower,
full of ravens    first thing each morning,

whose song is
            a sharpness

we quarreled so
               over the genius
of the heart
           *whose voice is capable*

they come on horseback
in the middle of the night,
two of them,    with a horse for me,
and we ride,      bareback
clinging to the white manes
at the edge of the sea-splash,

burst open,

           to divine
*the hidden and forgotten source,*
who is transparent
where the moon drops out of the fog
to bathe,
*but not to us*

the retired heart
           where the wind glitters

                                   *for Ellen Tallman*

# KENNETH KOCH (1925)

## PERMANENTLY

One day the Nouns were clustered in the street.
An Adjective walked by, with her dark beauty.
The Nouns were struck, moved, changed.
The next day a Verb drove up, and created the Sentence.

Each Sentence says one thing—for example, "Although it was a dark
      rainy day when the Adjective walked by, I shall remember the pure
      and sweet expression on her face until the day I perish from the green,
      effective earth."
Or, "Will you please close the window, Andrew?"
Or, for example, "Thank you, the pink pot of flowers on the window
      sill has changed color recently to a light yellow, due to the heat from
      the boiler factory which exists nearby."

In the springtime the Sentences and the Nouns lay silently on the grass.
A lonely Conjunction here and there would call, "And! But!"
But the Adjective did not emerge.

As the adjective is lost in the sentence,
So I am lost in your eyes, ears, nose, and throat—
You have enchanted me with a single kiss
Which can never be undone
Until the destruction of language.

## VARIATIONS ON A THEME BY
## WILLIAM CARLOS WILLIAMS

1

I chopped down the house that you have been saving to live in next summer.
I am sorry, but it was morning, and I had nothing to do
and its wooden beams were so inviting.

2

We laughed at the hollyhocks together
and then I sprayed them with lye.
Forgive me. I simply do not know what I am doing.


3

I gave away the money that you have been saving to live on for the next
    ten years.
The man who asked for it was shabby
and the firm March wind on the porch was so juicy and cold.


4

Last evening we went dancing and I broke your leg.
Forgive me. I was clumsy, and
I wanted you here in the wards, where I am the doctor!


## THANK YOU


Oh thank you for giving me the chance
Of being ship's doctor! I am sorry that I shall have to refuse—
But, you see, the most I know of medicine is orange flowers
Tilted in the evening light against a cashmere red
Inside which breasts invent the laws of light
And of night, where cashmere moors itself across the sea.
And thank you for giving me these quintuplets
To rear and make happy . . . My mind was on something else.

Thank you for giving me this battleship to wash,
But I have a rash on my hands and my eyes hurt,
And I know so little about cleaning a ship
That I should rather clean an island.
There one knows what one is about—sponge those palm trees, sweep up
    the sand a little, polish those coconuts;
Then take a rest for a while and it's time to trim the grass as well as
    separate it from each other where gummy substances have made
    individual blades stick together, forming an ugly bunch;
And then take the dead bark off the trees, and perfume these islands
    a bit with a song. . . . That's easy—but a battleship!
Where does one begin and how does one do? to batten the hatches?
    I would rather clean a million palm trees.

Now here comes an offer of a job for setting up a levee
In Mississippi. No thanks. Here it says *Rape or Worse.* I think they must
    want me to publicize this book.
On the jacket it says "Published in Boothbay Harbor, Maine"—what a
    funny place to publish a book!
I suppose it is some provincial publishing house
Whose provincial pages emit the odor of sails
And the freshness of the sea
Breeze. . . . But publicity!
The only thing I could publicize well would be my tooth,
Which I could say came with my mouth and in a most engaging manner
With my whole self, my body and including my mind,
Spirits, emotions, spiritual essences, emotional substances, poetry, dreams,
    and lords
Of my life, everything, all embraceleted with my tooth
In a way that makes one wish to open the windows and scream "Hi!" to
    the heavens,
And "Oh, come and take me away before I die in a minute!"

It is possible that the dentist is smiling, that he dreams of extraction
Because he believes that the physical tooth and the spiritual tooth are one.

Here is another letter, this one from a textbook advertiser;
He wants me to advertise a book on chopping down trees.
But how could I? I love trees! and I haven't the slightest sympathy with
    chopping them down, even though I know
We need their products for wood-fires, some houses, and maple syrup—
Still I like trees better
In their standing condition, when they sway at the beginning of evening . . .
And thank you for the pile of driftwood.
Am I wanted at the sea?

And thank you for the chance to run a small hotel
In an elephant stopover in Zambezi,
But I do not know how to take care of guests, certainly they would all
    leave soon
After seeing blue lights out the windows and rust on their iron beds—
    I'd rather own a bird-house in Jamaica:
Those people come in, the birds, they do not care how things are kept
    up . . .
It's true that Zambezi proprietorship would be exciting, with people
    getting off elephants and coming into my hotel,
But as tempting as it is I cannot agree.

And thank you for this offer of the post of referee
For the Danish wrestling championship—I simply do not feel qualified . . .

But the fresh spring air has been swabbing my mental decks
Until, although prepared for fight, still I sleep on land.
Thank you for the ostriches. I have not yet had time to pluck them,
But I am sure they will be delicious, adorning my plate at sunset,
My tremendous plate, and the plate
Of the offers to all my days. But I cannot fasten my exhilaration to
    the sun.

And thank you for the evening of the night on which I fell off my horse
    in the shadows. That was really useful.


## SLEEPING WITH WOMEN


Caruso: a voice.
Naples: sleeping with women.
Women: sleeping in the dark.
Voices: a music.
Pompeii: a ruin.
Pompeii: sleeping with women.
Men sleeping with women, women sleeping with women, sheep sleeping
    with women, everything sleeping with women.
The guard: asking you for a light.
Women: asleep.
Yourself: asleep.
Everything south of Naples: asleep and sleeping with them.
Sleeping with women: as in the poems of Pascoli.
Sleeping with women: as in the rain, as in the snow.
Sleeping with women: by starlight, as if we were angels, sleeping on the
    train,
On the starry foam, asleep and sleeping with them—sleeping with women.
Mediterranean: a voice.
Mediterranean: a sea. Asleep and sleeping.
Streetcar in Oslo, sleeping with women, Toonerville Trolley
In Stockholm asleep and sleeping with them, in Skansen
Alone, alone with women,

The rain sleeping with women, the brain of the dog-eyed genius
Alone, sleeping with women, all he has wanted,
The dog-eyed fearless man.
Sleeping with them: as in *The Perils of Pauline*
Asleep with them: as in Tosca
Sleeping with women and causing all that trouble
As in Roumania, as in Yugoslavia
Asleep and sleeping with them
Anti-Semitic, and sleeping with women,
Pro-canary, Rashomon, Shakespeare, tonight, sleeping with women
A big guy sleeping with women
A black seacoast's sleeve, asleep with them
And sleeping with women, and sleeping with them
The Greek islands sleeping with women
The muddy sky, asleep and sleeping with them.
Sleeping with women, as in a scholarly design
Sleeping with women, as if green polarity were a line
Into the sea, sleeping with women
As if wolverines, in a street line, as if sheep harbors
Could come alive from sleeping with women, wolverines
Greek islands sleeping with women, Nassos, Naxos, Kos,
Asleep with women, Mykonos, miotis,
And myositis, sleeping with women, blue-eyes
Red-eyed, green-eyed, yellow reputed, white-eyed women
Asleep and sleeping with them, blue, sleeping with women
As in love, as at sea, the rabbi, asleep and sleeping with them
As if that could be, the stones, the restaurant, asleep and sleeping with
    them
Sleeping with women, as if they were knee
Arm and thigh asleep and sleeping with them, sleeping with women.
And the iris peg of the sea
Sleeping with women
And the diet pill of the tree
Sleeping with women
And the apology the goon the candlelight
The groan: asking you for the night, sleeping with women
Asleep and sleeping with them, the green tree
The iris, the swan: the building with its mouth open
Asleep with women, awake with man,
The sunlight, asleep and sleeping with them, the moving gong
The abacus, the crab, asleep and sleeping with them
And moving, and the moving van, in London, asleep with women
And intentions, inventions for sleeping with them

Lands sleeping with women, ants sleeping with women, Italo-Greek or
      Anglo-French orchestras
Asleep with women, asleep and sleeping with them,
The foam and the sleet, asleep and sleeping with them,
The schoolboy's poem, the crippled leg
Asleep and sleeping with them, sleeping with women
Sleeping with women, as if you were a purist
Asleep and sleeping with them.
Sleeping with women: there is no known form for the future.
Of this undreamed-of view: sleeping with a chorus
Of highly tuned women, asleep and sleeping with them.
Bees, sleeping with women
And tourists, sleeping with them
Soap, sleeping with women; beds, sleeping with women
The universe: a choice
The headline: a voice, sleeping with women
At dawn, sleeping with women, asleep and sleeping with them.
Sleeping with women: a choice, as of a mule
As of an island, asleep or sleeping with them, as of a Russia,
As of an island, as of a drum: a choice of views: asleep and sleeping with
      them, as of high noon, as of a choice, as of variety, as of the sunlight,
      red student, asleep and sleeping with them,
As with an orchid, as with an oriole, at school, sleeping with women, and
      you are the one
The one sleeping with women, in Mexico, sleeping with women
The ghost land, the vectors, sleeping with women
The motel man, the viaduct, the sun
The universe: a question
The moat: a cathexis
What have we done? On Rhodes, man
On Samos, dog
Sleeping with women
In the rain and in the sun
The dog has a red eye, it is November
Asleep and sleeping with them, sleeping with women
This June: a boy
October: sleeping with women
The motto: a sign; the bridge: a definition.
To the goat: destroy; to the rain: be a settee.
O rain of joy: sleeping with women, asleep and sleeping with them.
Volcano, Naples, Caruso, asleep and sleeping, asleep and sleeping with them
The window, the windrow, the hedgerow, irretrievable blue,
Sleeping with women, the haymow, asleep and sleeping with them, the canal

Asleep and sleeping with them, the eagle's feather, the dock's weather, and
    the glue:
Sleeping with you; asleep and sleeping with you: sleeping with women.
Sleeping with women, charming aspirin, as in the rain, as in the snow,
Asleep and sleeping with you: as if the crossbow, as of the moonlight
Sleeping with women: as if the tractate, as if d'Annunzio
Asleep and sleeping with you, asleep with women
Asleep and sleeping with you, asleep with women, asleep and sleeping with
    you, sleeping with women
As if the sun, as of Venice and the Middle Ages' "true
Renaissance had just barely walked by the yucca
Forest" asleep and sleeping with you
In China, on parade, sleeping with women
And in the sun, asleep and sleeping with you, sleeping with women,
Asleep with women, the docks, the alley, and the prude
Sleeping with women, asleep with them.
The dune god: sleeping with women
The dove: asleep and sleeping with them
Dials sleeping with women; cybernetic tiles asleep and sleeping with them
Naples: sleeping with women; the short of breath
Asleep and sleeping with you, sleeping with women
As if I were you—moon idealism
Sleeping with women, pieces of stageboard, sleeping with women
The silent bus ride, sleeping with you.
The chore: sleeping with women
The force of a disaster: sleeping with you
The organ grinder's daughter: asleep with bitumen, sunshine, sleeping with
    women,
Sleeping with women: in Greece, in China, in Italy, sleeping with blue
Red green orange and white women, sleeping with two
Three four and five women, sleeping on the outside
And on the inside of women, a violin, like a vista, women, sleeping with
    women
In the month of May, in June, in July
Sleeping with women, "I watched my life go by" sleeping with women
A door of pine, a stormfilled valentine asleep and sleeping with them
"This Sunday heart of mine" profoundly dormoozed with them
They running and laughing, asleep and sleeping with them
"This idle heart of mine" insanely "shlamoozed" asleep and sleeping with
    them,
They running in laughter
To the nearest time, oh doors of eternity
Oh young women's doors of my own time! sleeping with women

Asleep and sleeping with them, all Naples asleep and sleeping with them,
Venice sleeping with women, Burgos sleeping with women, Lausanne
      sleeping with women, hail depth-divers
Sleeping with women, and there is the bonfire of Crete
Catching divorce in its fingers, purple sleeping with women
And the red lights of dawn, have you ever seen them, green ports sleeping
      with women, acrobats and pawns,
You had not known it ere I told it you asleep with women
The Via Appia Antica asleep with women, asleep and sleeping with them
All beautiful objects, each ugly object, the intelligent world,
The arena of the spirits, the dietetic whisky, the storms
Sleeping with women, asleep and sleeping with them,
Sleeping with women. And the churches in Antigua, sleeping with women
The stone: a vow
The Nereid: a promise—to sleep with women
The cold—a convention: sleeping with women
The carriage: sleeping with women
The time: sometimes
The certainty: now
The soapbox: sleeping with women
The time and again nubile and time, sleeping with women, and the time
      now
Asleep and sleeping with them, asleep and asleep, sleeping with women,
      asleep and sleeping with them, sleeping with women.

# JACK SPICER (1925-1965)


## FIVE WORDS FOR JOE DUNN ON HIS 22nd BIRTHDAY


I shall give you five words for your birthday.

The first is *anthropos*
Who celebrates birthdays.
He is withered and tough and blind, babbler
Of old wars and dead beauty.
He is there for the calmness of your heart as the days race
And the wars are lost and the roses wither.
No enemy can strike you that he has not defeated.
No beauty can die in your heart that he will not remember.

The second word is *andros*
Who is proud of his gender,
Wears it like a gamecock, erects it
Through the midnight of time
Like a birthday candle.
He will give you wisdom like a Fool
Hidden in the loins
Crying out against the inelegance
Of all that is not sacred.

The third word is *eros*
Who will cling to you every birthnight
Bringing your heart substance.
Whomever you touch will love you,
Will feel the cling of His touch upon you
Like sunlight scattered over an ancient mirror.

The fourth word is *thanatos*, the black belly
That eats birthdays.
I do not give you *thanatos*. I bring you a word to call Him
*Thanatos*, devourer of young men, heart-biter, bone-licker.
Look, He slinks away when you name Him.
Name Him! *Thanatos*.

The last word is *agape*,
The dancer that puts birthdays in motion.
She is there to lead words.
Counter to everything. She makes words
Circle around Her. Words dance.
See them. *Anthropos* ageless.
*Andros* made virgin, *Eros* unmirrored
*Thanatos* devoured.
*Agape*, *Agape*, ring-mistress,
Love
That comes from beyond birthdays,
That makes poetry
And moves stars.

## A BOOK OF MUSIC

Coming at an end, the lovers
Are exhausted like two swimmers. Where
Did it end? There is no telling. No love is
Like an ocean with the dizzy procession of the waves' boundaries
From which two can emerge exhausted, nor long goodbye
Like death.
Coming at an end. Rather, I would say, like a length
Of coiled rope
Which does not disguise in the final twists of its lengths
Its endings.
But, you will say, we loved
And some parts of us loved
And the rest of us will remain
Two persons. Yes,
Poetry ends like a rope.

## *from* THE HOLY GRAIL: THE BOOK OF GAWAIN


1

Tony
To be casual and have the wish to heal
Gawain, I think,
Had that when he saw the sick king squirming around like a half-cooked
      eel on a platter asking a riddle maybe only ghostmen could answer
His riddled body. Heal it how?
Gawain no ghostman, guest who could not gather
Anything
There was an easy grail.
Later shot a green knight
In a dead forest
That was an easy answer
No king
No riddle.


2

In some kind of castle some kind of knight played chess with an invisible
      chessplayer
A maiden, naturally.
You can hear the sound of wood on the board and some kind of knight
      breathing
It was another spoiled quest. George
Said to me that the only thing he thought was important in chess was
      killing the other king. I had accused him of lack of imagination.
I talked of fun and imagination but I wondered about the nature of poetry
      since there was some kind of knight and an invisible chessplayer and
      they had been playing chess in the Grail Castle.


3

The grail is the opposite of poetry
Fills us up instead of using us as a cup the dead drink from.
The grail the cup Christ bled into and the cup of plenty in Irish mythology
The poem. Opposite. Us. Unfullfilled.
These worlds make the friendliness of human to human seem close as cup
      to lip.
Savage in their pride the beasts pound around the forest perilous.

4

Everyone is impressed with courage and when he fought him he won
Who won?
I'm not sure but one was wearing red armor and one black armor
I'm not sure about the colors but they were looking for a cup or a poem
Everyone in each of the worlds is impressed with courage and I'm not sure
      if either of them were human or that what they were looking for
      could be described as a cup or a poem or why either of them fought
They made a loud noise in the forest and the ravens gathered in trees and
      you were almost sure they were ravens.

5

On the sea
(There is never an ocean in all Grail legend)
There is a boat.
There is always one lone person on it sailing
Widdershins.
His name is Kate or Bob or Mike or Dora and his sex is almost as obscure as
      his history.
Yet he will be met by a ship of singing women who will embalm him with
      nard and spice and all of the hallows
As the ocean
In the far distance.

6

They are still looking for it
Poetry and magic see the world from opposite ends
One cock-forward and the other ass-forward
All over Britain (but what a relief it would be to give all this up and find
      surcease in somebodyelse's soul and body)
Thus said Merlin
Unwillingly
Who saw through time.

7

Perverse
Turned against the light
The grail they said
Is achieved by steady compromise.
An unending
The prize is there at the bottom of the rainbow—follow the invisible
      markings processwise
I, Gawain, who am no longer human but a legend followed the markings

Did
More or less what they asked
My name is now a symbol for shame
I, Gawain, who once was a knight of the Grail in a dark forest.

End of Book of Gawain


# FOUR POEMS FOR *THE ST. LOUIS SPORTING NEWS*


1

Waiting like a trap-door spider for a rookie sell-out. Baseball or the name
    game?
When I was a catcher, you came to them. You said "Gee, Mr. Whilikers,
    I'd like to be a catcher." You worked out
With other unassigned players.
You had to make it or be signed down to Shenandoah or Rockport. Them
Was the days. Like
Now: the tigers treat the pigs real fine before they eat them: there is a
    pension for almost everything: very few and old pitchers throw
    screwballs. By request of the management.
Like kid, don't enter here or you'll become like a pop fly I lost in the sun
    but went back in the stands anyway. Foul.
"Learn
How to shoot fish in a barrel," someone said,
"People are starving."


2

I would like to beat my hands around your heart.
You are a young pitcher but you throw fast curve-balls, slow fast balls,
    change-ups that at the last moment don't change. Junk
The pitchers who are my age call it. And regret every forty years of their
    life when they have to use them.
If I were a catcher behind you, I'd make you throw real fast balls and a
    few sliders to keep them honest. But you're not on my team and
    when I face you as a pinch-hitter, I strike out.
Somebody so young being so cagy, I
Got three home-runs off of Warren Spahn but both of us understood where
    the ball was (or wasn't) going to go. You

Are a deceit and when you get to the age of thirty (and I live to see it)
     you're
Going to get knocked out of the box,
Baby.


     3

Pitchers are obviously not human. They have the ghosts of dead people in
     them. You wait there while they glower, put their hands to their
     mouths, fidget like puppets, while you're waiting to catch the ball.
You give them signs. They usually ignore them. A fast outside curve.
     High, naturally. And scientifically impossible. Where the batter
     either strikes out or he doesn't. You either catch it or you don't.
     You had called for an inside fast ball.
The runners on base either advance or they don't
In any case
The ghosts of the dead people find it mighty amusing. The pitcher, in
     his sudden humaness looks toward the dugout in either agony or
     triumph. You, in either case, have a pair of hot hands.
Emotion
Being communicated
Stops
Even when the game isn't over.


     4

God is a big white baseball that has nothing to do but go in a curve or a
     straight line. I studied geometry in highschool and know that this
     is true.
Given these facts the pitcher, the batter, and the catcher all look pretty
     silly. No Hail Marys
Are going to get you out of a position with the bases loaded and no outs,
     or when you're 0 and 2, or when the ball bounces out to the screen
     wildly. Off seasons
I often thought of praying to him but could not stand the thought of that
     big, white, round, omnipotent bastard.
Yet he's there. As the game follows rules he makes them.
I know
I was not the only one who felt these things.

# PAUL BLACKBURN (1926-1971)

## THE ASSISTANCE

On the farm it never mattered;
behind the barn, in any grass, against
any convenient tree,
                    the woodshed in winter, in a corner
if it came to that.

But in a city of eight million,      one
stands on the defensive.
                    In the West 59th St. parking lot
it has long since sunk into the cinders.

But in the shallow doorway of
a shop on Third Avenue, between
                    the dark and the streetlight,
it was the trail of the likewise drinking-man who preceded me
                    that gave me courage.

## THE ONCE-OVER

The tanned blonde
                    in the green print sack
in the center of the subway car
                              standing
tho there are seats
                    has had it from
1 teen-age hood
1 lesbian
1 envious housewife
4 men  over  fifty
(& myself),  in short
                    the contents of this half of the car

Our notations are:
long legs, long waist, high breasts (no bra), long
neck, the model slump
                        the handbag drape & how the skirt
cuts in under a very handsome
                                        set of cheeks
'stirring dull roots with spring rain'      sayeth the preacher

            Only a stolid young man—
         with a blue business suit and the New York Times
         does not know he is being assaulted

So.
She has us and we her
all the way to downtown Brooklyn
Over the tunnel and through the bridge
                        to DeKalb Avenue we go
all very chummy

She stares at the number over the door
                        and gives no sign
Yet the sign is on her

## SIRVENTES

*Un sirventes ai fach*
*Contra'l ciutat de Tolosa*
*On m'avia pretz ostalatge*
*D'un sen salvatge e famosa*
*Del mons . . .*

*PB / 1956*

I have made a sirventes against the city of Toulouse
                        and it cost me plenty garlic    :
and if I have a brother, say, or a cousin, or a 2nd cousin,
I'll tell him to stay out too.
                        As for me, Henri,

            I'd rather be in España
            pegging pernod thru a pajita

or yagrelling a luk
jedamput en Jugoslavije,
jowels wide & yowels not
permitted to emerge—
or even
in emergency
slopping slivovitsa thru
the brlog in the luk.
I mean I'm not particular,
but to be
in the Midi

now that rain is here,
to be sitting in Toulouse
for another year,
the slop tapping in the court
to stop typing just at ten
and the wet-rot setting in
and the price is always plus,
I mean, please,
must I?

Whole damn year teaching
trifles to these trout with trousers
tramping thru the damp
with gout up to my gut
taking all the guff, sweet
jesus crypt,
god of the he
brews, she blows, it bawls, & Boses
(by doze is stuffed)
by the balls of the livid saviour, lead be
back hindu eegypt-la-aad
before I'b canned for indisciblidnary reasons.

O god,
The hallowed halls
the ivy covered walls
the fishwife calls
& the rain falls

Bastal!

Jove, god of tourists, the whores in Barcelona are beautiful,
you would understand.
Weren't there Europa and Io? and Aegina, twin sister of Thebe
both daughters of Asopus?
and Maia and Antiope and
Niobe of the Thebans.
Eagle, ant, bull, beaver, flame, otter, how *not*?
Remember Leda?
I swan, you never felt old.
Your shower of rain at least was a shower of gold.
A gentle white bull with dewlaps.
The bulls in Barcelona are beautiful, Jove,
need no persuasion, are themselves as brave.

My old Guillem, who once stole this town,
thinking your wife's name enuf reason to . . .

St. Julian, patron of travellers, *mi des mercey*!

        Who else invoke?  Who else to save
          a damned poet impaled by a *beterave*?
Mercury!  Post of Heaven, you old thief, deliver me
from this ravel-streeted, louse-ridden, down-river,
gutter-sniping, rent-gouging, hard-hearted,
            complacent provincial town,
where they have forgotten all that made this country the
belly of courage, the body of beauty, the hands of heresy,
the legs of the individual spirit, the heart of song!

          That made Vidal would spit on it,
          that I as his maddened double
          do  —  too
          changed, too changed, o
          deranged master of song,
          master of the viol and the lute
          master of those sounds,
          I join you in public madness,
          in the street I piss
          on French politesse

that has wracked all passion from the sound of speech.
A leech that sucks the blood is less a lesion.  Speech!
this imposed imposing imported courtliness,   that

the more you hear it the more it's meaningless
                                    & without feeling.

          The peel is off the grape
          and there's not much left
          and what is left is soured
          if clean    :
          if I go off my beam, some
          small vengeance would be sweet,
          something definite and neat,
                              say total destruction.

Jove, father, cast your bolts
& down these bourgeois dolts    !

          Raise a wave, a glaive of light, Poseidon,
          inundate this fish bait    !

               Hermes, keep my song
               from the dull rhythms of rain.

                    Apollo, hurl your darts,
                    cleanse these abysmal farts
                    out from this dripping cave
                    in the name of Love.

## PHONE CALL TO RUTHERFORD

"It would be—
                    a mercy if
you did not come see me . . .

"I have dif-fi    /    culty
                    speak-ing, I
cannot count on it, I
am afraid it would be too em-
                    ba
                    rass-ing
for me        ."

>                    —Bill, can you still
>                    answer letters?

"No    .    my hands
are tongue-tied    .    You have . . . made

a record in my heart.
>                    Goodbye."

>                                             *October 1962*

## THE TIDES

>                         The girl with the beautiful legs
>                         walks down a Brooklyn street
>                         a hope-and-a-half away

Terrible indeed is the house of heaven in the mind
soft
giving back the quiver
deeper and deeper disclosed until the blind
sun bursts
into a close warm black behind the eyes
>                              yellow stars
>                              then the red

Light perspiration on bodies engraved as beads
>                         upon the stone mind
the heavy, delicate odor, the swift
calling by name, the pronouns
the arching back
a sky under which the blood speaks
its flood
>                         its ebb
what the man must do
what the woman must

# THE SLOGAN

Over the right
triangle formed
by Stuyvesant St. & Ninth, the
wellknit blonde in a blue knit dress &
the hair piled high

t
w
o

w
o
r
l
d
s

& several hemispheres as she walks.

                              The trajectory
causes a mass cessation of work
at a Con Edison encampment on
one of the other two sides, all
orange equipment with dark red flashers, flags
at the corners of the encampment wave cheerfully
in the Monday morning breeze, all the orange helmets
facing the same way, eyes right, and clearly

*everything else is right*

Click
click

the heels go at an easy pace across Stuyvesant
touch the curb at Ninth, jiggle-jiggle  .  The
          e x p l a n a t i o n

is printed on the sides of all the equipment, even on one flag    :

    DIG WE MUST

They dig   .




## 17.  IV.  71


My shoes  .
I have just taken them off,
                      my shoes.
Stare out the darkened window, damn, 've
forgotten the cigarettes in the car, empty
pack in my hand, crumple it, drop it in   .  2 points
Have to put my shoes back on   .  they
look at me reproachfully from the floor

            laces loose   .  their
            tongues slack.
so scruffed already they are   .
& had just relaxed

---

Cities & towns I have to give up this year
on account of my cancer:  Amster-
dam, Paris, Apt, Saignon and Aix,
(Toulouse I'll never loose), Perpignan and Dax,
Barcelona and south
                (or the other way,
            Catania   .  I warn ya)
The hell, I read a review of a reading in January.
They loved me in Shippensburg, Pennsylvania.

---

Top of the 8th, after
four fouled off Gentry, still
2 and 2    a plastic bag
blows over home plate, Dave
Cash of the Pirates steps
    out of the box, steps

back in, after speeding the plastic
    on its way
    with his bat, fouls
    two more off, then 3 & 2, then
infield bounce to the shortstop, out at first.

---

"Anything you want?"
    she asks, heading out the door, leading
    downstairs, get the bicycle out of the cellar  .
—No, nothing, thanks. The slacks are brown, she is
carrying anything I want downstairs to take it for
a ride on the bicycle  .

# ROBERT CREELEY (1926)

## THE IMMORAL PROPOSITION

If you never do anything for anyone else
you are spared the tragedy of human relation-

ships. If quietly and like another time
there is the passage of an unexpected thing:

to look at it is more
than it was. God knows

nothing is competent nothing is
all there is. The unsure

egoist is not
good for himself.

## I KNOW A MAN

As I sd to my
friend, because I am
always talking,—John, I

sd, which was not his
name, the darkness sur-
rounds us, what

can we do against
it, or else, shall we &
why not, buy a goddamn big car,

drive, he sd, for
christ's sake, look
out where yr going.

## THE WHIP

I spent a night turning in bed,
my love was a feather, a flat

sleeping thing. She was
very white

and quiet, and above us on
the roof, there was another woman I

also loved, had
addressed myself to in

a fit she
returned. That

encompasses it. But now I was
lonely, I yelled,

but what is that? Ugh,
she said, beside me, she put

her hand on
my back, for which act

I think to say this
wrongly.


## THE DOOR

*for Robert Duncan*


It is hard going to the door
cut so small in the wall where
the vision which echoes loneliness
brings a scent of wild flowers in a wood.

What I understood, I understand.
My mind is sometime torment,
sometimes good and filled with livelihood,
and feels the ground.

But I see the door,
and knew the wall, and wanted the wood,
and would get there if I could
with my feet and hands and mind.

Lady, do not banish me
for digressions. My nature
is a quagmire of unresolved
confessions. Lady, I follow.

I walked away from myself,
I left the room, I found the garden,
I knew the woman
in it, together we lay down.

Dead night remembers. In December
we change, not multiplied but dispersed,
sneaked out of childhood,
the ritual of dismemberment.

Mighty magic is a mother,
in her there is another issue
of fixture, repeated form, the race renewal,
the charge of the command.

The garden echoes across the room.
It is fixed in the wall like a mirror
that faces a window behind you
and reflects the shadows.

May I go now?
Am I allowed to bow myself down
in the ridiculous posture of renewal,
of the insistence of which I am the virtue?

Nothing for You is untoward.
Inside You would also be tall,
more tall, more beautiful.
Come toward me from the wall, I want to be with You.

So I screamed to You,
who hears as the wind, and changes
multiply, invariably,
changes in the mind.

Running to the door, I ran down
as a clock runs down. Walked backwards,
stumbled, sat down
hard on the floor near the wall.

Where were You.
How absurd, how vicious.
There is nothing to do but get up.
My knees were iron, I rusted in worship, of You.

For that one sings, one
writes the spring poem, one goes on walking.
The Lady has always moved to the next town
and you stumble on after Her.

The door in the wall leads to the garden
where in the sunlight sit
the Graces in long Victorian dresses,
of which my grandmother had spoken.

History sings in their faces.
They are young, they are obtainable,
and you follow after them also
in the service of God and Truth.

But the Lady is indefinable,
she will be the door in the wall
to the garden in sunlight.
I will go on talking forever.

I will never get there.
Oh Lady, remember me
who in Your service grows older
not wiser, no more than before.

How can I die alone.
Where will I be then who am now alone,
what groans so pathetically
in this room where I am alone?

I will go to the garden.
I will be a romantic. I will sell
myself in hell,
in heaven also I will be.

In my mind I see the door,
I see the sunlight before me across the floor
beckon to me, as the Lady's skirt
moves small beyond it.

## FOR MY MOTHER: GENEVIEVE JULES CREELEY

*April 8, 1887–October 7, 1972*

Tender, semi-
articulate flickers
of your

presence, all
those years
past

now, eighty-
five, impossible to
count them

one by one, like
addition, sub-
traction, missing

not one. The last
curled up, in
on yourself,

position you take
in the bed, hair
wisped up

on your head, a
top knot, body
skeletal, eyes

closed against,
it must be,
further disturbance—

breathing a skim
of time, lightly
kicks the intervals—

days, days and
years of it,
work, changes,

sweet flesh caught
at the edges,
dignity's faded

dilemma.  It
is *your* life, oh
no one's

forgotten anything
ever.  They want
to make you

happy when
they remember.  Walk
a little, get

up, now, die
safely,
easily, into

singleness, too
tired with it
to keep

on and on.
Waves break at
the darkness

under the road, sounds
in the faint
night's softness.  Look

at them, catching
the light, white
edge as they turn—

always again
and again.  Dead
one, two,

three hours—
all these minutes
pass.  Is it,

was it, ever
you alone
again, how

long you kept
at it, your
pride, your

lovely, confusing
discretion.  Mother, I
love you—for

whatever that
means,
meant—more

than I know, body
gave me my
own, generous,

inexorable place
of you.  I feel
the mouth's sluggish-

ness, slips on
turns of things
said, to you,

too soon, too late,
wants to
go back to beginning,

smells of the hospital
room, the doctor
she responds

to now, the
order—get me
there. "Death's

let you out—"
comes true,
this, that,

endlessly circular
life, and we
came back

to see you one
last
time, this

time?  Your head
shuddered,
it seemed, your

eyes wanted,
I thought,
to see

who it was.
I am here,
and will follow.

## PRAYER TO HERMES

*for Rafael Lopez-Pedraza*

Hermes, god
of crossed sticks,
crossed existence,
protect these feet

I offer.  Imagination
is the wonder
of the real, and I am
sore afflicted with

the devil's doubles,
the twos, of this
half-life,
this twilight.

Neither one nor two
but a mixture
walks here
in me—

feels forward,
finds behind
the track, yet
cannot stand

still or be here
elemental, be more
or less a man,
a woman.

What I understand
of this life,
what was right
in it, what was wrong,

I have forgotten
in these days
of physical change.
I see the ways

of knowing, of
securing, life grow
ridiculous.  A weakness,
a tormenting, relieving weakness

comes to me.  My hand
I see at arm's end—
five fingers, fist—
is not mine?

Then must I forever
walk on, *walk on*—
as I have and
as I can?

Neither truth, nor love,
nor body itself—
nor anyone of any—
become me?

Yet questions
are tricks,
for me—
and always will be.

This moment the grey,
suffusing fog
floats in the quiet courtyard
beyond the window—

this morning grows now
to noon, and somewhere above
the sun warms the air
and wetness drips as ever

under the grey, diffusing
clouds.  This weather,
this winter, comes closer.
This—*physical* sentence.

I give all
to you, hold
nothing back,
have no strength to.

My luck
is your gift,
my melodious
breath, my stumbling,

my twisted commitment,
my vagrant
drunkenness, my confused
flesh and blood.

All who know me
say, *why* this man's
persistent pain, the scarifying
openness he makes do with?

Agh! brother spirit,
what do they know
of whatever *is* the instant
cannot wait a minute—

*will* find heaven in hell,
*will* be there again even now,
and *will* tell of itself
all, *all* the world.

# ALLEN GINSBERG (1926)


## HOWL

*for Carl Solomon*

I

I saw the best minds of my generation destroyed by madness, starving
     hysterical naked,
dragging themselves through the negro streets at dawn looking for an
     angry fix,
angelheaded hipsters burning for the ancient heavenly connection to the
     starry dynamo in the machinery of night,
who poverty and tatters and hollow-eyed and high sat up smoking in the
     supernatural darkness of cold-water flats floating across the tops of
     cities contemplating jazz,
who bared their brains to Heaven under the El and saw Mohammedan
     angels staggering on tenement roofs illuminated,
who passed through universities with radiant cool eyes hallucinating
     Arkansas and Blake-light tragedy among the scholars of war,
who were expelled from the academies for crazy & publishing obscene
     odes on the windows of the skull,
who cowered in unshaven rooms in underwear, burning their money in
     wastebaskets and listening to the Terror through the wall,
who got busted in their pubic beards returning through Laredo with a
     belt of marijuana for New York,
who ate fire in paint hotels or drank turpentine in Paradise Alley, death,
     or purgatoried their torsos night after night
with dreams, with drugs, with waking nightmares, alcohol and cock and
     endless balls,
incomparable blind streets of shuddering cloud and lightning in the mind
     leaping toward poles of Canada & Paterson, illuminating all the
     motionless world of Time between,
Peyote solidities of halls, backyard green tree cemetery dawns, wine
     drunkenness over the rooftops, storefront boroughs of teahead
     joyride neon blinking traffic light, sun and moon and tree vibrations
     in the roaring winter dusks of Brooklyn, ashcan rantings and kind
     king light of mind,
who chained themselves to subways for the endless ride from Battery to
     holy Bronx on benzedrine until the noise of wheels and children
     brought them down shuddering mouth-wracked and battered bleak
     of brain all drained of brilliance in the drear light of Zoo,

who sank all night in submarine light of Bickford's floated out and sat
through the stale beer afternoon in desolate Fugazzi's, listening to
the crack of doom on the hydrogen jukebox,
who talked continuously seventy hours from park to pad to bar to
Bellevue to museum to the Brooklyn Bridge,
a lost battalion of platonic conversationalists jumping down the stoops
off fire escapes off windowsills off Empire State out of the moon,
yacketayakking screaming vomiting whispering facts and memories and
anecdotes and eyeball kicks and shocks of hospitals and jails and
wars,
whole intellects disgorged in total recall for seven days and nights with
brilliant eyes, meat for the Synagogue cast on the pavement,
who vanished into nowhere Zen New Jersey leaving a trail of ambiguous
picture postcards of Atlantic City Hall,
suffering Eastern sweats and Tangerian bone-grindings and migraines of
China under junk-withdrawal in Newark's bleak furnished room,
who wandered around and around at midnight in the railroad yard
wondering where to go, and went, leaving no broken hearts,
who lit cigarettes in boxcars boxcars boxcars racketing through snow
toward lonesome farms in grandfather night,
who studied Plotinus Poe St. John of the Cross telepathy and bop kaballa
because the cosmos instinctively vibrated at their feet in Kansas,
who loned it through the streets of Idaho seeking visionary indian angels
who were visionary indian angels,
who thought they were only mad when Baltimore gleamed in supernatural
ecstasy,
who jumped in limousines with the Chinaman of Oklahoma on the impulse
of winter midnight streetlight smalltown rain,
who lounged hungry and lonesome through Houston seeking jazz or sex or
soup, and followed the brilliant Spaniard to converse about America
and Eternity, a hopeless task, and so took ship to Africa,
who disappeared into the volcanoes of Mexico leaving behind nothing but
the shadow of dungarees and the lava and ash of poetry scattered in
fireplace Chicago,
who reappeared on the West Coast investigating the F.B.I. in beards and
shorts with big pacifist eyes sexy in their dark skin passing out
incomprehensible leaflets,
who burned cigarette holes in their arms protesting the narcotic tobacco
haze of Capitalism,
who distributed Supercommunist pamphlets in Union Square weeping and
undressing while the sirens of Los Alamos wailed them down, and
wailed down Wall, and the Staten Island ferry also wailed,
who broke down crying in white gymnasiums naked and trembling before
the machinery of other skeletons,

who bit detectives in the neck and shrieked with delight in policecars for
    committing no crime but their own wild cooking pederasty and
    intoxication,

who howled on their knees in the subway and were dragged off the roof
    waving genitals and manuscripts,

who let themselves be fucked in the ass by saintly motorcyclists, and
    screamed with joy,

who blew and were blown by those human seraphim, the sailors, caresses
    of Atlantic and Caribbean love,

who balled in the morning in the evenings in rosegardens and the grass of
    public parks and cemeteries scattering their semen freely to whom-
    ever come who may,

who hiccupped endlessly trying to giggle but wound up with a sob behind
    a partition in a Turkish Bath when the blonde & naked angel came
    to pierce them with a sword,

who lost their loveboys to the three old shrews of fate the one eyed shrew
    of the heterosexual dollar the one eyed shrew that winks out of the
    womb and the one eyed shrew that does nothing but sit on her ass
    and snip the intellectual golden threads of the craftsman's loom,

who copulated ecstatic and insatiate with a bottle of beer a sweetheart a
    package of cigarettes a candle and fell off the bed, and continued
    along the floor and down the hall and ended fainting on the wall
    with a vision of ultimate cunt and come eluding the last gyzym of
    consciousness,

who sweetened the snatches of a million girls trembling in the sunset, and
    were red eyed in the morning but prepared to sweeten the snatch of
    the sunrise, flashing buttocks under barns and naked in the lake,

who went out whoring through Colorado in myriad stolen night-cars, N.C.,
    secret hero of these poems, cocksman and Adonis of Denver—joy to
    the memory of his innumerable lays of girls in empty lots & diner
    backyards, moviehouses rickety rows, on mountaintops in caves or
    with gaunt waitresses in familiar roadside lonely petticoat upliftings
    & especially secret gas-station solipsisms of johns, & hometown
    alleys too,

who faded out in vast sordid movies, were shifted in dreams, woke on a
    sudden Manhattan, and picked themselves up out of basements
    hungover with heartless Tokay and horrors of Third Avenue iron
    dreams & stumbled to unemployment offices,

who walked all night with their shoes full of blood on the snowbank docks
    waiting for a door in the East River to open to a room full of
    steamheat and opium,

who created great suicidal dramas on the apartment cliff-banks of the
    Hudson under the wartime blue floodlight of the moon & their
    heads shall be crowned with laurel in oblivion,

who ate the lamb stew of the imagination or digested the crab at the muddy
    bottom of the rivers of Bowery,

who wept at the romance of the streets with their pushcarts full of onions
    and bad music,

who sat in boxes breathing in the darkness under the bridge, and rose up
    to build harpsichords in their lofts,

who coughed on the sixth floor of Harlem crowned with flame under the
    tubercular sky surrounded by orange crates of theology,

who scribbled all night rocking and rolling over lofty incantations which
    in the yellow morning were stanzas of gibberish,

who cooked rotten animals lung heart feet tail borsht & tortillas dreaming
    of the pure vegetable kingdom,

who plunged themselves under meat trucks looking for an egg,

who threw their watches off the roof to cast their ballot for Eternity
    outside of Time, & alarm clocks fell on their heads every day for
    the next decade,

who cut their wrists three times successively unsuccessfully, gave up and
    were forced to open antique stores where they thought they were
    growing old and cried,

who were burned alive in their innocent flannel suits on Madison Avenue
    amid blasts of leaden verse & the tanked-up clatter of the iron
    regiments of fashion & the nitroglycerine shrieks of the fairies of
    advertising & the mustard gas of sinister intelligent editors, or were
    run down by the drunken taxicabs of Absolute Reality,

who jumped off the Brooklyn Bridge this actually happened and walked
    away unknown and forgotten into the ghostly daze of Chinatown
    soup alleyways & firetrucks, not even one free beer,

who sang out of their windows in despair, fell out of the subway window,
    jumped in the filthy Passaic, leaped on negroes, cried all over the
    street, danced on broken wineglasses barefoot smashed phonograph
    records of nostalgic European 1930's German jazz finished the
    whiskey and threw up groaning into the bloody toilet, moans in
    their ears and the blast of colossal steamwhistles,

who barreled down the highways of the past journeying to each other's
    hotrod-Golgotha jail-solitude watch or Birmingham jazz incarnation,

who drove crosscountry seventytwo hours to find out if I had a vision or
    you had a vision or he had a vision to find out Eternity,

who journeyed to Denver, who died in Denver, who came back to Denver
    & waited in vain, who watched over Denver & brooded & loned in
    Denver and finally went away to find out the Time, & now Denver
    is lonesome for her heroes,

who fell on their knees in hopeless cathedrals praying for each other's
    salvation and light and breasts, until the soul illuminated its hair
    for a second,

who crashed through their minds in jail waiting for impossible criminals
    with golden heads and the charm of reality in their hearts who sang
    sweet blues to Alcatraz,
who retired to Mexico to cultivate a habit, or Rocky Mount to tender
    Buddha or Tangiers to boys or Southern Pacific to the black
    locomotive or Harvard to Narcissus to Woodlawn to the daisychain
    or grave,
who demanded sanity trials accusing the radio of hypnotism & were left
    with their insanity & their hands & a hung jury,
who threw potato salad at CCNY lecturers on Dadaism and subsequently
    presented themselves on the granite steps of the madhouse with
    shaven heads and harlequin speech of suicide, demanding
    instantaneous lobotomy,
and who were given instead the concrete void of insulin metrasol electricity
    hydrotherapy psychotherapy occupational therapy pingpong &
    amnesia,
who in humorless protest overturned only one symbolic pingpong table,
    resting briefly in catatonia,
returning years later truly bald except for a wig of blood, and tears and
    fingers, to the visible madman doom of the wards of the madtowns
    of the East,
Pilgrim State's Rockland's and Greystone's foetid halls, bickering with the
    echoes of the soul, rocking and rolling in the midnight solitude-bench
    dolmen-realms of love, dream of life a nightmare, bodies turned to
    stone as heavy as the moon,
with mother finally ******, and the last fantastic book flung out of the
    tenement window, and the last door closed at 4 AM and the last
    telephone slammed at the wall in reply and the last furnished room
    emptied down to the last piece of mental furniture, a yellow paper
    rose twisted on a wire hanger in the closet, and even that imaginary,
    nothing but a hopeful little bit of hallucination—
ah, Carl, while you are not safe I am not safe, and now you're really in the
    total animal soup of time—
and who therefore ran through the icy streets obsessed with a sudden flash
    of the alchemy of the use of the ellipse the catalog the meter & the
    vibrating plane,
who dreamt and made incarnate gaps in Time & Space through images
    juxtaposed, and trapped the archangel of the soul between 2 visual
    images and joined the elemental verbs and set the noun and dash of
    consciousness together jumping with sensation of Pater Omnipotens
    Aeterna Deus
to recreate the syntax and measure of poor human prose and stand before
    you speechless and intelligent and shaking with shame, rejected yet

confessing out the soul to conform to the rhythm of thought in his
   naked and endless head,
the madman bum and angel beat in Time, unknown, yet putting down here
   what might be left to say in time come after death,
and rose reincarnate in the ghostly clothes of jazz in the goldhorn shadow
   of the band and blew the suffering of America's naked mind for love
   into an eli eli lamma lamma sabacthani saxophone cry that shivered
   the cities down to the last radio
with the absolute heart of the poem of life butchered out of their own
   bodies good to eat a thousand years.


II

What sphinx of cement and aluminum bashed open their skulls and ate up
   their brains and imagination?
Moloch! Solitude! Filth! Ugliness! Ashcans and unobtainable dollars!
   Children screaming under the stairways! Boys sobbing in armies!
   Old men weeping in the parks!
Moloch! Moloch! Nightmare of Moloch! Moloch the loveless! Mental
   Moloch! Moloch the heavy judger of men!
Moloch the incomprehensible prison! Moloch the crossbone soulless
   jailhouse and Congress of sorrows! Moloch whose buildings are
   judgement! Moloch the vast stone of war! Moloch the stunned
   governments!
Moloch whose mind is pure machinery! Moloch whose blood is running
   money! Moloch whose fingers are ten armies! Moloch whose
   breast is a cannibal dynamo! Moloch whose ear is a smoking tomb!
Moloch whose eyes are a thousand blind windows! Moloch whose
   skyscrapers stand in the long streets like endless Jehovahs! Moloch
   whose factories dream and croak in the fog! Moloch whose
   smokestacks and antennae crown the cities!
Moloch whose love is endless oil and stone! Moloch whose soul is electricity
   and banks! Moloch whose poverty is the specter of genius! Moloch
   whose fate is a cloud of sexless hydrogen! Moloch whose name is
   the Mind!
Moloch in whom I sit lonely! Moloch in whom I dream Angels! Crazy in
   Moloch! Cocksucker in Moloch! Lacklove and manless in Moloch!
Moloch who entered my soul early! Moloch in whom I am a consciousness
   without a body! Moloch who frightened me out of my natural
   ecstasy! Moloch whom I abandon! Wake up in Moloch! Light
   streaming out of the sky!
Moloch! Moloch! Robot apartments! invisible suburbs! skeleton
   treasuries! blind capitals! demonic industries! spectral nations!
   invincible madhouses! granite cocks! monstrous bombs!

They broke their backs lifting Moloch to Heaven! Pavements, trees, radios,
    tons! lifting the city to Heaven which exists and is everywhere about
    us!
Visions! omens! hallucinations! miracles! ecstasies! gone down the
    American river!
Dreams! adorations! illuminations! religions! the whole boatload of
    sensitive bullshit!
Breakthroughs! over the river! flips and crucifixions! gone down the
    flood! Highs! Epiphanies! Despairs! Ten years' animal screams
    and suicides! Minds! New loves! Mad generation! down on the
    rocks of Time!
Real holy laughter in the river! They saw it all! the wild eyes! the holy
    yells! They bade farewell! They jumped off the roof! to solitude!
    waving! carrying flowers! Down to the river! into the street!


### III

Carl Solomon! I'm with you in Rockland
    where you're madder than I am
I'm with you in Rockland
    where you must feel very strange
I'm with you in Rockland
    where you imitate the shade of my mother
I'm with you in Rockland
    where you've murdered your twelve secretaries
I'm with you in Rockland
    where you laugh at this invisible humor
I'm with you in Rockland
    where we are great writers on the same dreadful typewriter
I'm with you in Rockland
    where your condition has become serious and is reported on the radio
I'm with you in Rockland
    where the faculties of the skull no longer admit the worms of the
    senses
I'm with you in Rockland
    where you drink the tea of the breasts of the spinsters of Utica
I'm with you in Rockland
    where you pun on the bodies of your nurses the harpies of the Bronx
I'm with you in Rockland
    where you scream in a straightjacket that you're losing the game of
    the actual pingpong of the abyss
I'm with you in Rockland
    where you bang on the catatonic piano the soul is innocent and
    immortal it should never die ungodly in an armed madhouse

I'm with you in Rockland
> where fifty more shocks will never return your soul to its body again
> from its pilgrimage to a cross in the void

I'm with you in Rockland
> where you accuse your doctors of insanity and plot the Hebrew
> socialist revolution against the fascist national Golgotha

I'm with you in Rockland
> where you will split the heavens of Long Island and resurrect your
> living human Jesus from the superhuman tomb

I'm with you in Rockland
> where there are twentyfive-thousand mad comrades all together
> singing the final stanzas of the Internationale

I'm with you in Rockland
> where we hug and kiss the United States under our bedsheets the
> United States that coughs all night and won't let us sleep

I'm with you in Rockland
> where we wake up electrified out of the coma by our own souls'
> airplanes roaring over the roof they've come to drop angelic bombs
> the hospital illuminates itself   imaginary walls collapse   O skinny
> legions run outside   O starry-spangled shock of mercy the eternal
> war is here   O victory forget your underwear we're free

I'm with you in Rockland
> in my dreams you walk dripping from a sea-journey on the highway
> across America in tears to the door of my cottage in the Western
> night

*San Francisco   1955-56*

# A SUPERMARKET IN CALIFORNIA

What thoughts I have of you tonight, Walt Whitman, for I walked
down the sidestreets under the trees with a headache self-conscious looking
at the full moon.

In my hungry fatigue, and shopping for images, I went into the neon
fruit supermarket, dreaming of your enumerations!

What peaches and what penumbras! Whole families shopping at
night! Aisles full of husbands! Wives in the avocados, babies in the
tomatoes!—and you, Garcia Lorca, what were you doing down by the
watermelons?

I saw you, Walt Whitman, childless, lonely old grubber, poking among the meats in the refrigerator and eyeing the grocery boys.

I heard you asking questions of each: Who killed the pork chops? What price bananas? Are you my Angel?

I wandered in and out of the brilliant stacks of cans following you, and followed in my imagination by the store detective.

We strode down the open corridors together in our solitary fancy tasting artichokes, possessing every frozen delicacy, and never passing the cashier.

Where are we going, Walt Whitman? The doors close in an hour. Which way does your beard point tonight?

(I touch your book and dream of our odyssey in the supermarket and feel absurd.)

Will we walk all night through solitary streets? The trees add shade to shade, lights out in the houses, we'll both be lonely.

Will we stroll dreaming of the lost America of love past blue automobiles in driveways, home to our silent cottage?

Ah, dear father, graybeard, lonely old courage-teacher, what America did you have when Charon quit poling his ferry and you got out on a smoking bank and stood watching the boat disappear on the black waters of Lethe?

*Berkeley 1955*

## AMERICA

America I've given you all and now I'm nothing.
America two dollars and twentyseven cents January 17, 1956.
I can't stand my own mind.
America when will we end the human war?
Go fuck yourself with your atom bomb.
I don't feel good don't bother me.
I won't write my poem till I'm in my right mind.
America when will you be angelic?
When will you take off your clothes?
When will you look at yourself through the grave?
When will you be worthy of your million Trotskyites?
America why are your libraries full of tears?

America when will you send your eggs to India?
I'm sick of your insane demands.
When can I go into the supermarket and buy what I need with my good
    looks?
America after all it is you and I who are perfect not the next world.
Your machinery is too much for me.
You made me want to be a saint.
There must be some other way to settle this argument.
Burroughs is in Tangiers I don't think he'll come back it's sinister.
Are you being sinister or is this some form of practical joke?
I'm trying to come to the point.
I refuse to give up my obsession.
America stop pushing I know what I'm doing.
America the plum blossoms are falling.
I haven't read the newspapers for months, everyday somebody goes on
    trial for murder.
America I feel sentimental about the Wobblies.
America I used to be a communist when I was a kid I'm not sorry.
I smoke marijuana every chance I get.
I sit in my house for days on end and stare at the roses in the closet.
When I go to Chinatown I get drunk and never get laid.
My mind is made up there's going to be trouble.
You should have seen me reading Marx.
My psychoanalyst thinks I'm perfectly right.
I won't say the Lord's Prayer.
I have mystical visions and cosmic vibrations.
America I still haven't told you what you did to Uncle Max after he came
    over from Russia.

I'm addressing you.
Are you going to let your emotional life be run by Time Magazine?
I'm obsessed by Time Magazine.
I read it every week.
Its cover stares at me every time I slink past the corner candystore.
I read it in the basement of the Berkeley Public Library.
It's always telling me about responsibility. Businessmen are serious.
    Movie producers are serious. Everybody's serious but me.
It occurs to me that I am America.
I am talking to myself again.

Asia is rising against me.
I haven't got a chinaman's chance.
I'd better consider my national resources.

My national resources consist of two joints of marijuana millions of
    genitals an unpublishable private literature that goes 1400 miles
    an hour and twentyfive-thousand mental institutions.
I say nothing about my prisons nor the millions of underprivileged who
    live in my flowerpots under the light of five hundred suns.
I have abolished the whorehouses of France, Tangiers is the next to go.
My ambition is to be President despite the fact that I'm a Catholic.

America how can I write a holy litany in your silly mood?
I will continue like Henry Ford my strophes are as individual as his
    automobiles more so they're all different sexes.
America I will sell you strophes $2500 apiece $500 down on your old
    strophe
America free Tom Mooney
America save the Spanish Loyalists
America Sacco & Vanzetti must not die
America I am the Scottsboro boys.
America when I was seven momma took me to Communist Cell meetings
    they sold us garbanzos a handful per ticket a ticket costs a nickel
    and the speeches were free everybody was angelic and sentimental
    about the workers it was all so sincere you have no idea what a good
    thing the party was in 1835 Scott Nearing was a grand old man a
    real mensch Mother Bloor made me cry I once saw Israel Amter
    plain. Everybody must have been a spy.
America you don't really want to go to war.
America it's them bad Russians.
Them Russians them Russians and them Chinamen. And them Russians.
The Russia wants to eat us alive. The Russia's power mad. She wants to
    take our cars from out our garages.
Her wants to grab Chicago. Her needs a Red Readers' Digest. Her wants
    our auto plants in Siberia. Him big bureaucracy running our
    fillingstations.
That no good. Ugh. Him make Indians learn read. Him need big black
    niggers. Hah. Her make us all work sixteen hours a day. Help.
America this is quite serious.
America this is the impression I get from looking in the television set.
America is this correct?
I'd better get right down to the job.
It's true I don't want to join the Army or turn lathes in precision parts
    factories, I'm nearsighted and psychopathic anyway.
America I'm putting my queer shoulder to the wheel.

## from KADDISH

*for Naomi Ginsberg 1894-1956*

I

Strange now to think of you, gone without corsets & eyes, while I walk
   on the sunny pavement of Greenwich Village.
downtown Manhattan, clear winter noon, and I've been up all night,
      talking, talking, reading the Kaddish aloud, listening to Ray Charles
      blues shout blind on the phonograph
the rhythm the rhythm—and your memory in my head three years after—
      And read Adonais' last triumphant stanzas aloud—wept, realizing
      how we suffer—
And how Death is that remedy all singers dream of, sing, remember,
      prophesy as in the Hebrew Anthem, or the Buddhist Book of
      Answers—and my own imagination of a withered leaf—at dawn—
Dreaming back thru life, Your time—and mine accelerating toward
      Apocalypse,
the final moment—the flower burning in the Day—and what comes after,
looking back on the mind itself that saw an American city
a flash away, and the great dream of Me or China, or you and a phantom
      Russia, or a crumpled bed that never existed—
like a poem in the dark—escaped back to Oblivion—
No more to say, and nothing to weep for but the Beings in the Dream,
      trapped in its disappearance,
sighing, screaming with it, buying and selling pieces of phantom,
      worshipping each other,
worshipping the God included in it all—longing or inevitability?—while it
      lasts, a Vision—anything more?
It leaps about me, as I go out and walk the street, look back over my
      shoulder, Seventh Avenue, the battlements of window office
      buildings shouldering each other high, under a cloud, tall as the sky
      an instant—and the sky above—an old blue place.
or down the Avenue to the South, to—I walk toward the Lower East Side—
      where you walked 50 years ago, little girl—from Russia, eating the
      first poisonous tomatoes of America—frightened on the dock—
the struggling in the crowds of Orchard Street toward what?—toward
      Newark—
toward candy store, first home-made sodas of the century, handchurned
      ice cream in backroom on musty brownfloor boards—
Toward education marriage nervous breakdown, operation, teaching
      school, and learning to be mad, in a dream—what is this life?
Toward the Key in the window—and the great Key lays its head of light

on top of Manhattan, and over the floor, and lays down on the
   sidewalk—in a single vast beam, moving, as I walk down First toward
   the Yiddish Theater—and the place of poverty
you knew, and I know, but without caring now—Strange to have moved
   thru Paterson, and the West, and Europe and here again,
with the cries of Spaniards now in the doorstoops doors and dark boys
   on the street, fire escapes old as you
—Tho you're not old now, that's left here with me—
Myself, anyhow, maybe as old as the universe—and I guess that dies with
   us—enough to cancel all that comes—What came is gone forever
   every time—
That's good! That leaves it open for no regret—no fear radiators, lacklove,
   torture even toothache in the end—
Though while it comes it is a lion that eats the soul—and the lamb, the
   soul, in us, alas, offering itself in sacrifice to change's fierce hunger—
   hair and teeth—and the roar of bonepain, skull bare, break rib, rot-
   skin, braintricked Implacability.
Ai! ai! we do worse! We are in a fix! And you're out, Death let you
   out, Death had the Mercy, you're done with your century, done
   with God, done with the path thru it—Done with yourself at last—
   Pure—Back to the Babe dark before your Father, before us all—
   before the world—
There, rest. No more suffering for you. I know where you've gone, it's
   good.
No more flowers in the summer fields of New York, no joy now, no more
   fear of Louis,
and no more of his sweetness and glasses, his high school decades, debts,
   loves, frightened telephone calls, conception beds, relatives, hands—
No more of sister Elanor,—she gone before you—we kept it secret—you
   killed her—or she killed herself to bear with you—an arthritic heart—
   But Death's killed you both—No matter—
Nor your memory of your mother, 1915 tears in silent movies weeks and
   weeks—forgetting, agrieve watching Marie Dressler address humanity,
   Chaplin dance in youth,
or Boris Godinov, Chaliapin's at the Met, halling his voice of a weeping
   Czar—by standing room with Elanor & Max—watching also the
   Capitalists take seats in Orchestra, white furs, diamonds,
with the YPSL's hitch-hiking thru Pennsylvania, in black baggy gym skirts
   pants, photograph of 4 girls holding each other round the waist, and
   laughing eye, too coy, virginal solitude of 1920
all girls grown old, or dead, now, and that long hair in the grave—lucky to
   have husbands later—
You made it—I came too—Eugene my brother before (still grieving now

and will gream on to his last stiff hand, as he goes thru his cancer—or
  kill—later perhaps—soon he will think—)
And it's the last moment I remember, which I see them all, thru myself,
  now—tho not you
I didn't foresee what you felt—what more hideous gape of bad mouth came
  first—to you—and were you prepared?
To go where? In that Dark—that—in that God? a radiance? A Lord in the
  Void? Like an eye in the black cloud in a dream? Adonoi at last,
  with you?
Beyond my remembrance! Incapable to guess! Not merely the yellow
  skull in the grave, or a box of worm dust, and a stained ribbon—
  Deathshead with Halo? can you believe it?
Is it only the sun that shines once for the mind, only the flash of existence,
  than none ever was?
Nothing beyond what we have—what you had—that so pitiful—yet Triumph,
to have been here, and changed, like a tree, broken, or flower—fed to the
  ground—but mad, with its petals, colored, thinking Great Universe,
  shaken, cut in the head, leaf stript, hid in an egg crate hospital, cloth
  wrapped, sore—freaked in the moon brain, Naughtless.
No flower like that flower, which knew itself in the garden, and fought the
  knife—lost
Cut down by an idiot Snowman's icy—even in the Spring—strange ghost
  thought—some Death—Sharp icicle in his hand—crowned with old
  roses—a dog for his eyes—cock of a sweatshop—heart of electric irons.
All the accumulations of life, that wear us out—clocks, bodies, consciousness,
  shoe, breasts—begotten sons—your Communism—'Paranoia' into
  hospitals.
You once kicked Elanor in the leg, she died of heart failure later. You of
  stroke. Asleep? within a year, the two of you, sisters in death. Is
  Elanor happy?
Max grieves alive in an office on Lower Broadway, lone large mustache
  over midnight Accountings, not sure. His life passes—as he sees—
  and what does he doubt now? Still dream of making money, or
  that might have made money, hired nurse, had children, found
  even your Immortality, Naomi?
I'll see him soon. Now I've got to cut through—to talk to you—as I didn't
  when you had a mouth.
Forever. And we're bound for that, Forever—like Emily Dickinson's
  horses—headed to the End.
They know the way—These Steeds—run faster than we think—it's our own
  life they cross—and take with them.

Magnificent, mourned no more, marred of heart, mind behind,
married dreamed, mortal changed—Ass and face done with murder.

In the world, given, flower maddened, made no Utopia, shut under
pine, almed in Earth, balmed in Lone, Jehovah, accept.

Nameless, One Faced, Forever beyond me, beginningless, endless,
Father in death. Tho I am not there for this Prophecy, I am unmarried,
I'm hymnless, I'm Heavenless, headless in blisshood I would still adore

Thee, Heaven, after Death, only One blessed in Nothingness, not
light or darkness, Dayless Eternity—

Take this, this Psalm, from me, burst from my hand in a day, some
of my Time, now given to Nothing—to praise Thee—But Death

This is the end, the redemption from Wilderness, way for the
Wonderer, House sought for All, black handkerchief washed clean by
weeping—page beyond Psalm—Last change of mine and Naomi—to God's
perfect Darkness—Death, stay thy phantoms!

# KRAL MAJALES

And the Communists have nothing to offer but fat cheeks and eyeglasses
        and lying policemen
and the Capitalists proffer Napalm and money in green suitcases to the
        Naked,
and the Communists create heavy industry but the heart is also heavy
and the beautiful engineers are all dead, the secret technicians conspire for
        their own glamor
in the Future, in the Future, but now drink vodka and lament the Security
        Forces,
and the Capitalists drink gin and whiskey on airplanes but let Indian brown
        millions starve
and when Communist and Capitalist assholes tangle the Just man is arrested
        or robbed or had his head cut off,
but not like Kabir, and the cigarette cough of the Just man above the
        clouds
in the bright sunshine is a salute to the health of the blue sky.
For I was arrested thrice in Prague, once for singing drunk on Narodni
        street,
once knocked down on the midnight pavement by a mustached agent who
        screamed out BOUZERANT,

once for losing my notebooks of unusual sex politics dream opinions,
and I was sent from Havana by plane by detectives in green uniform,
and I was sent from Prague by plane by detectives in Czechoslovakian
    business suits,
Cardplayers out of Cézanne, the two strange dolls that entered Joseph
    K's room at morn
also entered mine, and ate at my table, and examined my scribbles,
and followed me night and morn from the houses of lovers to the cafés of
    Centrum—
And I am the King of May, which is the power of sexual youth,
and I am the King of May, which is industry in eloquence and action in
    amour,
and I am the King of May, which is long hair of Adam and the Beard of
    my own body
and I am the King of May, which is Kral Majales in the Czechoslovakian
    tongue,
and I am the King of May, which is old Human poesy, and 100,000 people
    chose my name,
and I am the King of May, and in a few minutes I will land at London
    Airport,
and I am the King of May, naturally, for I am of Slavic parentage and a
    Buddhist Jew
who worships the Sacred Heart of Christ the blue body of Krishna the
    straight back of Ram
the beads of Chango the Nigerian   singing Shiva Shiva in a manner which
    I have invented,
and the King of May is a middleeuropean honor, mine in the XX century
despite space and the Time Machine, because I heard the voice of Blake in
    a vision,
and repeat that voice. And I am King of May that sleeps with teenagers
    laughing.
And I am the King of May, that I may be expelled from my Kingdom with
    Honor, as of old,
To shew the difference between Caesar's Kingdom and the Kingdom of
    the May of Man—
and I am the King of May, the paranoid, for the Kingdom of May is too
    beautiful to last for more than a month—
and I am the King of May because I touched my finger to my forehead
    saluting
a luminous heavy girl trembling hands who said "one moment Mr.
    Ginsberg"
before a fat young Plainclothesman stepped between our bodies—I was
    going to England—

and I am the King of May, returning to see Bunhill Fields and walk on
      Hampstead Heath,
and I am the King of May, in a giant jetplane touching Albion's airfield
      trembling in fear
as the plane roars to a landing on the grey concrete, shakes & expells
      air,
and rolls slowly to a stop under the clouds with part of blue heaven still
      visible.
And *tho* I am the King of May, the Marxists have beat me upon the street,
      kept me up all night in Police Station, followed me thru Springtime
      Prague, detained me in secret and deported me from our kingdom
      by airplane.
Thus I have written this poem on a jet seat in mid Heaven.

*May 7, 1965*

## ON NEAL'S ASHES

Delicate eyes that blinked blue Rockies all ash
nipples, Ribs I touched w/ my thumb are ash
mouth my tongue touched once or twice all ash
bony cheeks soft on my belly are cinder, ash
earlobes & eyelids, youthful cock tip, curly pubis
breast warmth, man palm, high school thigh,
baseball bicept arm, asshole anneal'd to silken skin
             all ashes, all ashes again.

*August 1968*

# FRANK O'HARA (1926-1966)

## ON RACHMANINOFF'S BIRTHDAY

Quick! a last poem before I go
off my rocker. Oh Rachmaninoff!
Onset, Massachusetts. Is it the fig-newton
playing the horn? Thundering windows
of hell, will your tubes ever break
into powder? Oh my palace of oranges,
junk shop, staples, umber, basalt;
I'm a child again when I was really
miserable, a grope pizzicato. My pocket
of rhinestone, yoyo, carpenter's pencil,
amethyst, hypo, campaign button,
is the room full of smoke? Shit
on the soup, let it burn. So it's back.
You'll never be mentally sober.

## TO THE HARBORMASTER

I wanted to be sure to reach you;
though my ship was on the way it got caught
in some moorings. I am always tying up
and then deciding to depart. In storms and
at sunset, with the metallic coils of the tide
around my fathomless arms, I am unable
to understand the forms of my vanity
or I am hard alee with my Polish rudder
in my hand and the sun sinking. To
you I offer my hull and the tattered cordage
of my will. The terrible channels where
the wind drives me against the brown lips
of the reeds are not all behind me. Yet
I trust the sanity of my vessel; and

if it sinks, it may well be in answer
to the reasoning of the eternal voices,
the waves which have kept me from reaching you.


# IN MEMORY OF MY FEELINGS

*to Grace Hartigan*

1

My quietness has a man in it, he is transparent
and he carries me quietly, like a gondola, through the streets.
He has several likenesses, like stars and years, like numerals.

My quietness has a number of naked selves,
so many pistols I have borrowed to protect myselves
from creatures who too readily recognize my weapons
and have murder in their heart!
                              though in winter
they are warm as roses, in the desert
taste of chilled anisette.
                         At times, withdrawn,
I rise into the cool skies
and gaze on at the imponderable world with the simple identification
of my colleagues, the mountains. Manfred climbs to my nape,
speaks, but I do not hear him,
                              I'm too blue.
An elephant takes up his trumpet,
money flutters from the windows of cries, silk stretching its mirror
across shoulder blades. A gun is "fired."
                                        One of me rushes
to window #13 and one of me raises his whip and one of me
flutters up from the center of the track amidst the pink flamingoes,
and underneath their hooves as they round the last turn my lips
are scarred and brown, brushed by tails, masked in dirt's lust,
definition, open mouths gasping for the cries of the bettors for the lungs
of earth.
         So many of my transparencies could not resist the race!
Terror in earth, dried mushrooms, pink feathers, tickets,
a flaking moon drifting across the muddied teeth,
the imperceptible moan of covered breathing,
                                           love of the serpent!

I am underneath its leaves as the hunter crackles and pants
and bursts, as the barrage balloon drifts behind a cloud
and animal death whips out its flashlight,

                        whistling
and slipping the glove off the trigger hand. The serpent's eyes
redden at sight of those thorny fingernails, he is so smooth!

                            My transparent selves
flail about like vipers in a pail, writhing and hissing
without panic, with a certain justice of response
and presently the aquiline serpent comes to resemble the Medusa.


       2
The dead hunting
and the alive, ahunted.

                   My father, my uncle,
my grand-uncle and the several aunts. My
grand-aunt dying for me, like a talisman, in the war,
before I had even gone to Borneo
her blood vessels rushed to the surface
and burst like rockets over the wrinkled
invasion of the Australians, her eyes aslant
like the invaded, but blue like mine.
An atmosphere of supreme lucidity,

                       humanism,
the mere existence of emphasis,

                      a rusted barge
painted orange against the sea
full of Marines reciting the Arabian ideas
which are a proof in themselves of seasickness
which is a proof in itself of being hunted.
A hit? *ergo* swim.

                My 10     my 19,
my 9,          and the several years. My
12 years since they all died, philosophically speaking.
And now the coolness of a mind
like a shuttered suite in the Grand Hotel
where mail arrives for my incognito,

                       whose façade
has been slipping into the Grand Canal for centuries;
rockets splay over a *sposalizio*,

                   fleeing into night
from their Chinese memories, and it is a celebration,
the trying desperately to count them as they die.

But who will stay to be these numbers
when all the lights are dead?


3

The most arid stretch is often richest,
the hand lifting towards a fig tree from hunger
                                                    digging
and there is water, clear, supple, or there
deep in the sand where death sleeps, a murmurous bubbling
proclaims the blackness that will ease and burn.
You preferred the Arabs? but they didn't stay to count
their inventions, racing into sands, converting themselves into
so many,
            embracing, at Ramadan, the tenderest effigies of
themselves with penises shorn by the hundreds, like a camel
ravishing a goat.
            And the mountainous-minded Greeks could speak
of time as a river and step across it into Persia, leaving the pain
at home to be converted into statuary. I adore the Roman copies.
And the stench of the camel's spit I swallow,
and the stench of the whole goat. For we have advanced, France,
together into a new land, like the Greeks, where one feels nostalgic
for mere ideas, where truth lies on its deathbed like an uncle
and one of me has a sentimental longing for number,
as has another for the ball gowns of the Directoire and yet
another for "Destiny, Paris, destiny!"
                                    or "Only a king may kill a king."


How many selves are there in a war hero asleep in names? under
a blanket of platoon and fleet, orderly. For every seaman
with one eye closed in fear and twitching arm at a sigh for Lord Nelson,
he is all dead; and now a meek subaltern writhes in his bedclothes
with the fury of a thousand, violating an insane mistress
who has only herself to offer his multitudes.
                                    Rising,
he wraps himself in the burnoose of memories against the heat of life
and over the sands he goes to take an algebraic position *in re*
a sun of fear shining not too bravely. He will ask himselves to
vote on fear before he feels a tremor,
                        as runners arrive from the mountains
bearing snow, proof that the mind's obsolescence is still capable
of intimacy. His mistress will follow him across the desert
like a goat, towards a mirage which is something familiar about

one of his innumerable wrists,

                      and lying in an oasis one day,
playing catch with coconuts, they suddenly smell oil.


     4
Beneath these lives
the ardent lover of history hides,

                  tongue out
leaving a globe of spit on a taut spear of grass
and leaves off rattling his tail a moment
to admire this flag.
              I'm looking for my Shanghai Lil.
Five years ago, enamored of fire-escapes, I went to Chicago,
an eventful trip: the fountains! the Art Institute, the Y
for both sexes, absent Christianity.
              At 7, before Jane
was up, the copper lake stirred against the sides
of a Norwegian freighter; on the deck a few dirty men,
tired of night, watched themselves in the water
as years before the German prisoners on the *Prinz Eugen*
dappled the Pacific with their sores, painted purple
by a Naval doctor.
             Beards growing, and the constant anxiety
over looks. I'll shave before she wakes up. Sam Goldwyn
spent $2,000,000 on Anna Sten, but Grushenka left America.
One of me is standing in the waves, an ocean bather,
or I am naked with a plate of devils at my hip.
              Grace
to be born and live as variously as possible. The conception
of the masque barely suggests the sordid identifications.
I am a Hittite in love with a horse. I don't know what blood's
in me I feel like an African prince I am a girl walking downstairs
in a red pleated dress with heels I am a champion taking a fall
I am a jockey with a sprained ass-hole I am the light mist
              in which a face appears
and it is another face of blonde I am a baboon eating a banana
I am a dictator looking at his wife I am a doctor eating a child
and the child's mother smiling I am a Chinaman climbing a mountain
I am a child smelling his father's underwear I am an Indian
sleeping on a scalp
           and my pony is stamping in the birches,
and I've just caught sight of the *Nina*, the *Pinta* and the *Santa Maria*.
           What land is this, so free!

                                        I watch
the sea at the back of my eyes, near the spot where I think
in solitude as pine trees groan and support the enormous winds,
they are humming *L'Oiseau de feu!*
                        They look like gods, these whitemen,
and they are bringing me the horse I fell in love with on the frieze.


        5
And now it is the serpent's turn.
I am not quite you, but almost, the opposite of visionary.
You are coiled around the central figure,
                                    the heart
that bubbles with red ghosts, since to move is to love
and the scrutiny of all things is syllogistic,
the startled eyes of the dikdik, the bush full of white flags
fleeing a hunter,
                which is our democracy
                                    but the prey
is always fragile and like something, as a seashell can be
a great Courbet, if it wishes. To bend the ear of the outer world.


                        When you turn your head
can you feel your heels, undulating? that's what it is
to be a serpent. I haven't told you of the most beautiful things
in my lives, and watching the ripple of their loss disappear
along the shore, underneath ferns,
                            face downward in the ferns
my body, the naked host to my many selves, shot
by a guerrilla warrior or dumped from a car into ferns
which are themselves *journalières.*
                        The hero, trying to unhitch his parachute,
stumbles over me. It is our last embrace.
                            And yet
I have forgotten my loves, and chiefly that one, the cancerous
statue which my body could no longer contain,
                                against my will
                                against my love
become art,
            I could not change it into history
and so remember it,
                    and I have lost what is always and everywhere
present, the scene of my selves, the occasion of these ruses,
which I myself and singly must now kill
                        and save the serpent in their midst.

## WHY I AM NOT A PAINTER

I am not a painter, I am a poet.
Why? I think I would rather be
a painter, but I am not. Well,

For instance, Mike Goldberg
is starting a painting   I drop in.
"Sit down and have a drink" he
says. I drink; we drink. I look
up. "You have SARDINES in it."
"Yes, it needed something there."
"Oh." I go and the days go by
and I drop in again. The painting
is going on, and I go, and the days
go by. I drop in. The painting is
finished. "Where's SARDINES?"
All that's left is just
letters, "It was too much," Mike says.

But me? One day I am thinking of
a color: orange. I write a line
about orange. Pretty soon it is a
whole page of words, not lines.
Then another page. There should be
so much more, not of orange, of
words, of how terrible orange is
and life. Days go by. It is even in
prose, I am a real poet. My poem
is finished and I haven't mentioned
orange yet. It's twelve poems, I call
it ORANGES. And one day in a gallery
I see Mike's painting, called SARDINES.

# ODE:  SALUTE TO THE FRENCH NEGRO POETS

From near the sea, like Whitman my great predecessor, I call
to the spirits of other lands to make fecund my existence

do not spare your wrath upon our shores, that trees may grow
upon the sea, mirror of our total mankind in the weather

one who no longer remembers dancing in the heat of the moon may call
across the shifting sands, trying to live in the terrible western world

here where to love at all's to be a politician, as to love a poem
is pretentious, this may sound tendentious but it's lyrical

which shows what lyricism has been brought to by our fabled times
where cowards are shibboleths and one specific love's traduced

by shame for what you love more generally and never would avoid
where reticence is paid for by a poet in his blood or ceasing to be

blood!  blood that we have mountains in our veins to stand off jackals
in the pillaging of our desires and allegiances, Aimé Césaire

for if there is fortuity it's in the love we bear each other's differences
in race which is the poetic ground on which we rear our smiles

standing in the sun of marshes as we wade slowly toward the culmination
of a gift which is categorically the most difficult relationship

and should be sought as such because it is our nature, nothing
inspires us but the love we want upon the frozen face of earth

and utter disparagement turns into praise as generations read the message
of our hearts in adolescent closets who once shot at us in doorways

or kept us from living freely because they were too young then to know
what they would ultimately need from a barren and heart-sore life

the beauty of America, neither cool jazz nor devoured Egyptian heroes, lies in
lives in the darkness I inhabit in the midst of sterile millions

the only truth is face to face, the poem whose words become your mouth
and dying in black and white we fight for what we love, not are

## THE DAY LADY DIED

It is 12:20 in New York a Friday
three days after Bastille day, yes
it is 1959 and I go get a shoeshine
because I will get off the 4:19 in Easthampton
at 7:15 and then go straight to dinner
and I don't know the people who will feed me

I walk up the muggy street beginning to sun
and have a hamburger and a malted and buy
an ugly NEW WORLD WRITING to see what the poets
in Ghana are doing these days
                              I go on to the bank
and Miss Stillwagon (first name Linda I once heard)
doesn't even look up my balance for once in her life
and in the GOLDEN GRIFFIN I get a little Verlaine
for Patsy with drawings by Bonnard although I do
think of Hesiod, trans. Richmond Lattimore or
Brendan Behan's new play or *Le Balcon* or *Les Nègres*
of Genet, but I don't, I stick with Verlaine
after practically going to sleep with quandariness

and for Mike I just stroll into the PARK LANE
Liquor Store and ask for a bottle of Strega and
than I go back where I came from to 6th Avenue
and the tobacconist in the Ziegfeld Theatre and
casually ask for a carton of Gauloises and a carton
of Picayunes, and a NEW YORK POST with her face on it

and I am sweating a lot by now and thinking of
leaning on the john door in the 5 SPOT
while she whispered a song along the keyboard
to Mal Waldron and everyone and I stopped breathing

## POEM

Khrushchev is coming on the right day!
                            the cool graced light
is pushed off the enormous glass piers by hard wind
and everything is tossing, hurrying on up
                     this country
has everything but *politesse*, a Puerto Rican cab driver says
and five different girls I see
                   look like Piedie Gimbel
with her blonde hair tossing too,
                        as she looked when I pushed
her little daughter on the swing on the lawn it was also windy

last night we went to a movie and came out,
                        Ionesco is greater
than Beckett, Vincent said, that's what I think, blueberry blintzes
and Khrushchev was probably being carped at
                      in Washington, no *politesse*
Vincent tells me about his mother's trip to Sweden
                            Hans tells us
about his father's life in Sweden, it sounds like Grace Hartigan's
painting *Sweden*
               so I go home to bed and names drift through my head
Purgatorio Merchado, Gerhard Schwartz and Gaspar Gonzales, all
        unknown figures of the early morning as I go to work

where does the evil of the year go
                     when September takes New York
and turns it into ozone stalagmites
               deposits of light
               so I get back up
make coffee, and read François Villon, his life, so dark
   New York seems blinding and my tie is blowing up the street
I wish it would blow off
                 though it is cold and somewhat warms my neck
as the train bears Khrushchev on to Pennsylvania Station
    and the light seems to be eternal
    and joy seems to be inexorable
    I am foolish enough always to find it in wind

# HÔTEL TRANSYLVANIE

Shall we win at love or shall we lose
                can it be
that hurting and being hurt is a trick forcing the love
we want to appear, that the hurt is a card
and is it black? is it red? is it a paper, dry of tears
*chevalier*, change your expression! the wind is sweeping over
the gaming tables ruffling the cards/they are black and red
like Futurist torture and how do you know it isn't always there
waiting while doubt is the father that has you kidnapped by friends

        yet you will always live in a jealous society of accident
you will never know how beautiful you are or how beautiful
the other is, you will continue to refuse to die for yourself
you will continue to sing on trying to cheer everyone up
and they will know as they listen with excessive pleasure that you're dead
        and they will not mind that they have let you entertain
at the expense of the only thing you want in the world/you are amusing
as a game is amusing when someone is forced to lose as in a game I must

        oh *hôtel*, you should be merely a bed
surrounded by walls where two souls meet and do nothing but breathe
breathe in breathe out fuse illuminate confuse *stick* dissemble
but not as cheaters at cards have something to win/you have only to be
as you are being, as you must be, as you always are, as you shall be forever
no matter what fate deals you or the imagination discards like a tyrant
as the drums descend and summon the hatchet over the tinselled realities

you know that I am not here to fool around, that I must win or die
I expect you to do everything because it is of no consequence/no duel
you must rig the deck you must make me win at whatever cost to the
        reputation
of the establishment/sublime moment of dishonest hope/I must win
for if the floods of tears arrive they will wash it all away
                       and then
you will know what it is to want something, but you may not be allowed
to die as I have died, you may only be allowed to drift downstream
to another body of inimical attractions for which you will substitute/distrust
and I will have had my revenge on the black bitch of my nature which you
        love as I have never loved myself

but I hold on/I am lyrical to a fault/I do not despair being too foolish
where will you find me, projective verse, since I will be gone?
for six seconds of your beautiful face I will sell the hotel and commit
an uninteresting suicide in Louisiana where it will take them a long time
to know who I am/why I came there/what and why I am and made to happen


## AVE MARIA


Mothers of America
               let your kids go to the movies!
get them out of the house so they won't know what you're up to
it's true that fresh air is good for the body
                           but what about the soul
that grows in darkness, embossed by silvery images
and when you grow old as grow old you must
                       they won't hate you
they won't criticize you they won't know
                       they'll be in some glamorous country
they first saw on a Saturday afternoon or playing hookey
they may even be grateful to you
                 for their first sexual experience
which only cost you a quarter
                and didn't upset the peaceful home
they will know where candy bars come from
                   and gratuitous bags of popcorn
as gratuitous as leaving the movie before it's over
with a pleasant stranger whose apartment is in the Heaven on Earth Bldg
near the Williamsburg Bridge
                oh mothers you will have made the little tykes
so happy because if nobody does pick them up in the movies
they won't know the difference
                and if somebody does it'll be sheer gravy
and they'll have been truly entertained either way
instead of hanging around the yard
             or up in their room
                hating you
prematurely since you won't have done anything horribly mean yet
except keeping them from the darker joys

it's unforgivable the latter
so don't blame me if you won't take this advice
and the family breaks up
and your children grow old and blind in front of a TV set
seeing
movies you wouldn't let them see when they were young


# ANSWER TO VOZNESENSKY & EVTUSHENKO


We are tired of your tiresome imitations of Mayakovsky
we are tired
of your dreary tourist ideas of our Negro selves
our selves are in far worse condition than the obviousness
of your color sense
your general sense of Poughkeepsie is
a gaucherie no American poet would be guilty of in Tiflis
thanks to French Impressionism
we do not pretend to know more
than can be known
how many sheets have you stained with your semen
oh Tartars, and how many
of our loves have you illuminated with
your heart your breath
as we poets of America have loved you
your countrymen, our countrymen, our lives, your lives, and
the dreary expanses of your translations
your idiotic manifestos
and the strange black cock which has become ours despite your envy

we do what we feel
you do not even do what you must or can
I do not love you any more since Mayakovsky died and Pasternak
theirs was the death of my nostalgia for your tired ignorant race
since you insist on race
you shall not take my friends away from me
because they live in Harlem
you shall not make Mississippi into Sakhalin
you came too late, a lovely talent doesn't make a ball

I consider myself to be black and you not even part
where you see death
                          you see a dance of death
                                            which is
imperialist, implies training, requires techniques
our ballet does not employ
                          you are indeed as cold as wax
as your progenitor was red, and how greatly we loved his redness
in the fullness of our own idiotic sun! what
"roaring universe" outshouts his violent triumphant sun!
        you are not even speaking
                              in a whisper
        Mayakovsky's hat worn by a horse

                                                *1963*

# LEW WELCH (1926-1971)

## CHICAGO POEM

I lived here nearly 5 years before I could
    meet the middle western day with anything approaching
Dignity.  It's a place that lets you
    understand why the Bible is the way it is:
Proud people cannot live here.

The land's too flat.  Ugly sullen and big it
    pounds men down past humbleness.  They
Stoop at 35 possibly cringing from the heavy and
    terrible sky.  In country like this there
Can be no God but Jahweh.

In the mills and refineries of its south side Chicago
    passes its natural gas in flames
Bouncing like bunsens from stacks a hundred feet high.
    The stench stabs at your eyeballs.
The whole sky green and yellow backdrop for the skeleton
    steel of a bombed-out town.

Remember the movies in grammar school?  The goggled men
    doing strong things in
Showers of steel-spark?  The dark screen cracking light
    and the furnace door opening with a
Blast of orange like a sunset?  Or an orange?

It was photographed by a fairy, thrilled as a girl, or
    a Nazi who wished there were people
Behind that door (hence the remote beauty), but Sievers,
    whose old man spent most of his life in there,
Remembers a "nigger in a red T-shirt pissing into the
    black sand."

It was 5 years until I could afford to recognize the ferocity.
    Friends helped me.  Then I put some
Love into my house.  Finally I found some quiet lakes
    and a farm where they let me shoot pheasant.

Standing in the boat one night I watched the lake go absolutely
    flat. Smaller than raindrops, and only
Here and there, the feeding rings of fish were visible 100 yards
    away—and the Blue Gill caught that afternoon
Lifted from its northern lake like a tropical! Jewel at its ear
    Belly gold so bright you'd swear he had a
Light in there. His color faded with his life. A small
    green fish . . .

All things considered, it's a gentle and undemanding
    planet, even here. Far gentler
Here than any of a dozen other places. The trouble is
    always and only with what we build on top of it.

There's nobody else to blame. You can't fix it and you
    can't make it go away. It does no good appealing
To some ill-invented Thunderer
    Brooding above some unimaginable crag . . .

It's ours. Right down to the last small hinge it
    all depends for its existence
Only and utterly upon our sufferance.

Driving back I saw Chicago rising in its gases and I
    knew again that never will the
Man be made to stand against this pitiless, unparalleled
    monstrocity. It
Snuffles on the beach of its Great Lake like a
    blind, red, rhinoceros.
It's already running us down.

You can't fix it. You can't make it go away.
    I don't know what you're going to do about it,
But I know what I'm going to do about it. I'm just
    going to walk away from it. Maybe
A small part of it will die if I'm not around

    feeding it anymore.

## *from* TAXI SUITE: AFTER ANACREON

When I drive cab
    I am moved by strange whistles and wear a hat.

When I drive cab
    I am the hunter. My prey leaps out from where it
    hid, beguiling me with gestures.

When I drive cab
    all may command me, yet I am in command of all who do.

When I drive cab
    I am guided by voices descending from the naked air.

When I drive cab
    A revelation of movement comes to me. They wake now.
    Now they want to work or look around. Now they want
    drunkenness and heavy food. Now they contrive to love.

When I drive cab
    I bring the sailor home from the sea. In the back of
    my car he fingers the pelt of his maiden.

When I drive cab
    I watch for stragglers in the urban order of things.

When I drive a cab
    I end the only lit and waitful thing in miles of
    darkened houses.

# WOBBLY ROCK

*for Gary Snyder*

*"I think I'll be the Buddha. of this place"*

*and sat himself*
*down*

1
It's a real rock

(believe this first)

Resting on actual sand at the surf's edge:
Muir Beach, California

(like everything else I have
somebody showed it to me and I found it by myself)

Hard common stone
Size of the largest haystack
It moves when hit by waves
Actually shudders

(even a good gust of wind will do it
if you sit real still and keep your mouth shut)

Notched to certain center it
Yields and then comes back to it:

Wobbly tons

2
Sitting here you look below to other rocks
Precisely placed as rocks of Ryoanji:
Foam like swept stones

(the mind getting it all confused again:
"snow like frosting on a cake"
"rose so beautiful it don't look real")

Isn't there a clear example here—
Stone garden shown to me by

Berkeley painter I never met
A thousand books and somebody else's boatride ROCKS

       (garden)

EYE

       (nearly empty despite this clutter-image all
       the opposites cancelling out a
       CIRCULAR process: *Frosting-snow*)

Or think of the monks who made it 4 hundred 50 years ago
Lugged the boulders from the sea
Swept to foam original gravelstone from sea

       (first saw it, even then, when finally they
       all looked up the
       instant AFTER it was made)

And now all rocks are different and
All the spaces in between

       (which includes about everything)

The instant
After it is made


    3
*I have been in many shapes before I attained congenial form*
All those years on the beach, lifetimes . . .

When I was a boy I used to watch the Pelican:
It always seemed his wings broke
And he dropped, like scissors, in the sea . . .
Night fire flicking the shale cliff
Balls tight as a cat after the cold swim
Her young snatch sandy . . .

       *I have travelled*
       *I have made a circuit*
       *I have lived in 14 cities*
       *I have been a word in a book*
       *I have been a book originally*

*Dychymig Dychymig:* (riddle me a riddle)

>    Waves and the sea.  If you
>    take away the sea

Tell me what it is


    4
Yesterday the weather was nice there were lots of people
Today it rains, the only other figure is far up the beach

>        (by the curve of his body I know he leans against the
>        tug of his fishingline:  there is no separation)

Yesterday they gathered and broke gathered and broke like
Feeding swallows dipped down to pick up something ran back to
Show it
And a young girl with jeans rolled to mid-thigh ran
Splashing in the rain creek

>        *"They're all so damned happy—*
>        *why can't they admit it?"*

Easy enough until a little rain shuts beaches down . . .


Did it mean nothing to you Animal that turns this
Planet to a smoky rock?
Back among your quarrels
How can I remind you of your gentleness?

>        Jeans are washed
>        Shells all lost or broken
>        Driftwood sits in shadow boxes on a tracthouse wall

Like swallows you were, gathering
Like people I wish for . . .


>        cannot even tell this to that fisherman

5

3 of us in a boat the size of a bathtub . pitching in
slow waves . fish poles over the side . oars

We rounded a point of rock and entered a small cove

Below us:
            fronds of kelp
            fish
            crustaceans
            eels
Then us
            then rocks at the cliff's base
            starfish
            (hundreds of them sunning themselves)
            final starfish on the highest rock then
Cliff
            4 feet up the cliff a flower
            grass
            further up more grass
            grass over the cliff's edge
            branch of pine then
Far up the sky

            a hawk

Clutching to our chip we are jittering in a spectrum
Hung in the film of this narrow band
Green
            to our eyes only


6
On a trail not far from here
Walking in meditation
We entered a dark grove
And I lost all separation in step with the
Eucalyptus as the trail walked back beneath me

Does it need to be that dark or is
Darkness only its occasion
Finding it by ourselves knowing
Of course
Somebody else was there before . . .

I like playing that game
Standing on a high rock looking way out over it all:

> *"I think I'll call it the Pacific"*

Wind water
Wave rock
Sea sand

> (there is no separation)

Wind that wets my lips is salt
Sea breaking within me balanced as the
Sea that floods these rocks.  Rock
Returning to the sea, easily, as
Sea once rose from it.  It
Is a sea rock

> (easily)

I am
Rocked by the sea


## SONG OF THE TURKEY BUZZARD

> *For Rock Scully who heard it the first time*

*Praises, Tamalpais,*
> *Perfect in Wisdom and Beauty,*
*She of the Wheeling Birds*


### I.
The rider riddle is easy to ask,
but the answer might surprise you.

How desperately I wanted Cougar
(I, Leo, etc.)
> brilliant proofs:  terrain,
color, food, all
nonsense.  All made up.

*They were always there, the*
*laziest high-flyers, bronze-winged,*
*the silent ones*

"A cunning man always laughs and smiles,
even if he's desperately hungry,
while a good bird always flies like a vulture,
even if it is starving."

(Milarepa sang)

Over and over again, that sign:

I hit one once, with a .22
heard the "flak" and a feather flew off, he
flapped his wings just once and
went on sailing.  Bronze
(when seen from above)

as I have seen them, all day sitting
on a cliff so steep they
circled below me, in the up-draft
passed so close I could see this
eye.

*Praises Tamalpais,*
*Perfect in Wisdom and Beauty,*
*She of the Wheeling Birds*

Another time the vision was so clear another saw it, too. Wet, a
hatching bird, the shell of the egg streaked with dry scum, exhausted, wet,
too weak to move the shriveled wings, fierce sun-heat, sand. Twitching, as
with elbows (we all have the same parts). Beak open, neck stretched,
gasping for air. O how we want to live!

"Poor little bird," she said, "he'll never make it."

*Praises, Tamalpais,*
*Perfect in Wisdom & Beauty,*
*She of the Wheeling Birds*

Even so, I didn't get it for a long long while. It finally came in a
trance, a coma, half in sleep and half in fever-mind. A Turkey Buzzard,
wounded, found by a rock on the mountain. He wanted to die alone. I
had never seen one, wild, so close. When I reached out, he sidled away,

head drooping, as dizzy as I was. I put my hands on his wing-shoulders and lifted him. He tried, feebly, to tear at my hands with his beak. He tore my flesh too slightly to make any difference. Then he tried to heave his great wings. Weak as he was, I could barely hold him.

A drunken veterinarian found a festering bullet in his side, a .22 that slid between the great bronze scales his feathers were. We removed it and cleansed the wound.

Finally he ate the rotten gophers I trapped and prepared for him. Even at first, he drank a lot of water. My dog seemed frightened of him.

> They smell sweet
> > meat is dry on their talons
>
> They very opposite of
> > death
>
> birth of re-birth
> > Buzzard
>
> meat is rotten meat made
> > sweet again and
>
> lean, unkillable, wing-locked
> > soarer till he's but a
>
> speck in the highest sky
> > infallible
>
> eye finds Feast!  on
> > baked concrete
>
> > free!
>
> squashed rabbit ripened:
> > our good cheese

(to keep the highways clean, and bother no Being)

II.

> *Praises Gentle Tamalpais*
> *Perfect in Wisdom and Beauty of the*
> *sweetest water*
> *and the soaring birds*
>
> *great seas at the feet of thy cliffs*

Hear my last Will & Testament:

Among my friends there shall always be
one with proper instructions
for my continuance.

> Let no one grieve.
> I shall have used it all up
> used up every bit of it.
>
> What an extravagance!
> What a relief!

On a marked rock, following his orders,
place my meat.

> All care must be taken not to
> frighten the natives of this
> barbarous land, who
> will not let us die, even,
> as we wish.

With proper ceremony disembowel what I
no longer need, that it might more quickly
rot and tempt

my new form

NOT THE BRONZE CASKET BUT THE BRAZEN WING

SOARING FOREVER ABOVE THEE O PERFECT

O SWEETEST WATER O GLORIOUS

WHEELING

BIRD

# JOHN ASHBERY (1927)

## THE INSTRUCTION MANUAL

As I sit looking out of a window of the building
I wish I did not have to write the instruction manual on the uses of a new
    metal.
I look down into the street and see people, each walking with an inner
    peace,
And envy them—they are so far away from me!
Not one of them has to worry about getting out this manual on schedule.
And, as my way is, I begin to dream, resting my elbows on the desk and
    leaning out of the window a little,
Of dim Guadalajara! City of rose-colored flowers!
City I wanted most to see, and most did not see, in Mexico!
But I fancy I see, under the press of having to write the instruction manual,
Your public square, city, with its elaborate little bandstand!
The band is playing *Scheherazade* by Rimsky-Korsakov.
Around stand the flower girls, handing out rose- and lemon-colored flowers,
Each attractive in her rose-and-blue striped dress (Oh! such shades of rose
    and blue),
And nearby is the little white booth where women in green serve you
    green and yellow fruit.
The couples are parading; everyone is in a holiday mood.
First, leading the parade, is a dapper fellow
Clothed in deep blue. On his head sits a white hat
And he wears a mustache, which has been trimmed for the occasion.
His dear one, his wife, is young and pretty; her shawl is rose, pink, and white
Her slippers are patent leather, in the American fashion,
And she carries a fan, for she is modest, and does not want the crowd to
    see her face too often
But everybody is so busy with his wife or loved one.
I doubt they would notice the mustachioed man's wife.
Here come the boys! They are skipping and throwing little things on the
    sidewalk
Which is made of gray tile. One of them, a little older, has a toothpick in
    his teeth.
He is silenter than the rest, and affects not to notice the pretty young girls
    in white.
But his friends notice them, and shout their jeers at the laughing girls.

Yet soon all this will cease, with the deepening of their years,
And love bring each to the parade grounds for another reason.
But I have lost sight of the young fellow with the toothpick.
Wait—there he is—on the other side of the bandstand,
Secluded from his friends, in earnest talk with a young girl
Of fourteen or fifteen. I try to hear what they are saying
But it seems they are just mumbling something—shy words of love,
    probably.
She is slightly taller than he, and looks quietly down into his sincere eyes.
She is wearing white. The breeze ruffles her long fine black hair against
    her olive cheek.
Obviously she is in love. The boy, the young boy with the toothpick, he
    is in love too;
His eyes show it. Turning from this couple,
I see there is an intermission in the concert.
The paraders are resting and sipping drinks through straws
(The drinks are dispensed from a large glass crock by a lady in dark blue),
And the musicians mingle among them, in their creamy white uniforms,
    and talk
About the weather, perhaps, or how their kids are doing at school.

Let us take this opportunity to tiptoe into one of the side streets.
Here you may see one of those white houses with green trim
That are so popular here. Look—I told you!
It is cool and dim inside, but the patio is sunny.
An old woman in gray sits there, fanning herself with a palm leaf fan.
She welcomes us to her patio, and offers us a cooling drink.
"My son is in Mexico City," she says. "He would welcome you too
If he were here. But his job is with a bank there.
Look, here is a photograph of him."
And a dark-skinned lad with pearly teeth grins out at us from the worn
    leather frame.
We thank her for her hospitality, for it is getting late
And we must catch a view of the city, before we leave, from a good high
    place.
That church tower will do—the faded pink one, there against the fierce
    blue of the sky. Slowly we enter.
The caretaker, an old man dressed in brown and gray, asks us how long
    we have been in the city, and how we like it here.
His daughter is scrubbing the steps—she nods to us as we pass into the
    tower.
Soon we have reached the top, and the whole network of the city extends
    before us.

There is the rich quarter, with its houses of pink and white, and its
    crumbling, leafy terraces.
There is the poorer quarter, its homes a deep blue.
There is the market, where men are selling hats and swatting flies
And there is the public library, painted several shades of pale green and
    beige.
Look! There is the square we just came from, with the promenaders.
There are fewer of them, now that the heat of the day has increased,
But the young boy and girl still lurk in the shadows of the bandstand.
And there is the home of the little old lady—
She is still sitting in the patio, fanning herself.
How limited, but how complete withal, has been our experience of
    Guadalajara!
We have seen young love, married love, and the love of an aged mother for
    her son.
We have heard the music, tasted the drinks, and looked at colored houses.
What more is there to do, except stay? And that we cannot do.
And as a last breeze freshens the top of the weathered old tower, I turn
    my gaze
Back to the instruction manual which has made me dream of Guadalajara.

### "HOW MUCH LONGER WILL I BE ABLE TO INHABIT THE DIVINE SEPULCHER . . ."

How much longer will I be able to inhabit the divine sepulcher
Of life, my great love? Do dolphins plunge bottomward
To find the light? Or is it rock
That is searched? Unrelentingly? Huh. And if some day

Men with orange shovels come to break open the rock
Which encases me, what about the light that comes in then?
What about the smell of the light?
What about the moss?

In pilgrim times he wounded me
Since then I only lie
My bed of light is a furnace choking me
With hell (and sometimes I hear salt water dripping).

I mean it—because I'm one of the few
To have held my breath under the house. I'll trade
One red sucker for two blue ones. I'm
Named Tom. The

Light bounces off mossy rocks down to me
In this glen (the neat villa! which
When he'd had he would not had he of
And jests under the smarting of privet

Which on hot spring nights perfumes the empty rooms
With the smell of sperm flushed down toilets
On hot summer afternoons within sight of the sea.
If you knew why then professor) reads

To his friends: Drink to me only with
And the reader is carried away
By a great shadow under the sea.
Behind the steering wheel

The boy took out his own forehead.
His girlfriend's head was a green bag
of narcissus stems. "OK you win
But meet me anyway at Cohen's Drug Store

In 22 minutes." What a marvel is ancient man!
Under the tulip roots he has figured out a way to be a religious animal
And would be a mathematician. But where in unsuitable heaven
Can he get the heat that will make him grow?

For he needs something or will forever remain a dwarf,
Though a perfect one, and possessing a normal-sized brain
But he has got to be released by giants from things.
And as the plant grows older it realizes it will never be a tree,

Will probably always be haunted by a bee
And cultivates stupid impressions
So as not to become part of the dirt. The dirt
Is mounting like a sea. And we say goodbye

Shaking hands in front of the crashing of the waves
That give our words lonesomeness, and make these flabby hands seem
    ours—

Hands that are always writing things
On mirrors for people to see later—

Do you want them to water
Plant, tear listlessly among the exchangeable ivy—
Carrying food to mouth, touching genitals—
But no doubt you have understood

It all now and I am a fool. It remains
For me to get better, and to understand you so
Like a chair-sized man. Boots
Were heard on the floor above. In the garden the sunlight was still purple

But what buzzed in it had changed slightly
But not forever . . . but casting its shadow
On sticks, and looking around for an opening in the air, was quite as if it
          had never refused to exist differently. Guys
In the yard handled the belt he had made

Stars
Painted the garage roof crimson and black
He is not a man
Who can read these signs . . . his bones were stays . . .

And even refused to live
In a world and refunded the hiss
Of all that exists terribly near us
Like you, my love, and light.

For what is obedience but the air around us
To the house? For which the federal men came
In a minute after the sidewalk
Had taken you home? ("Latin . . . blossom . . .")

After which you led me to water
And bade me drink, which I did, owing to your kindness.
You would not let me out for two days and three nights,
Bringing me books bound in wild thyme and scented wild grasses

As if reading had any interest for me, you . . .
Now you are laughing.
Darkness interrupts my story
Turn on the light.

Meanwhile what am I going to do?
I am growing up again, in school, the crisis will be very soon.
And you twist the darkness in your fingers, you
Who are slightly older . . .

Who are you, anyway?
And it is the color of sand,
The darkness, as it sifts through your hand
Because what does anything mean,

The ivy and the sand?  That boat
Pulled up on the shore?  Am I wonder,
Strategically, and in the light
Of the long sepulcher that hid death and hides-me?


## A LAST WORLD


These wonderful things
Were planted on the surface of a round mind that was to become our
     present time.
The mark of things belongs to someone
But if that somebody was wise
Then the whole of things might be different
From what it was thought to be in the beginning, before an angel bandaged
     the field glasses.
Then one could say nothing hear nothing
Of what the great time spoke to its divisors.
All borders between men were closed.
Now all is different without having changed
As though one were to pass through the same street at different times
And nothing that is old can prefer the new.
An enormous merit has been placed on the head of all things
Which, bowing down, arrive near the region of their feet
So that the earth-stone has stared at them in memory at the approach of
     an error.
Still it is not too late for these things to die
Provided that an anemone will grab them and rush them to the wildest
     heaven.

But having plucked oneself, who could live in the sunlight?
And the truth is cold, as a giant's knee
Will seem cold.

Yet having once played with tawny truth
Having once looked at a cold mullet on a plate on a table supported by the
    weight of the inconstant universe
He wished to go far away from himself.
There were no baskets in those jovial pine-tree forests, and the waves
    pushed without whitecaps
In that foam where he wished to be.

Man is never without woman, the neuter sex
Casting up her equations, looks to her lord for loving kindness
For man smiles never at woman.
In the forests a night landslide could disclose that she smiled.
Guns were fired to discourage dogs into the interior
But woman—never. She is completely out of this world.
She climbs a tree to see if he is coming
Sunlight breaks at the edges of the wet lakes
And she is happy, if free
For the power he forces down at her like a storm of lightning.

Once a happy old man
One can never change the core of things, and light burns you the harder
    for it.
Glad of the changes already and if there are more it will never be you
    that minds
Since it will not be you to be changed, but in the evening in the severe
    lamplight doubts come
From many scattered distances, and do not come too near.
As it falls along the house, your treasure
Cries to the other men; the darkness will have none of you, and you are
    folded into it like mint into the sound of haying.
It was ninety-five years ago that you strolled in the serene little port; under
    an enormous cornice six boys in black slowly stood.
Six frock coats today, six black fungi tomorrow,
And the day after tomorrow—but the day after tomorrow itself is blackening
    dust.
You court obsidian pools
And from a tremendous height twilight falls like a stone and hits you.

You who were always in the way
Flower
Are you afraid of trembling like breath
But there is no breath in seriousness; the lake howls for it.
Swiftly sky covers earth, the wrong breast for a child to suck, and that,
What have you got there in your hand?
It is a stone
So the passions are divided into tiniest units
And of these many are lost, and those that remain are given at nightfall to
    the uneasy old man
The old man who goes skipping along the roadbed.
In a dumb harvest
Passions are locked away, and states of creation are used instead, that is to
    say synonyms are used.


Honey
On the lips of elders is not contenting, so
A firebrand is made. Woman carries it,
She who thought herself good only for bearing children is decked out in
    the lace of fire
And this is exactly the way she wanted it, the trees coming to place
    themselves in her
In a rite of torpor, dust.
A bug carries the elixir
Naked men pray the ground and chew it with their hands
The fire lives
Men are nabbed
She her bonnet half off is sobbing there while the massacre yet continues
    with a terrific thin energy
A silver blaze calms the darkness.


Rest undisturbed on the dry of the beach
Flower
And night stand suddenly sideways to observe your bones
Vixen


Do men later go home
Because we wanted to travel
Under the kettle of trees
We thought the sky would melt to see us
But to tell the truth the air turned to smoke,
We were forced back onto a foul pillow that was another place.
Or were lost by our comrades

Somewhere between heaven and no place, and were growing smaller.
In another place a mysterious mist shot up like a wall, down which
      trickled the tears of our loved ones.
Bananas rotten with their ripeness hung from the leaves, and cakes and
      jewels covered the sand.
But these were not the best men
But there were moments of the others
Seen through indifference, only bare methods
But we can remember them and so we are saved.

A last world moves on the figures;
They are smaller than when we last saw them caring about them.
The sky is a giant rocking horse
And of the other things death is a new office building filled with modern
      furniture,
A wide thing, but which has no purpose for us.

Everything is being blown away;
A little horse trots up with a letter in its mouth, which is read with
      eagerness
As we gallop into the flame.

# A BLESSING IN DISGUISE

Yes, they are alive and can have those colors,
But I, in my soul, am alive too.
I feel I must sing and dance, to tell
Of this in a way, that knowing you may be drawn to me.

And I sing amid despair and isolation
Of the chance to know you, to sing of me
Which are you. You see,
You hold me up to the light in a way

I should never have expected, or suspected, perhaps
Because you always tell me I am you,
And right. The great spruces loom.
I am yours to die with, to desire.

I cannot ever think of me, I desire you
For a room in which the chairs ever
Have their backs turned to the light
Inflicted on the stone and paths, the real trees

That seem to shine at me through a lattice toward you.
If the wild light of this January day is true
I pledge me to be truthful unto you
Whom I cannot ever stop remembering.

Remembering to forgive. Remember to pass beyond you into the day
On the wings of the secret you will never know.
Taking me from myself, in the path
Which the pastel girth of the day has assigned to me.

I prefer "you" in the plural, I want "you,"
You must come to me, all golden and pale
Like the dew and the air.
And then I start getting this feeling of exaltation.


## THESE LACUSTRINE CITIES


These lacustrine cities grew out of loathing
Into something forgetful, although angry with history.
They are the product of an idea: that man is horrible,
        for instance.
Though this is only one example.

They emerged until a tower
Controlled the sky, and with artifice dipped back
Into the past for swans and tapering branches,
Burning, until all that hate was transformed into useless love.

Then you are left with an idea of yourself
And the feeling of ascending emptiness of the afternoon
Which must be charged to the embarrassment of others
Who fly by you like beacons.

The night is a sentinel.
Much of your time has been occupied by creative games
Until now, but we have all-inclusive plans for you.
We had thought, for instance, of sending you to the middle
        of the desert.

To a violent sea, or of having the closeness of the others be air
To you, pressing you back into a startled dream
As sea-breezes greet a child's face.
But the past is already here, and you are nursing some private project.

The worst is not over, yet I know
You will be happy here. Because of the logic
Of your situation, which is something no climate can outsmart.
Tender and insouciant by turns, you see.

You have built a mountain of something.
Thoughtfully pouring all your energy into this single monument,
Whose wind is desire starching a petal,
Whose disappointment broke into a rainbow of tears.


## DECOY

We hold these truths to be self-evident:
That ostracism, both political and moral, has
Its place in the twentieth-century scheme of things;
That urban chaos is the problem we have been seeing into and seeing into,
For the factory, deadpanned by its very existence into a
Descending code of values, has moved right across the road from total
        financial upheaval
And caught regression head-on. The descending scale does not imply
A corresponding deterioration of moral values, punctuated
By acts of corporate vandalism every five years,
Like a bunch of violets pinned to a dress, that knows and ignores its own
        standing.
There is every reason to rejoice with those self-styled prophets of
        commercial disaster, those harbingers of gloom,
Over the imminent lateness of the denouement that, advancing slowly,
        never arrives,

At the same time keeping the door open to a tongue-and-cheek attitude
      on the part of the perpetrators,
The men who sit down to their vast desks on Monday to begin planning
      the week's notations, jotting memoranda that take
Invisible form in the air, like flocks of sparrows
Above the city pavements, turning and wheeling aimlessly
But on the average directed by discernible motives.

To sum up: We are fond of plotting itineraries
And our pyramiding memories, alert as dandelion fuzz, dart from one
      pretext to the next
Seeking in occasions new sources of memories, for memory is profit
Until the day it spreads out all its accumulation, delta-like, on the plain
For that day no good can come of remembering, and the anomalies cancel
      each other out.
But until then foreshortened memories will keep us going, alive, one to
      the other.

There was never any excuse for this and perhaps there need be none,
For kicking out into the morning, on the wide bed,
Waking far apart on the bed, the two of them:
Husband and wife
Man and wife

## PYROGRAPHY

Out here on Cottage Grove it matters. The galloping
Wind balks at its shadow. The carriages
Are drawn forward under a sky of fumed oak.
This is America calling:
The mirroring of state to state,
Of voice to voice on the wires,
The force of colloquial greetings like golden
Pollen sinking on the afternoon breeze.
In service stairs the sweet corruption thrives;
The page of dusk turns like a creaking revolving stage in Warren, Ohio.

If this is the way it is let's leave,
They agree, and soon the slow boxcar journey begins,

Gradually accelerating until the gyrating fans of suburbs
Enfolding the darkness of cities are remembered
Only as a recurring tic.  And midway
We meet the disappointed, returning ones, without its
Being able to stop us in the headlong night
Toward the nothing of the coast.  At Bolinas
The houses doze and seem to wonder why through the
Pacific haze, and the dreams alternately glow and grow dull.
Why be hanging on here?  Like kites, circling,
Slipping on a ramp of air, but always circling?

But the variable cloudiness is pouring it on,
Flooding back to you like the meaning of a joke,
The land wasn't immediately appealing; we built it
Partly over with fake ruins, in the image of ourselves:
An arch that terminates in mid-keystone, a crumbling stone pier
For laundresses, an open-air theater, never completed
And only partially designed.  How are we to inhabit
This space from which the fourth wall is invariably missing,
As in a stage-set or dollhouse, except by staying as we are,
In lost profile, facing the stars, with dozens of as yet
Unrealized projects, and a strict sense
Of time running out, of evening presenting
The tactfully folded-over bill?  And we fit
Rather too easily into it, become transparent,
Almost ghosts.  One day
The birds and animals in the pasture have absorbed
The color, the density of the surroundings,
The leaves are alive, and too heavy with life.

A long period of adjustment followed.
In the cities at the turn of the century they knew about it
But were careful not to let on as the iceman and the milkman
Disappeared down the block and the postman shouted
His daily rounds.  The children under the trees knew it
But all the fathers returning home
On streetcars after a satisfying day at the office undid it:
The climate was still floral and all the wallpaper
In a million homes all over the land conspired to hide it.
One day we thought of painted furniture, of how
It just slightly changes everything in the room
And in the yard outside, and how, if we were going
To be able to write the history of our time, starting with today,

It would be necessary to model all these unimportant details
So as to be able to include them; otherwise the narrative
Would have that flat, sandpapered look the sky gets
Out in the middle west toward the end of summer,
The look of wanting to back out before the argument
Has been resolved, and at the same time to save appearances
So that tomorrow will be pure. Therefore, since we have to do our
    business
In spite of things, why not make it in spite of everything?
That way, maybe the feeble lakes and swamps
Of the back country will get plugged into the circuit
And not just the major events but the whole incredible
Mass of everything happening simultaneously and pairing off,
Channeling itself into history, will unroll
As carefully and as casually as a conversation in the next room,
And the purity of today will invest us like a breeze,
Only be hard, spare, ironical: something one can
Tip one's hat to and still get some use out of.

The parade is turning into our street.
My stars, the burnished uniforms and prismatic
Features of this instant belong here. The land
Is pulling away from the magic, glittering coastal towns
To an aforementioned rendezvous with August and December.
The hunch is it will always be this way,
The look, the way things first scared you
In the night light, and later turned out to be,
Yet still capable, all the same, of a narrow fidelity
To what you and they wanted to become:
No sighs like Russian music, only a vast unravelling
Out toward the junctions and to the darkness beyond
To these bare fields, built at today's expense.

# WET CASEMENTS

*When Eduard Raban, coming along the passage, walked into the open doorway, he saw that it was raining. It was not raining much.*

— Kafka, *Wedding Preparations in the Country*

The conception is interesting: to see, as though reflected
In streaming windowpanes, the look of others through
Their own eyes. A digest of their correct impressions of
Their self-analytical attitudes overlaid by your
Ghostly transparent face. You in falbalas
Of some distant but not too distant era, the cosmetics,
The shoes perfectly pointed, drifting (how long you
Have been drifting; how long I have too for that matter)
Like a bottle-imp toward a surface which can never be approached,
Never pierced through into the timeless energy of a present
Which would have its own opinions on these matters,
Are an epistemological snapshot of the processes
That first mentioned your name at some crowded cocktail
Party long ago, and someone (not the person addressed)
Overheard it and carried that name around in his wallet
For years as the wallet crumbled and bills slid in
And out of it. I want that information very much today,

Can't have it, and this makes me angry.
I shall use my anger to build a bridge like that
Of Avignon, on which people may dance for the feeling
Of dancing on a bridge. I shall at last see my complete face
Reflected not in the water but in the worn stone floor of my bridge.

I shall keep to myself.
I shall not repeat others' comments about me.

## LARRY EIGNER (1927)

## "FROM THE SUSTAINING AIR"

from the sustaining air

fresh air

There is the clarity of a shore
And shadow,   mostly,   brilliance

summer
            the billows of August

When, wandering, I look from my page

I say nothing

      when asked

I am, finally, an incompetent, after all

## DO IT YRSELF

Now they have two cars to clean
the front and back lawns
bloom in the drought

                        why not turn the other radio on the
            pious hopes of the Red Sox

yes, that's a real gangling kid coming down the street

he'll grow up

He'll fill out

sponges with handles

we got trinaural hearing

—they are taller than their cars

## "THE DARK SWIMMERS"

the dark swimmers
  their heads in the sun

        If time shd stand still
you can't see it move

which way does the river go
  partially the

    wind,      and light,      Down waves
            the indefinite flooring

the toppled clouds
the squared mountain

## "THE WIND LIKE AN OCEAN"

the wind like an ocean
but sometimes the sun stills it
and the surface is solid

why shouldn't life pass as in a dream
or a dream itself,    there are different degrees

or different dreams    reality
at one with a dream

   the naked sea
     stinking
  is fresh
     in time,

       (o shut your eyes against the wind


## LETTER FOR DUNCAN


 just because I forget
to perch different ways
       the fish
  go monotonous

     the
   sudden hulks of the trees
    in a glorious summer
you don't realize
  how mature you get
    at 21

  but you look back

    wherever a summer
     continue 70 seasons

     this one
      has been so various

      was the spring hot?

every habit

 to read

nothing you've done you have

    older

        the fish
     can't bother screaming

     flap by hook

      the working pain

          jaws by trying a head    bodies

     you'll always go to sleep
      more times than you'll wake

## "FLAKE DIAMOND OF / THE SEA"

     flake diamond of
             the sea

    the shimmering sand
      dilation    shadow in rain

blank   the somehow disfiguring
     weed   or the smell from
       some damp childhood

      clogged dry   strings   the
           periwinkle crust

     of sewage   newspulp   the sea breathing
         out   and in

       to high air

       not visible

        sprays   mountain
          flower in storms

    when under the surface
       the fish bank

         and give murk

   stems   knuckled formicant ice
      water       down

     grass by the sea
       in quiet   smells
         a little way

## "THAT THE NEIGHBORHOOD MIGHT BE COVERED"

That the neighborhood might be covered
by one roof, occurred
this morning,     Snow on the ground
         phonepoles, flagpoles,
windows,     so many chimneys,

    even up the hill

        grass smoking out west
     the tides, clouds from the past
    vanishing rain
         the base

    beaten out,

    death when you don't want it    what you like
    is a plain object

          the long-trunked clouds
     a weltered event

          shale    fish broken off

      a spiderweb hitched the dictionary
      overnight, I left it out there, well

screens in summer to keep the flies out

            into the dark sea

    the open garage doors
          under the vine which in autumn
          looks as if it still might hold

        shingles, encroached saw, horses
   somebody's back yard
            angling out

  you want the hills to rise

    twigs
      levelled on against the sky

           After 3 days   the air
           empty from the rain


## "I HAVE FELT IT AS THEY'VE SAID"

I have felt it as they've said
there is nothing to say

there is everything to speak of
  but the words are words

When you speak that is a sound
what have you done, when you have spoken

of nothing
  or something I will remember

After trying my animal noise
i break out with a man's cry


## "DON'T GO"

don't go
   see
it backwards

      time or space

      the crickets match
      the morning

         silence

      birds dreamed there
            hungry

         the trees in wait
         for food

            stars shone
            on deadly fish


## "THE BARE TREE / ALTERNATE"

the bare tree
      alternate
winds shake it
   cupfuls of leaves
      bright rain

     in the eye
        water continues
  time spreads
  the sea
        humid is it
       taking the present in

in imagination   an old man
    looking back,    young

or what night restored
in a dream, not
   adamant sleep

       twigs make a circle
              things

atmosphere of seasons

        and then the individual
            identity

     clearing

# EDWARD DORN (1929)


## THE RICK OF GREEN WOOD


In the woodyard were green and dry
woods fanning out, behind
                              a valley below
a pleasure for the eye to go.

Woodpile by the buzzsaw. I heard
the woodsman down in the thicket. I don't
want a rick of green wood, I told him
I want cherry or alder or something strong
and thin, or thick if dry, but I don't
want the green wood, my wife would die

Her back is slender
and the wood I get must not
bend her too much through the day.

Aye, the wood is some green
and some dry, the cherry thin of bark
cut in July.

My name is Burlingame
said the woodcutter.
My name is Dorn, I said.
I buzz on Friday if the weather cools
said Burlingame, enough of names.

        Out of the thicket my daughter was walking
singing—
        backtracking the horse hoof
        gone in earlier this morning, the woodcutter's horse
        pulling the alder, the fir, the hemlock
        above the valley
                        in the november

air, in the world, that was getting colder
as we stood there in the woodyard talking
pleasantly, of the green wood and the dry.

*[1956]*


# VAQUERO


The cowboy stands beneath
a brick-orange moon. The top
of his oblong head is blue, the sheath
of his hips
is too.

In the dark brown night
your delicate cowboy stands quite still.
His plain hands are crossed.
His wrists are embossed white.

In the background night is a house,
has a blue chimney top,
Yi Yi, the cowboy's eyes
are blue. The top of the sky
is too.


# ARE THEY DANCING


There is a sad carnival up the valley
The willows flow it seems on trellises of music
Everyone is there today, everyone I love.

There is a mad mad fiesta along the river
Thrilling ladies sing in my ear, where
Are your friends, lost? They were to come

And banjoes were to accompany us all
And our feet were to go continually
The sound of laughter was to flow over the water

What was to have been, is something else
I am afraid.  Only a letter from New Mexico
And another from a mountain by Pocatello,

I wonder, what instruments are playing
And whose eyes are straying over the mountain
Over the desert
And are they dancing:  or gazing at the earth.

## THE AIR OF JUNE SINGS

Quietly and while at rest on the trim grass I have gazed,
admonished myself for having never been here
at the grave-side and read the names of my Time Wanderers.
And now, the light noise of the children at play on the inscribed stone

jars my ear and they whisper and laugh covering their mouths. "My
        Darling"
my daughter reads, some of the markers
reflect such lightness to her reading eyes, yea, as I rove
among these polished and lime blocks I am moved to tears and I hear
the depth in "Darling, we love thee," and as in "Safe in Heaven."

I am going off to heaven and I won't see you anymore. I am
going back into the country and I won't be here anymore. I am
going to die in 1937.  But where did you die my Wanderer?
You, under the grave-grass, with the tin standard whereat
I look, and try to read the blurred ink.  I cannot believe
you were slighted knowing what I do of cost and evil
yet tin is less than granite.  Those who buried you should have known
a 6 inch square of sandstone, flush with the earth
is more proper for the gone than blurred and faded flags.

Than the blurred and faded flags I am walking with in the graveyard.

Across the road in the strawberry field two children are stealing
their supper fruit, abreast in the rows, in the fields of the overlord,
Miller his authentic name, and I see that name represented here,
there is that social side of burial too, long residence,
and the weight of the established local dead. My eyes avoid
the largest stone, larger than the common large, Goodpole Matthews,
Pioneer, and that pioneer sticks in me like a wormed black cherry
in my throat, No Date, nothing but that zeal, that trekking
and Business, that presumption in a sacred place, where children
are buried, and where peace, as it is in the fields and the country
should reign. A wagon wheel is buried there. Lead me away
to the small quiet stones of the unpreposterous dead and leave
me my tears for Darling we love thee, for Budded on earth and
　　　blossomed
in heaven, where the fieldbirds sing in the fence rows,
and there is possibility, where there are not the loneliest of all.

Oh, the stones not yet cut.


## LOS MINEROS


Now it is winter and the fallen snow
has made its stand on the mountains, making dunes
of white on the hills, drifting over
the flat valley floors, and the cold cover
has got us out to look for fuel.

First to Madrid which is 4 miles beyond Cerillos
close to the Golden Mountains
a place whose business once throve like the clamor in Heorot Hall;
but this was not sporting business, The Mine Explosion of 1911.
And on the wall in the mine office

　　　　　　　there in Madrid

are two pictures of those blackbirds, but a time later;
the thirties, and the bite of the depression is no bleaker
on their faces than is the coming morning of the day they were took.
These men whom we will never know are ranged 14 in number
in one of those pictures that are very long, you've seen them.

And the wonder is five are smiling Mexicanos, the rest
could be English or German, blown to New Mexico on another
winter's snow.  Hard to imagine Spanish as miners, their
sense is good-naturedly above ground (and their cruelty).
In a silly way they know their pictures are being taken,

and know it isn't necessary honor standing in line with their hands hiding
in their pockets.  I was looking to see if they are short
as Orwell says miners must be, but they aren't save two
little Mexican boys.  What caught my eye at first was the way
they were so finely dressed in old double-breasted suit coats, ready for  work.

Then I looked into their faces and the races separated.
The English or Germans wear a look which is mystic in its expectancy;
able men underground,
but the Spanish face carries no emergency
and one of the little boys, standing behind a post
looks right out of the picture faintly smiling:  even today. Martinez
whom I had gone with was waiting for the weight slip.
When we got over to the giant black chute the man above waved
as from the deck of a troubled ship and said no carbon
amigos, and then climbed down the ladder.

Madrid is a gaunt town now.  Its houses stand unused
along the entering road, and they are all green and white,
every window has been abused with the rocks of departing children.


## FROM GLOUCESTER OUT


It has all
come back today.
That memory for me is nothing
there ever was,
                    That man

so long,
when stretched out
and so bold

              on his ground
and so much
lonely anywhere.

But never to forget
                    that moment

when we came out of the tavern
and wandered through the carnival.
They were playing
the washington post march
but I mistook it for manhattan beach
for all around were the colored lights
of delirium
                to the left the boats
of Italians
and ahead of us, past the shoulders
of St. Peter the magician of those fishermen

the bay
stood, and immediately in it the silent
inclined pole where tomorrow the young men
of this colony
so dangerous on the street
will fall harmlessly
into the water.

They are not the solid
but are the solidly built
citizens, and they are about us
as we walk across
                    the square
with their black provocative
women
slender, like whips of
sex in the sousa filled night.

Where edged
by that man in the music
of a transplanted time and
enough of drunkenness
to make you senseless of all
but virtue

(there is never
no, there is never a small complaint)
(that all things shit poverty,
and Life, one wars on with
many embraces) oh it was a time that was perfect
but for my own hesitating
to know all I had not known.
Pure existence, even in the crowds
I love
will never be possible for me

even with the men I love
                              This is
the guilt
that kills me
                My adulterated presence

but please believe with all men
I love to be

●

That memory
of how he lay out
on the floor in his great length
and when morning came,
late,
we lingered
in the vastest of all cities
in this hemisphere
                      and all other movement
stopped, nowhere
else was there a stirring known to us

yet that morning I stood
by the window up 3 levels
and watched a game
of stick ball, thinking of going away,
and wondering what would befall that man
when he returned to his territory.
The street as you could guess
was thick with their running
and cars,
themselves, paid that activity

such respect I thought a ritual
in the truest sense,
where all time and all motion
part around the space of men
in that act
as does a river flow past
the large rock.

●

And he slept.
in the next room, waiting
in an outward slumber
                    for the time

we climbed into the car, accepting all things
from love, the currency of which is
parting, and glancing.

Then went
out of that city to jersey
where instantly we could not find our way
and the maze of the outlands west
starts that quick
where you may touch
your finger to liberty
and look so short a space
to the columnar bust
of New York
and know those people exist
as a speck in your own lonely heart
who will shortly depart,
taking a conveyance for the
radial stretches
past girls on corners
past drugstores, tired hesitant
creatures who I also love
in all their alienation were it not so
past all equipment of country side
to temporary homes
where the wash of sea and other
populations come
once more to whisper only one thing
for all people: a late and far-away

night yearning for
and when he gets there
I want him to stay away
from the taverns of familiarity
I want him to walk by the seashore alone
in all height
which is nothing more than
a mountain.  Or the hailing of a mast
with big bright eyes.

So rushing,
        all the senses
come to him
as a swarm of golden bees
and their sting is the power
he uses as parts of
the oldest brain.  He hears
the delicate thrush
of the water attacking
He hears the cries, falling gulls
and watches silently the gesture of grey
bygone people.  He hears their cries
and messages, he never

ignores any sound.
As they come to him he places them
puts clothes upon them
and gives them their place
in their new explanation, there is never
a lost time, nor any inhabitant
of that time to go split by prisms or unplaced
and unattended,
        that you may believe

is the breath he gives
the great already occurred and nightly beginning world.
So with the populace of his mind
you think his nights? are not
lonely.  My God.  Of his
loves, you know nothing and of his
false beginnning
you can know nothing,
        but this thing to be marked

again

    only

he who worships the gods with his strictness
can be of their company
the cat and the animals, the bird he took
from the radiator
of my car saying it had died
a natural death, rarely seen in a bird.

To play, as areal particulars can out of the span
of Man, and of all, this man
does not
      he, does, he
   walks
      by the sea
in my memory

and sees all things and to him
are presented at night
the whispers of the most flung shores
from Gloucester out

                       *[1964]*

## FOR THE NEW UNION DEAD IN ALABAMA

The Rose of Sharon
      I lost in the tortured night
 of this banished place
  the phrase
    and the rose
    from wandering
away, down the lanes
   in all their abstract directions
     a worry about the peninsula
  of the east,
       and the grim territories

of the west
here in the raw greed
of the frontier my soul can find
no well of clear water
it is pressed
as a layer
between unreadable concerns,
a true sandwich, a true
grave, like a performance
in an utterly removed theater
is a grave, the unreachable action makes
a crypt
of distance,
a rose of immense beauty
to yearn for.
the cutting of it
cutting off the world
the thorn however
remains, in the desert
in the throat of our national hypocrisy
strewn we are along all the pathways
of our exclusively gelding mentality
we stride in
our gelding culture.
oh rose
of priceless beauty
refrain from our shores
suffocate the thin isthmus
of our mean land.
cast us back
into isolation

# LA MÁQUINA A HOUSTON

The train has come to rest and ceased its creaking
We hear the heavy breathing of the máquina
A relic in its own time
Like all the manifestations of technical art

And without real gender
And hidden from direct appeal
By the particulates of the English language
Itself the agent of frag mentation
And lonely accuser of the generic lines
The heavy breathing of the lonely máquina
Stopped in its tracks waiting for the photograph.


The Apache are prodded out into the light
Remember, there are still dark places then
Even in the solar monopoly of Arizona and Tejas


We are with the man with the camera
They step off the train and wait among the weeds
They never take their eyes off of us, wise practice
We motioned the way with our shotguns
They are almost incredibly beautiful


We are struck and thrilled
With the completeness of their smell
To them we are weird while to us
They are not weird, to them we are undeniable
And they stop only before that, they are like us
Yet we are not like them
Since we dont recognize that. We say:
One cannot have a piece of what is indivisible
Is natural Apache policy
Where for us, that is a philosophical implication
We are alike, but we see things
From behind dis-simular costumes,
The first principle of warfare
Where *All of Us* is the Army, and they are the people
Precisely they step off the train
And this is an important terminal moment
In the Rush Hour begun in this hemisphere


This is the moment before the leg irons
They look Good. They look better than we do.
They will look better than we look forever.
We will never really look very good
We are too far gone on thought, and its rejections
The two actions of a Noos

Natches sits alone in the center
Because he is the elegant one among them
Hereditary, proper as a dealer
He is inherent and most summary of themselves
Supple, graceful, flexible hands
Goodnatured, fond of women


As the train moves off at the first turn of the wheel
With its cargo of florida bound exiles
Most all of whom had been put bodily
Into the coaches, their 3000 dogs,
Who had followed them like a grand party
To the railhead at Holbrook
                          began to cry
When they saw the smoking creature resonate
With their masters,
And as the máquina acquired speed they howled and moaned
A frightening noise from their great mass
And some of them followed the cars
For forty miles
Before they fell away in exhaustion

# JONATHAN WILLIAMS (1929)

## OVID, MEET A METAMORPHODITE

Hermaphroditus, a delight, a
dreamboat on Lake Salmacis,

a dazzling dud
what wist not whut luv wuz

alas, a lout, the lass aloud allowed,
                                        so far beside herself

that scarcely could she stay

so Sister Salmacis hides her in
a bushy queach
to glim the scene at Muscle-Beach
as Hermes, Junior, doffs
his dongarees

no fenny sedge, nor barren reek, no reed
nor rush, just

            SPLASH!

—and passion's double-clutched!

strive, writhe, wrest and struggle, unsnugglin' stranger, grins she
snake-like,
applyin' the boa bit . . .

Hermaphroditus?/Hismaphroditus?
butch?/bitch?
which twain has the gonē?

o, one'll get you two:  a toy of double-shape—

the cream of
genes!

## THE HONEY LAMB

the boysick (by gadzooks thunderstruck)
Rex Zeus, sex
expert, erects
a couple temples
            and cruises the Trojan Coast . . .

eagle-eyed, spies,
swoops,
swishes into town

ponders, whether tis nobler
to bullshit, brown
or go down
on
    that catamite cat, Kid Ganymedes,
                    mead-mover,

erstwhile eagle-scout
bed-mate

## THE ADHESIVE AUTOPSY OF WALT WHITMAN

"Gentlemen, look on this wonder . . .
and wonders within there yet":

"pleurisy of the left side, consumption
of the right lung,

general miliary tuberculosis
and parenchymatous nephritis . . . a fatty

liver, a huge stone
filling the gall,

a cyst in the adrenal, tubercular abcesses
involving the bones,

and pachymeningitis"

"that he was a Kosmos is a piece of news we were
hardly prepared for . . ."

---

Verbatim quotations from the Philadelphia and Camden newspapers.

## A VULNERARY

*(for Robert Duncan)*

one comes to language from afar, the ear
fears for its sound-barriers—

but one 'comes'; the language 'comes' for
*The Beckoning Fair One*

*plant you now, dig you
later*, the plaint stirs winter
earth . . .

air in a hornets' nest
over the water makes a
solid, six-sided music . . .

a few utterly quiet scenes, things
are very far away—*'form
is emptiness'*

comely, comely, love trembles

and the sweet-shrub

## THE BITCH-KITTY

O Quondam Pre-and-Post-Bellum
Finger-Lickin Late Georgian Gentility!

this Lady thinks on Beauty, yes,
high cottons of Beauty up to
and including
the kazoo, bless
her Cottonpickin
Soul indeed
on its avoidance . . .

hast thou not never,
O Nouveau-Riche Peach-Queen, yet paused
to smile upon the blooming earth?

not 'just divine' but *green*

(*I find you highly offensive, suh,* she
said)

O green as goslinshit, and fertile
to the poorest Muse!


## A LITTLE TUMESCENCE

this time, I mean it:
twice tonight!

                    (*omne animal*, always
                    The Hope

*triste, triste*
situation, such outrageous
limitation,
limp,

      simply

## THE HERMIT CACKLEBERRY BROWN, ON HUMAN VANITY:

caint call your name
but your face is easy

come sit

now some folks figure theyre
bettern
cowflop they
aint

not a bit

just good to hold the world together
like hooved up ground

thats what

# GREGORY CORSO (1930)

## BIRTHPLACE REVISITED

I stand in the dark light in the dark street
and look up at my window, I was born there.
The lights are on; other people are moving about.
I am with raincoat; cigarette in mouth,
hat over eye, hand on gat.
I cross the street and enter the building.
The garbage cans haven't stopped smelling.
I walk up the first flight; Dirty Ears
aims a knife at me . . .
I pump him full of lost watches.

## HELLO

It is disastrous to be a wounded deer.
I'm the most wounded, wolves stalk,
and I have my failures, too.
My flesh is caught on the Inevitable Hook!
As a child I saw many things I did not want to be.
Am I the person I did not want to be?
That talks-to-himself person?
That neighbors-make-fun-of person?
Am I he who, on museum steps, sleeps on his side?
Do I wear the cloth of a man who has failed?
Am I the looney man?
In the great serenade of things,
    am I the most cancelled passage?

# UCCELLO

They will never die on that battlefield
nor the shade of wolves recruit their hoard like brides of
wheat on all horizons   waiting there to consume battle's end
    There will be no dead to tighten their loose bellies
no heap of starched horses to redsmash their bright eyes
        or advance their eat of dead
    They would rather hungersulk with mad tongues
than believe that on that field no man dies

    They will never die who fight so embraced
breath to breath   eye knowing eye   impossible to die
or move   no light seeping through   no maced arm
nothing but horse outpanting horse   shield brilliant upon
shield   all made starry by the dot ray of a helmeted eye
ah   how difficult to fall between those knitted lances
And those banners!   angry as to flush insignia across its
        erasure of sky
    You'd think he'd paint his armies by the coldest rivers
have rows of iron skulls flashing in the dark
    You'd think it impossible for any man to die
each combatant's mouth is a castle of song
each iron fist a dreamy gong   flail resounding flail
                    like cries of gold
how I dream to join such battle!
a silver man on a black horse with red standard and striped
        lance        never to die but to be endless
        a golden prince of pictorial war

# POETS HITCHHIKING ON THE HIGHWAY

Of course I tried to tell him
but he cranked his head
        without an excuse.
I told him the sky chases
        the sun

And he smiled and said:
    'What's the use.'
I was feeling like a demon
    again
So I said: 'But the ocean chases
    the fish.'
This time he laughed
    and said: 'Suppose the
      strawberry were
        pushed into a mountain.'
After that I knew the
    war was on—
So we fought:
He said: 'The apple-cart like a
        broomstick-angel
     snaps & splinters
       old dutch shoes.'
I said: 'Lightning will strike the old oak
     and free the fumes!'
He said: 'Mad street with no name.'
I said: 'Bald killer! Bald killer! Bald killer!'
He said, getting real mad,
    'Firestoves! Gas! Couch!'
I said, only smiling,
    'I know God would turn back his head
    if I sat quietly and thought.'
We ended by melting away,
    hating the air!

## A DREAMED REALIZATION

The carrion-eater's nobility calls back from God;
Never was a carrion-eater *first* a carrion-eater—
Back there in God creatures sat like stone
—no light in their various eyes.

Life. It was Life jabbed a spoon in their mouths.
Crow jackal hyena vulture worm woke to necessity
—dipping into Death like a soup.

## SPONTANEOUS REQUIEM FOR
## THE AMERICAN INDIAN

Wakonda! Talako! deathonic turkey gobbling in the soft-footpatch night!
Blue-tipped yellow-tipped red-tipped feathers of whort dye fluffing in fire
    mad dance whaa whaa dead men red men feathers-in-their-head-men
    night!
Deerskin rage of flesh on the bone on the hot tobacco ground!
Muskhogean requiems america southeastern, O death of Creeks, Choctaws,
The youthful tearful Brave, in his dying hand trout, well-caught proud
    trout,
Softest of feet, fleet, o america dirge, o america norwegians swedes of quid
    and murder and boots and slaughter and God and rot-letters,
O pinto brays! O deatheme sled mourning the dying chief!
Berries, spruce, whortle, cranky corn, bitter wheat; o scarcity of men!
High-throttled squawlark, sister warrior, teepee maid, scar lover, crash
    down thy muskrat no longer thy flesh hand and rage and writhe
    and pound thy Indianic earth with last pang of love of love,
o america, o requiems—

Ghost-herds of uneaten left to rot animals thundering across the plains
Chasing the ghost of England across the plains forever ever, pompous
    Kiwago raging in the still Dakotas, o america—
America o mineral scant america o mineralize america o conferva of that
    once
great lovely Muskhogean pool, o oil-suck america despite, oil from forgetive
    days, hare to arrow, muskellunge to spear, fleet-footed know ye
    speed-well the tribes thence outraced the earth to eat to love to die,
o requiems, Hathor off-far bespeaks Wakonda,
heraldic henequen tubas whittled in coyote tune to mourn the death of
    the going sun the going sled of each dying, sad and dying, shake of
    man, the tremble of men, of each dying chief slow and red and
    leather fur hot—
Shake slow the rattler, the hawk-teeth, the bettle-bells, shake slow dirge, o
    dirge, shake slow the winds of winds, o feathers withered and blown,
Dirge the final pinto-led sled, the confused hurt sad king of Montanas,
Strike dumb the French fur trappers in their riverboat brool mockery, no
    chant of death in such a wealth of muskrat and beaver, shun them,
O slam squaw hysteria down on america, the covered wagon america, the
    arrow flamed wagons of conquest, the death stand of quakers and
    white-hooded hags and proud new men, young and dead,
O Geronimo! hard nickel faced Washington Boliva of a dying city that

never was, that monster-died, that demons gathered to steal and did,
O Sitting Bull pruneman Jefferson Lenin Lincoln reddeadman, force thy
    spirit to wings, cloud the earth to air, o the condor the vulture the
    hawk fat days are gone, and you are gone, o america, o requiems,
Dry valleys, deathhead stones, high Arizonas, red sun earth, the sled,
The weeping bray, the ponymarenight, the slow chief of death, wrinkled
    and sad and manless, vistaless, smokeless, proud sad dying—
Toward the coyote reach of peak and moon, howl of heyday, laugh proud
    of men and men, Blackfoot, Mohawk, Algonquin, Seneca, all men,
    o american, peaked there then bow
Thy white-haired straw head and, pinto imitated, die with the rising moon,
    hotnight, lost, empty, unseen, musicless, mindless; no wind—
In the grim dread light of the Happy Hunting Ground
A century of chiefs argue their many scalps, whacking the yellow strands
    of a child against the coaly misty harsh of tent;
It falls apart in a scatter of strewn, away, gone, no more, back free out of
    the quay, into the bladder seep of the bald dead seeking the hairless
    rawhead child of whiteman's grave;
O there is more an exact sorrow in this Indianical eternity,
Sure o america woof and haw and caw and wooooo whirl awhirl here o
    weep!
Indianhill woe!  never was the scalp of men the prime knife in the heart
    of a savagengence era, Clevelandestroyer of manland, o requiems,
O thundercloud, thunderbird, rain-in-the-face, hark in the gloom, death,
And blankets and corn, and peaceful footings of man in quest of Kiwago,
    america, Kiwago, america, corn america, earthly song of a sad boy's
    redfleshed song in the night before the peered head intrusive head
    of laughing thunderbolt Zeus, o the prank, o the death, o the night,
Requiem, america, sing a dirge that might stalk the white wheat black in
    praise of Indianever again to be, gone, gone, desolate, and gone;
Hear the plains, the great divide, hear the wind of this night Oklahoma
    race to weep first in the dirge of mountains and streams and trees and
    birds and day and night and the bright yet lost apparitional sled,
The bowed head of an Indian is enough to bow the horse's head and both
    in unison die and die and die and never again die for once the night
    eats up the dying it eats up the pain and there is no Indian pain no
    pregnant squaw no wild-footed great-eyed boy no jolly stern fat
    white-furred chief of tobacco damp and sweet, o america america—
Each year Kiwago must watch its calves thin out; must watch with all its
    natural killers dead, the new marksmen of machines and bullets and
    trained studied eyes aim and fire and kill the oldest bull, the king,
    the Kiwago of the reminiscent plain—
Each year Wakonda must watch the motionless desert, the dry tearless

childless desert, the smokeless desert, the Indianlessadly desert—
Each year Talako must watch the bird go arrowless in his peace of sky in his
 freedom of the mouth of old america, raw wild calm america,
O america, o requiem, o tumbleweed, o Western Sky, each year is another
 year the soft football doesn't fall, the thin strong arm of spear never
 raised, the wise council of gathered kings no longer warm with life
 and fur and damp and heat and hotcorn and dry jerky meat, each
 year no squaw titters her moony lover of hard love and necessary
 need of man and wife and child child, each year no child, no mien
 of life, good life, no, no, america, but the dead stones, the dry trees,
 the dusty going winded earth—requiem.

Pilgrim blunderbuss, buckles, high hat, Dutch, English, patent leather
shoes, Bible, pray, snow, careful, careful, o but feast, turkey, corn,
pumpkin, sweet confused happy hosty guests, Iroquois, Mohawk, Oneida,
Onondaga, Thanksgiving!
O joy! o angels! o peace! o land! land land land, o death,
O fire and arrow and buckshot and whisky and rum and death and land,
O witches and taverns and quakers and Salem and New Amsterdam and
 corn,
And night, softfeet, death, massacre, massacre, o america, o requiem—
Log-cabins, forts, outposts, trading-posts, in the distance, clouds,
Dust, hordes, tribes, death, death, blonde girls to die, gowns of ladies to
 burn, men of redcoats and bluecoats to die, boys to drum and fife
 and curse and cry and die, horses. . . to die, babies. . . to die;
Yeeeeeeeeeeeeeeeeooooooooooooo! Harrrrrrrrrrrrrrraaaaaaaaaa!
EEEEEEEEeeeeeeeeEEEEEEaaaaaaaaaaaaaaah!
To die to die to die to die to die to die . . . america, requiem.
Corn, jerky, whortly, the Seneca in a deacon's suit, gawky, awkward,
 drunk,
Tired, slouched—the gowns and bright boots pass, the quick take-your-
partner-swing-to-the-left-swing-to-the-right hums all is over, done, the
Seneca sleeps, no sled, no pinto, no end, but sleep, and a new era, a new
day, a new light and the corn grows plenty, and the night is forever, and
the day;

The jetliner streams down upon Texas,
 Requiem.

Motorcyclist Blackfoot his studded belt at night wilder than bright hawk-
eyes sits on his fat bike black smelly brusqued assy about to goggleeye
himself down golden ventures whizzing faster than his ancestral steed past
smokestacks bannershacks O the timid shade of Kiwago now! the mad

roar exhaustpipe Indian like a fleeing oven clanking weeeeee weeeeeee no
feathers in his oily helmet O he's a fast engine of steam zooming unlaurelled
by but he's stupid he sits in Horn & Hardart's his New York visit and he's
happy with his short girls with pink faces and bright hair talking about his
big fat bike and their big fat bike, O he's an angel there though sinister
sinister in shape of Steel Discipline smoking a cigarette in a fishy corner in
the night, waiting, america, waiting the end, the last Indian, mad Indian of
no fish or foot or proud forest haunt, mad on his knees ponytailing &
rabbitfooting his motorcycle, his the final requiem the final america
READY THE FUNERAL STOMP goodluck charms on, tires aired, spikes
greased, morose goggles on, motor gas brakes checked! 1958 Indians,
heaps of leather—ZOOM down the wide amber speedway of Death, Little
Richard, tuba mirum, the vast black jacket brays in the full forced fell.

## JOEL OPPENHEIMER (1930)

## THE LOVE BIT

the colors we depend on are
red for raspberry jam, white
of the inside thigh, purple as
in deep, the blue of moods, green
cucumbers (cars), yellow stripes down
the pants, orange suns on ill-
omened days, and black as the
dirt in my fingernails.
also, brown, in the night,
appearing at its best when
the eyes turn inward, seeking
seeking, to dig everything but
our own. i.e. we make it crazy or
no, and sometimes in the afternoon.

## THE INNOCENT BREASTS

the innocence of her
breasts. the way in
the soft morning, as
she leaned over him,
reaching to see the
time, they hung tender
and innocent.
                just
six hours earlier, as
in many other beds,
they had been hard
and passionate as
pomegranates, and a
few hours before

that, every man at
the party wanted them.
go further back: ten
months ago they had
been filled with
milk, and the boy
suckled, and the
man held back his
hands and lips—now
they were not his.

we are all, we know
now, bone-pickers after
darwin, rag-pickers after
marx, brain-pickers
after freud—we are
trying to reconstruct
our history. breasts
are a sexual attribute.
the chimpanzee's flat
chest with long nipple
is more efficient for
feeding. the breast is
a sexual attribute. they
hang warm and innocent
in the morning.
                    four
hours later, at the
forum, fortunately or
not, those breasts took
over the conversation.
after all man is a
political animal also,
and can figure a way
to breasts even with
war. but she was embarrassed,
saying, they/re not
even that good. and he:
you didn/t think it/d
mention your ass, did you?
and the politics of
breasts leads men into
madness, tumbling over

each other in a
mad race for a
sight, touch, taste.
i won/t be blamed
for it—i unabashedly
stare through every
see-through blouse,
look down every low
neckline, peer carefully
through the right
kind of armhole. it
is nobody/s fault, we
are born to love them,
even though they are
difficult to make
love to.
     the buttocks
at least are truly
functional, allowing
man mobility, agility,
speed. the breasts hang
innocent in the morning
light. at night they
tighten in desire; in
the evening they peep
provocatively. the
young man asked plaintively
whether lenin had ever
wondered about the cup-sizes
of fellow revolutionaries.
i hope so—this is how
the revolution gets
made.

     in the morning light
he ached to touch them,
catch the weight and the
softness in his hand, but
could not. some obscure
idea made him just watch,
while she thought him
still asleep. they were
too innocent in the

morning light. he thought
it no time for the carnal,
though he laughed as he
thought that. he preferred
the thoughts he was
having, to the action—
not perversely, but as
a special delight.
                besides,
after the forum, they
would nap, in the warm
afternoon, and the meat
of it, the true carnality,
would carry them. the
breasts hung innocent
in the morning light.


## MOTHER POEM


the first cries were
pain, the next anger,
the next, demands. ma
ma, each time different,
the succession of the
waking up. i went to
him to soothe him, to
put him back to sleep.
he was ready. he asked
ma ma quizzically, this
time for information.
falling asleep three
times he moaned ma ma.
this time it was loss,
this time it was
not consolable except
by sleep. holy mother
you know this having
heard it all your life.

do i fall asleep any
differently? does any
man? crying for you,
knowing we have not
touched you all day
long though our fingers
rake your breasts and
face, knowing we will
never touch you, missing
you, missing
what is within you,
in the slow creaking
rock of our cradles
or our heads. in our
dreams you dance before
us, in our lives we
turn away. holy
mother hold us
holy mother even if
we turn away, even if
we strike out at you,
hold us hold us hold us.
you will listen to our
cries every day and
night you live, and
we will continue
crying while we breathe.
a small child taught
me this, what has he
not taught you, what
have you not taught
him, what is it he
will forget when he
grows to my age, when
he becomes me, lashing
out at your dancing
figure, turning his
head, refusing the
only thing that will
comfort him at all.

## FATHER POEM

i have fathered
four sons, they surround
me in an age of
women, they will
have to fight like
hell to find the
action, i have laid
something very heavy
on their heads. the
youngest, perhaps,
will survive into
the new world.
                    myself,
like always and always,
i will be defeated, they
will carry me ball-less and
regal into the house of
the dead where i will
pay for this sin, having
fathered only sons,
having brought no young
women into this world.
but this is in me rock-
like, to do the wrong
thing, to pick the
wrong time. it is
obduracy, pride, a
need to go the wrong way.
yet they are strong.
it is the first time
i have seen them all
together.
                    i await
my golden throne,
defeated, regal, honored.
when i get there i
will have a drink and
let them do the fighting.
the fathers of daughters
cannot say this.

# GARY SNYDER (1930)


## *from* MYTHS & TEXTS:  BURNING


1. *second shaman song*

Squat in swamp shadows.
  mosquitoes sting;
   high light in cedar above.
Crouched in a dry vain frame
  —thirst for cold snow
  —green slime of bone marrow
Seawater fills each eye

Quivering in nerve and muscle
Hung in the pelvic cradle
Bones propped against roots
A blind flicker of nerve

Still hand moves out alone
Flowering and leafing
   turning to quartz
Streaked rock  congestion of karma
The long body of the swamp.
A mud-streaked thigh.

Drying carp biting air
   in the damp grass,
River recedes.  No matter.

Limp fish sleep in the weeds
The sun dries me as I dance


3. *Maudgalyâyana saw hell*

Under the shuddering eyelid
Dreams gnawing the nerve-strings,
The mind grabs and the shut eye sees:
Down dimensions floating below sunlight,

Worlds of the dead, Bardo, mind-worlds
& horror of sunless cave-ritual
Meeting conscious monk bums
Blown on winds of karma from hell
To endless changing hell,
Life and death whipped
On this froth of reality (wind & rain
Realms human and full of desire) over the cold
Hanging enormous unknown, below
Art and History and all mankind living thoughts,
Occult & witchcraft evils each all true.
The thin edge of nature rising fragile
And helpless with its love and sentient stone
And flesh, above dark drug-death dreams.

Clouds I cannot lose, we cannot leave.
We learn to love, horror accepted.
Beyond, within, all normal beauties
Of the science-conscious sex and love-receiving
Day-to-day got vision of this sick
Sparkling person at the inturned dreaming
Blooming human mind
Dropping it all, and opening the eyes.

4. *Maitreya the future Buddha*

He's out stuck in a bird's craw
                              last night
Wildcat vomited his pattern on the snow.

Who refused to learn to dance, refused
To kiss you long ago. You fed him berries
But fled, the red stain on his teeth;
And when he cried, finding the world a Wheel—
                    you only stole his rice,
Being so small and gray. He will not go,
But wait through fish scale, shale dust, bone
            of hawk and marmot,
                caught leaves in ice,
Till flung on a new net of atoms:
Snagged in flight
Leave you hang and quiver like a gong

Your empty happy body
Swarming in the light


5. *jimson weed*

Now both
Being persons—alive
We sit here
The wind
Whirls
      "Don't kill it man,
The roach is the best part"
        still an incessant chatter
On Vulture Peak
Crack of dawn/       calor/canor/dulcor   faugh

I hold it
I tell of it, standing
I look here
I look there
Standing
       great limp mouth
       hanging loose in air
       quivers, turns in upon itself,
       gone
       with a diabolical laugh
The night bat
Rising flies, I tell it
I sing it

"Jesus was a great doctor, I guess he was
the best gambler in the United States"
At Hakwinyava
Imagine a dark house
Blue


14.

A skin-bound bundle of clutchings
      unborn and with no place to go
Balanced on the boundless compassion
Of diatoms, lava, and chipmunks.

Love, let it be,
Is a sacrifice
            knees, the cornered eyes
Tea on a primus stove after a cold swim
Intricate doors and clocks, the clothes
        we stand in—
Gaps between seedings, the right year,
Green shoots in the marshes
Creeks in the proper directions
Hills in proportion,
Astrologers, go-betweens present,
                a marriage has been.


Walked all day through live oak and manzanita,
Scrabbling through dust down Tamalpais—
Thought of high mountains;
Looked out on a sea of fog.
Two of us, carrying packs.


15.


Stone-flake and salmon.
The pure, sweet, straight-splitting
                with a ping
Red cedar of the thick coast valleys
Shake-blanks on the mashed ferns
                the charred logs
Fireweed and bees
An old burn, by new alder
Creek on smooth stones,
Back there a Tarheel logger farm.
(High country fir still hunched in snow)


From Siwash strawberry-pickers in the Skagit
Down to the boys at Sac,
Living by the river
            riding flatcars to Fresno,
Across the whole country
Steep towns, flat towns, even New York,
And oceans and Europe & libraries & galleries
And the factories they make rubbers in
This whole spinning show

(among others)
Watched by the Mt. Sumeru L.O.

From the middle of the universe
& them with no radio.
"What is imperfect is best"
               silver scum on the trout's belly
               rubs off on your hand.
It's all falling or burning—
               rattle of boulders—
               steady dribbling of rocks down cliffs
               bark chips in creeks
Porcupine chawed here—
                              Smoke
From Tillamook a thousand miles
Soot and hot ashes.  Forest fires.
Upper Skagit burned I think 1919
Smoke covered all northern Washington.
               lightning strikes, flares,
Blossoms a fire on the hill.
Smoke like clouds.  Blotting the sun
Stinging the eyes.
The hot seeds steam underground
               still alive.


17. *the text*

Sourdough mountain called a fire in:
Up Thunder Creek, high on a ridge.
Hiked eighteen hours, finally found
A snag and a hundred feet around on fire:
All afternoon and into night
Digging the fire line
Falling the burning snag
It fanned sparks down like shooting stars
Over the dry woods, starting spot-fires
Flaring in wind up Skagit valley
From the Sound.
Toward morning it rained.
We slept in mud and ashes,
Woke at dawn, the fire was out,
The sky was clear, we saw
The last glimmer of the morning star.

*the myth*

Fire up Thunder Creek and the mountain—
                troy's burning!
The cloud mutters
The mountains are your mind.
The woods bristle there,
Dogs barking and children shrieking
Rise from below.

Rain falls for centuries
Soaking the loose rocks in space
Sweet rain, the fire's out
The black snag glistens in the rain
& the last wisp of smoke floats up
Into the absolute cold
Into the spiral whorls of fire
The storms of the Milky Way
"Buddha incense in an empty world"
Black pit cold and light-year
Flame tongue of the dragon
Licks the sun

The sun is but a morning star

# FOR A FAR-OUT FRIEND

Because I once beat you up
Drunk, stung with weeks of torment
And saw you no more,
And you had calm talk for me today
        I now suppose
I was less sane than you,
You hung on dago red,
        me hooked on books,
You once ran naked toward me
Knee deep in cold March surf
On a tricky beach between two
        pounding seastacks—

I saw you as a Hindu Deva-girl
Light legs dancing in the waves,
Breasts like dream-breasts
Of sea, and child, and astral
       Venus-spurting milk.
And traded our salt lips.

Visions of your body
Kept me high for weeks, I even had
       a sort of trance for you
A day in a dentist's chair.
I found you again, gone stone,
In Zimmer's book of Indian Art:
Dancing in that life with
Grace and love, with rings
And a little golden belt, just above
       your naked snatch
And I thought—more grace and love
In that wild Deva life where you belong
Than in this dress-and-girdle life
You'll ever give
Or get.

# RIPRAP

Lay down these words
Before your mind like rocks.
       placed solid, by hands
In choice of place, set
Before the body of the mind
       in space and time:
Solidity of bark, leaf, or wall
       riprap of things:
Cobble of milky way,
       straying planets,
These poems, people,
       lost ponies with
Dragging saddles—
       and rocky sure-foot trails.

The worlds like an endless
                    four-dimensional
Game of *Go*.
                    ants and pebbles
In the thin loam, each rock a word
                    a creek-washed stone
Granite:  ingrained
                    with torment of fire and weight
Crystal and sediment linked hot
                    all change, in thoughts,
As well as things.


## THROUGH THE SMOKE HOLE

*for Don Allen*

I

There is another world above this one; or outside of this one; the way to
   it is thru the smoke of this one, & the hole that smoke goes through.
   The ladder is the way through the smoke hole; the ladder holds up,
   some say, the world above; it might have been a tree or pole; I think
   it is merely a way.

Fire is at the foot of the ladder. The fire is in the center. The walls are
   round. There is also another world below or inside this one. The
   way there is down thru smoke. It is not necessary to think of a series.

Raven and Magpie do not need the ladder. They fly thru the smoke holes
   shrieking and stealing. Coyote falls thru; we recognize him only as a
   clumsy relative, a father in old clothes we don't wish to see with our
   friends.

It is possible to cultivate the fields of our own world without much
   thought for the others. When men emerge from below we see them
   as the masked dancers of our magic dreams. When men disappear
   down, we see them as plain men going somewhere else. When men
   disappear up we see them as great heroes shining through the smoke.
   When men come back from above they fall thru and tumble; we don't
   really know them; Coyote, as mentioned before.

II

Out of the kiva come
masked dancers or
plain men.
        plain men go into the ground.


out there out side all the chores
        wood and water, dirt,
wind, the view across the flat,
here, in the round
                        no corners
head is full of magic figures—

woman your secrets aren't my secrets
what I cant say I wont
walk round
put my hand flat down.
you in the round too.
gourd vine blossom.
walls and houses drawn up
from the same soft soil.


thirty million years gone
                drifting sand.
    cool rooms pink stone
worn down fort floor, slat sighting
    heat shine on jumna river


dry wash, truck tracks in the riverbed
coild sand pinyon.


            seabottom
            riverbank
            sand dunes
the floor of a sea once again.


            human fertilizer
            underground water tunnels
            skinny dirt gods
            grandmother berries
                            out
through the smoke hole.
        (for childhood and youth *are* vanity)

a Permian reef of algae,

*out* through the smoke hole
swallowd sand
           salt mud
swum bodies,      flap
to the limestone blanket—

lizzard tongue,      lizzard tongue

     *wha, wha, wha*    flying
*in* and *out* thru the smoke hole

          plain men
come out of the ground.

# WHAT YOU SHOULD KNOW TO BE A POET

all you can about animals as persons.
the names of trees and flowers and weeds.
names of stars, and the movements of the planets
               and the moon.

your own six senses, with a watchful and elegant mind.

at least one kind of traditional magic:
divination, astrology, the *book of changes*, the tarot;

dreams.
the illusory demons and illusory shining gods;

kiss the ass of the devil and eat shit;
fuck his horny barbed cock,
fuck the hag,
and all the celestial angels
               and maidens perfum'd and golden—

& then love the human: wives    husbands    and friends.

children's games, comic books, bubble-gum,
the weirdness of television and advertising.

work, long dry hours of dull work swallowed and accepted
and livd with and finally lovd.        exhaustion,
                        hunger, rest.

the wild freedom of the dance, *extasy*
silent solitary illumination, *enstasy*

real danger.  gambles.  and the edge of death.




# LMFBR


Death himself,
            (Liquid Metal Fast Breeder Reactor)
            stands grinning, beckoning.
Plutonium tooth-glow.
Eyebrows buzzing.
Strip-mining scythe.

Kālī dances on the dead stiff cock.


        Aluminum beer cans, plastic spoons,
plywood veneer, PVC pipe, vinyl seat covers,
            don't exactly burn, don't quite rot,
            flood over us,


        robes and garbs
        of the Kālī-yūga

        end of days.

## WHAT HAPPENED HERE BEFORE

−300,000,000

First a sea:  soft sands, muds, and marls
    —loading, compressing, heating, crumpling,
        crushing, recrystallizing, infiltrating,
several times lifted and submerged.
intruding molten granite magma
        deep-cooled and speckling,
            gold quartz fills the cracks—

−80,000,000−

sea-bed strata raised and folded,
        granite far below.
warm quiet centuries of rains
        (make dark red tropic soils)
        wear down two miles of surface,
lay bare the veins and tumble heavy gold
        in steambeds
                slate and schist rock-riffles catch it—
volcanic ash floats down and dams the streams,
        piles up the gold and gravel—

−3,000,000

flowing north, two rivers joined,
        to make a wide long lake.
and then it tilted and the rivers fell apart
        all running west
        to cut the gorges of the Feather,
            Bear, and Yuba.
Ponderosa pine, manzanita, black oak, mountain yew.
        deer, coyote, bluejay, gray squirrel,
        ground squirrel, fox, blacktail hare,
            ringtail, bobcat, bear,
            all came to live here.

−40,000−

And human people came with basket hats and nets
     winter-houses underground
     yew bows painted green,
     feasts and dances for the boys and girls
        songs and stories in the smoky dark.

                    —125—

Then came the white man: tossed up trees and
     boulders with big hoses,
     going after that old gravel and the gold.
horses, apple-orchards, card-games,
     pistol-shooting, churches, county jail.

We asked, who the land belonged to.
     and where one pays tax.
(two gents who never used it twenty years,
and before them the widow
     of the son of the man
     who got him a patented deed
     on a worked-out mining claim,)
laid hasty on land that was deer and acorn
     grounds of the Nisenan?
     branch of the Maidu?
(they never had a chance to speak, even,
     their name.)
(and who remembers the Treaty of Guadalupe Hidalgo.)

     the land belongs to itself.
     "no self in self; no self in things"

     Turtle Island swims
     in the ocean-sky swirl-void
     biting its tail while the worlds go
       on-and-off
         winking

& Mr. Tobiassen, a Cousin Jack,
     assesses the county tax.
(the tax is our body-mind, guest at the banquet)
     Memorial and Annual, in honor
     of sunlight grown heavy and tasty
     while moving up food-chains

in search of a body with eyes and a fairly large
        brain—
    to look back at itself
        on high.)


                *now,*


we sit here near the diggings
in the forest, by our fire, and watch
the moon and planets and the shooting stars—

my sons ask, who are we?
drying apples picked from homestead trees
drying berries, curing meat,
shooting arrows at a bale of straw.

military jets head northeast, roaring, every dawn.

my sons ask, who are they?

    *WE SHALL SEE*
    *WHO KNOWS*
    *HOW TO BE*

Bluejay screeches from a pine.

# JEROME ROTHENBERG (1931)


## POLAND/1931    "The Wedding"


my mind is stuffed with tablecloths
& with rings but my mind
is dreaming of poland stuffed with poland
brought in the imagination
to a black wedding
a naked bridegroom hovering above
his naked bride     mad poland
how terrible thy jews at weddings
thy synagogues with camphor smells & almonds
thy thermos bottles thy electric fogs
thy braided armpits
thy underwear alive with roots o poland
poland poland poland poland poland
how thy bells wrapped in their flowers toll
how they do offer up their tongues to kiss the moon
old moon old mother stuck in thy sky thyself
an old bell with no tongue a lost udder
o poland thy beer is ever made of rotting bread
thy silks are linens merely thy tradesmen
dance at weddings where fanatic grooms
still dream of bridesmaids still are screaming
past their red moustaches poland
we have lain awake in thy soft arms forever
thy feathers have been balm to us
thy pillows capture us like sickly wombs & guard us
let us sail through thy fierce weddings poland
let us tread thy markets where thy sausages grow ripe & full
let us bite thy peppercorns let thy oxen's dung be sugar to thy dying jews
o poland o sweet resourceful restless poland
o poland of the saints unbuttoned poland repeating endlessly the triple
     names of mary
poland poland poland poland poland
have we not tired of thee poland no for thy cheeses
shall never tire us nor the honey of thy goats
thy grooms shall work ferociously upon their looming brides
shall bring forth executioners

shall stand like kings inside thy doorways
shall throw their arms around thy lintels poland
& begin to crow


## THE OTHERS    HUNTERS IN THE NORTH    THE CREE

*for Howard Norman*


1
the photo shows me
bearded man with hand
over one eye
they say    he pulls his eye out
now the shadow
—death's line—
's at my gut
flower in the soup
2 flowers now
2 eyes
the hunters watch
I take them
& place a stem in each socket
sharp as wires
the flowers dance on ends of
we remember
in the movie you were watching with
the others    hunters in the north    the Cree
sweet music over Tundra
lovely as the lady
Harpo saw & plucked
both eyes
to juggle & never
got them back in straight
much to their laughter    doomed
to double vision
men with eyebrows of crows
whose women swim in them
were Trickster's boys
among the fjords & flows

we share
somehow in a hut of dreams
he leaves for us


    2
lately I saw
my eye over ocean
tipped with red
my blood the seashell held
in drops
so red the sun was
drew out our organs to the light
the madman cloud
has spoken
"when we leave this world we walk
"under another sun
"the language changes
"slowly
"frees us at last to speak
the stranger wanders thru the message room
my captain    he is half asleep
half swedish
the hair grows even to his toes
but soon forgotten shy
"I try to make things right (he tells us)
"sometimes it doesn't work
& sleeps first in a hammock that becomes
a valley
the ends held up by pine trees
hanging upside down
no animals left in that world
but dreaming
each eye now sees a different shape
a porcupine stuck to a cloud
by quills
a bird
—a footprint—
worms inside it
crowing
"fill up your ears with whitefish oil
"with mud
"so not to listen
"to the windigo who sits

"still on my tongue
"the way it always was
"& chews my heart
"the liver in my only cave
I WANT THIS AS A NAME:
HE-PULLS-HIS-EYE-OUT


     3
the body of a Seneca
fell once
down from the overpass
onto the highway
same year that Gary Gordon
flew from his car to heaven
didn't make it
the roads are haunted now
that cross the woods
we do not know these windigo
—ice hearts that melt—
we feel them everywhere
blue lights
we see them floating
down Allegany
call them our deaths




# 48 WORDS FOR A WOMAN'S DANCE SONG


playing the 7th
rattle
on the bench
my feet tucked in against
the wood
right foot tapping
hard
old rattle slaps
my hand
zat why you're smiling at me
brother Lyford

let's make this one real loud
(he says)
"what kind of Indian are you?"
"a fuzzy Indian"

## THE STRUCTURAL STUDY OF MYTH

*for Barbara Kirshenblatt-Gimblett*

the thief became the rabbi
in that old story
others would say he was his father
all along      the way the moon
reflected in the water
is the water
maybe the master gonnif come to earth
old Trickster brother Jesus
didn't us Jews tell stories of his magic
"because we are like him"
the Crow Indian had said about Coyote
hitting the nail at last

## A POEM IN YELLOW AFTER TRISTAN TZARA

(Invocation):

angel slide your hand
into my basket      eat my yellow fruit
my eye is craving it
my yellow tires screech
o dizzy human heart
my yellow dingdong

# MICHAEL McCLURE (1932)


## CANTICLE


The sharks tooth is perfect for biting. The intent
matters. / I am sick of beautiful things
/ and I would make a robe of gestures

without beauty except for the beauty inherent
in words and motion.

Listen / Listen / listen / Listen / Listen

to the words as waves / pressures
all is destruction—without it there is
no strength.      The muscle builds
itself double      by destruction of cells.

The tendons whisper to the skeleton

Listen / Listen / listen / Listen / Listen
and only the nerves hear.
The field and seed are one thing destroying
the other.  Intent, enwrapped with one another

Erethism is love.  Love

Inventing a thing of leaves and flowers

'retractions devour' the thing burgeoning
is the thing intent / Love / Strength / Light
and Dark / spring to blossoms.

## PEYOTE POEM

I

Clear — the senses bright — sitting in the black chair — Rocker —
 the white walls reflecting the color of clouds
 moving over the sun. Intimacies! The rooms

  not important — but like divisions of all space
   of all hideousness and beauty. I hear
   the music of myself and write it down

   for no one to read. I pass fantasies as they
    sing to me with Circe-Voices. I visit
   among the peoples of myself and know all
     I need to know.

I KNOW EVERYTHING! I PASS INTO THE ROOM

   there is a golden bed radiating all light

   the air is full of silver hangings and sheathes

    I smile to myself. I know

   all that there is to know. I see all there

    is to feel. I am friendly with the ache
     in my belly. The answer

   to love is my voice. There is no Time!
No answers. The answer to feeling is my feeling.

   The answer to joy is joy without feeling.

    The room is a multicolored cherub
of air and bright colors. The pain in my stomach

   is warm and tender. I am smiling. The pain
    is many pointed, without anguish.

Light changes the room from yellows to violet!

The dark brown space behind the door is precious
intimate, silent and still. The birthplace
of Brahms. I know

all that I need to know. There is no hurry.

I read the meanings of scratched walls and cracked ceilings.

I am separate. I close my eyes in divinity and pain.

I blink in solemnity and unsolemn joy.

I smile at myself in my movements. Walking
I step higher in carefulness. I fill

space with myself. I see the secret and distinct
patterns of smoke from my mouth

I am without care part of all. Distinct.
I am separate from gloom and beauty. I see all.

---

(SPACIOUSNESS


And grim intensity — close within myself. No longer
a cloud
but flesh real as rock. Like Herakles
of primordial substance and vitality.
And not even afraid of the thing shorn of glamor

but accepting.
The beautiful things are not of ourselves

but I watch them. Among them.

---

And the Indian thing. It is true!
Here in my Apartment I think tribal thoughts.)

---

## STOMACHE!!!

There is no time. I am visited by a man
who is the god of foxes
there is dirt under the nails of his paw
fresh from his den.
We smile at one another in recognition.

I am free from Time. I accept it without triumph

— a fact.

Closing my eyes there are flashes of light.

My eyes won't focus but leap. I see that I have three feet.
I see seven places at once!
The floor slants — the room slopes
things melt
into each other. Flashes
of light
and meldings. I wait

seeing the physical thing pass.

I am on a mesa of time and space.

## ! STOM-ACHE !

Writing the music of life
in words.
Hearing the round sounds of the guitar
as colors.
Feeling the touch of flesh.

Seeing the loose chaos of words
on the page.
(ultimate grace)
(Sweet Yeats and his ball of hashish.)

My belly and I are two individuals
joined together
in life.

---

THIS IS THE POWERFUL KNOWLEDGE

we smile with it.

---

At the window I look into the blue-gray
gloom of dreariness.
I am warm.  Into the dragon of space.
I stare into clouds seeing
their misty convolutions.

The whirls of vapor

I will small clouds out of existence.

They become fish devouring each other.

And change like Dante's holy spirits

becoming an osprey frozen skyhigh

to challenge me.

## THE AELF-SCIN

### THE AELF-SCIN, THE SHINING SCIMMER THE GLEAM, THE SHINING

color of walls of scratches of cracks of brightness
the cold mystery the (Philip calls it) Weir.  The deja
vu of the forest-sorrel, tiny, leaves sun-folded
bent like a head in uniqueness.  Animal in look
to fold so.  The moment I

leave what I am in aelf-scin. Stand
in wonder. Lose myself. Even to fear.
A difference. Aelf-scin, Weir. But
similar. Knowing its name the horror
of void is gone. Knowing it almost
with my ash spear over my arm in the black
FOREST CLEAR WATER AND AIR SEA

The Anglo Saxons build huge boats fight battles
and rejoice in what they see,
see beauty more clearly
have words for what
I forget. Live in
liberty. For.
ever. !!!!

CALL IT FEAR NOW-GONE
the whole thing a star
breathing.

# MAD SONNET 1

THE PLUMES OF LOVE ARE BLACK! THE PLUMES OF LOVE
[ARE BLACK
AND DELICATE! OH!
and shine like moron-eyed plumes of a peacock
with violetshine and yellow on shadowy black.
They spray SPRAY from the body of the Beloved. Vanes shaking in air!

---

AND I DO NOT WANT BLACK PLUMES OR AGONY ... AND I DO
NOT SURRENDER. And I ask for noble combat!!
to give pure Love
as best I can
with opened heart
LOVE!!

I have not seen you before and you're
more beautiful than a plume!

Stately, striding in Space and warm... (Your
human breasts!)
LET ME MAKE YOUR SMILE AND HEARTSHAPED FACE IMMORTAL

— — — — — — — — — — — — — — — — — — — — — — — — — — — — — — — — —

YOUR GRAY EYES ARE WHAT I FINALLY COME TO WITH MY BROWN!
AND YOUR HIGH CHEEKS, and your hair rough
for a woman's—like a lamb. And the walking Virtue
that you are!

## WITH TENDRILS OF POEMS

WITH TENDRILS OF POEMS,
WITH PERCEPTIONS
LIKE AMINO ACIDS,
the gray plateau is eaten away
and becomes humus for the senses
to feel. Space
is created in the solid dullness.
Scents appear.

Beauteous mephitic odors from green flowers.
Dust in the beard.
Art Nouveau butterflies.
Cliffs shaggy with gardens.
Marble.
Pearls.
Lilies.
Jade.
Song sparrows. Flames.
And the WHOLE BEAST self
laughing and slouching and striding.
SEPTEMBER BLACKBERRIES!

## THE JUNGLE

1

time & time again the laughter after the footsteps
in the snow, the moths walk stiffly
dont palm off yr deathshead on me, man,
or yr horse with the broken leg
         on stilts
         always on stilts
hair brushing the stars, the hair ends cracking

and this is NY    nothing but sleet & foghorns
we'd have to answer the door again someday you know:
the sleet, kissing the window like a goldfish
like a sick goldfish, a goldfish gone to seed;
300 watts in my ceiling, 3 eyes regard me;
the claw lowered behind me on a web.
where's the cellar where you never wet yr feet?
         whose sound is it?

dont come in no cravat to this falling door
two deathblows it had
I shall stop shaking someday
         the beasts cry out:
lushpadded, making it, the growth slimy
they walk, paths never crossing, like dancers
their tails erect, or swishing, or they droop
but their eyes
         the rain falls on the leaves
         the leaves
fall; tenderfooted they walk, tendergrowling, all of love
in the deathspring

2

tomatoes on the vine,
         but that green fruit
juggled too soon,
         it rots before it ripes

its sweet all in its seed
                    its gay tomorrows.
who says we shall not die, the sleet counts off
that Mr. Goldberg has the cheapest tombstones
on Rivington, but Schultz, he does the carving
makes you cry.
I shall put on my seven league boots
and go out picking daisies.
Bullshit.
I shall sit in a freezing pad
while my door gets deathblows.
                    how my window's bruised
blue fleshmarks on the glass.
the wind ignores me, glances off my cunt
            my knuckles
            & the corners of my mouth
the wind is pink, it makes the snow obscene.


            3
tomorrow the fire went out, under the small porch, the snail
regarded the matter, retreated,
            backing into an asymmetrical web
a foot came thru the ceiling, someone turned the knob
on the cancerous door.
I will let you lay yr hand on my head again
but in another fashion.
            Rape of the spirit,
that was
& this a holiday for pears
            if only banners streamed
in different directions
            if only a single face
were turned away . . .


            4
to drop the fucking thing & watch it burn
if it were in my hands, the atomic war wd be past history.
how cosmic chill
passes from one to other as we kiss.
I walk with every beast that walks in me
more catfooted than they
but at the kill, exultant, all of wind
is nothing to this.

It's a losing game.
I walk with every beast that walks
        to take the dragon
thru the city gates
        neck with the cyclops,
etc.
        Eumenides, if one face turns
away
        and the wind, which we must
swallow, whatever we will.


        5
that the sea shd only pay us a flying visit
that the flowers scattered on it do not change
the least of its plans.
my hands are in the wind's mouth, I am led
my eyes are blank,
        nothing is in my hands.
the wall in front of me cuts off sound & sight
my head is chained
nothing is in my hands.
no vines grow on the wall, from time to time
the rain
brings down a rumor of the sky.
that we have floated together away from the fire
that the castle has turned to cardboard, that the air
        will not go near us.
*somewhere the wind plays only on the grass*
*dark and light the turning in the air*

that the block of ice which binds us
                        binds us both.

## THE PRACTICE OF MAGICAL EVOCATION

> *The female is fertile, and discipline*
> *(contra naturam) only*
> *confuses her.*
> —*Gary Snyder*

i am a woman and my poems
are woman's:  easy to say
this.  the female is ductile
and
    (stroke after stroke)
built for masochistic
calm.    The deadened nerve
is part of it:
awakened sex, dead retina
fish eyes;       at hair's root
minimal feeling

and pelvic architecture functional
assailed inside & out
(bring forth)   the cunt gets wide
and relatively sloppy
bring forth men children only
                female
                is
                ductile

woman, a veil thru which the fingering Will
twice torn
twice torn
        inside & out
the flow
what rhythm add to stillness
what applause?

# IN MEMORY OF MY FIRST CHAPATIS

If we had dope for an excuse, or love,
something bumpier, with ups and downs
(like the chapatis, puffing & going stiff—
I probably overcooked them) to account for
your incessant displeasures.

You stalk around the house, brandishing T-squares
you dream of drowning the children
you tell me nine days of the week that you are leaving
but you're still here. I can tell by the lump in my stomach
my unreasonable desire to sleep all the time

so as not to hear you starting the Volkswagen Bus
as if it were a Mercedes, zooming out of the driveway

The women of the rest of the world have so much to teach me!
Them in their saris so cool, kneading chapatis
or tortillas, depending on where, kneeling by their fires
or by their hibachis, or standing by their wood stoves
the women of the rest of the world plait their hair as I do
but they have more patience, they have put up a screen

behind which they only dimly discern their menfolk
bursting the air with perennial desperations.

# GOODBYE NKRUMAH

And yet, where would we be without the American culture
Bye bye blackbird, as Miles plays it, in the '50's
Those coffee malteds?
When the radio told me there was dancing in the streets,
I knew we had engineered another coup;
Bought off another army. And I wondered
what the boys at the Black Arts Theatre were saying
and sent them my love, and my help, which they would not accept
Why should they? It's their war, all I can do is wait

Is not put detergents in the washingmachine, so the soil will still
be productive
when the black men, or the Chinese, come to cultivate it.

I remember a news photo of you stepping off a plane somewhere,
so cool, so straight a look, and so black.
There was nothing we could do but do you in.
You understand, of course.  There is nothing we can do

but shoot students
buy armies
like the British before us killing the Zulus—
now they are fat and placid
their country a shambles.
Well, for us it won't end like that
not quite so simply:
when the Nevele Country Club, the Hotel Americana
when Beverly Hills and the Cliff House
come crashing down, it will be Shiva who dances,
the sky behind him orange (saffron) a great black mushroom
painted on it somewhere
(it was a mushroom killed Buddha)
will kill him again, compassion has to go

a few of us tried it, we tried to stop it with printing
we tried to protect you with mimeograph machines
green posters LUMUMBA LIVES flooded Harlem in those days
well, the best thing to do with a mimeograph is to drop it
from a five story window, on the head of a cop

we buy the arms and the armed men, we have placed them
on all the thrones of South America
we are burning the jungles, the beasts will rise up against us
even now those small jungle people with black eyes
look calmly at us out of their photographs
and it is their calm that will finish us, it is the calm
of the earth itself.

*Mar 1966*

# ANSELM HOLLO (1934)


## THAT OLD SAUNA HIGH

to make the vapor bath
a frame   three sticks
meet at the top

stretch woollen cloth
take care
the seams are tight

a tent   & into it
a dish
with red-hot stones

then take some hemp-seed
& creep in

the seed
onto those stones:
at once
great smoke!
"gives off a vapor
unsurpassed
by any bath
we have in greece"

410 b.c.
eyes watering
by candlelight
uncle herodotus
penned these instructions

adding "the scythians
enjoy it so
they *howl* with pleasure"

getting so clean
all clean   inside

## LE JAZZ HOT

talked to my father again in a dream he seemed happy
perhaps a little older than the last time    told me
he had discovered something called *'le jazz hot'*
& found it of some interest

*(1967)*

## BUFFALO–ISLE OF WIGHT POWER CABLE

1
writing a letter he said
"this instant in time"
but what was that instant
if not where they were

she & the three
like plants with platinum petal hair
sprung from his head

2
in the neverness motels of the bitter country
lovers lie sleeping & loving in fits & starts

3
empty    milky sky
above the building-brick town with its captive dogs
baying at night & in the mornings
the radiation
you opened the door & it hit you

air of metal & transmutations

4
the cars kept flowing past & into the tower courtyard
but when they stopped no one got out of them
he was waiting for no one
whom did he want to hold

                    here in the next town
far away too

he had won the race but no one was cheering
slowly he drove up to the starting line

                                                    *(1967)*

# RAIN

one evening when we were lounging in his apartment in a relaxed mood,
smoking a little hashish, charles baudelaire said to me: "you know, every-
body has seen rain falling—most people have, at one time or another,
actually noticed it."

i agreed with a chuckle. he continued: "you know, i think we can be
fairly confident that it has been raining, on & off, for a very long time!"

having said this, he collapsed on the *chaise-longue*, in a veritable *paroxysme*;
but as always, there was a tinge, a definite tinge of bitterness in his
merriment.

"it would be absurd to imagine," he said, "that rain could ever have
behaved in any way different from that which we observe today. . ."

after a moment's crystalline silence our conversation drifted to other topics—
the day's gossip, the inexhaustible genius of edgar poe. but when we stood
on the fire escape, taking leave, he gazed over my left shoulder into some
indefinable distance or abyss and said, almost dreamily: "it is for ever
washing the substance of the land into the sea."

                                                    *(1968)*

## AMAZING GRACE

people going straight up to heaven


forty of them, in three hours

8-12-72
6-9:00 a.m.
indianola, iowa

*(1972)*


## WASP SEX MYTH (ONE)


when he comes home at night
sue greets her husband jack
in exotic costumes
one evening she may be a harem girl
the next a lolita
a ziegfield follies showgirl
an eighteenth century courtesan a gypsy
fortune teller a prim schoolteacher
who has to be coaxed into unwinding
a roman slave girl an indian maiden
playing these glamorous roles
makes sue less irritable
if while she is scrubbing & waxing the kitchen floor
she is also plotting
in her mind
a geisha costume & a beautiful japanese dinner
then that floor will be done more cheerfully
she loves getting away from the humdrum
& stepping into other worlds
you'll never find jack lingering at the office
for a drink or two with the boys

he can hardly wait to get home
he'll never be on the prowl for other women
he has so many at home

*(1973)*

# WASP SEX MYTH (TWO)

ted & marge had been married eight years. the first three, ted was insane
about marge in bed, but during the fourth year marge became aware that
ted didn't devote as much time to sex. where they used to spend maybe
an hour making love, they now had somehow slipped back to about half
an hour. instinctively marge knew that ted was ripe to fall into the bed
of another woman because he needed the stimulation of a new experience.
she determined that, to keep that other woman's hands off her ted, she
would rekindle his sex drive.
the next week ted had to go to pittsburgh
on company business & while he was away marge worked like a fiend.
first she went to the beauty salon & had her marvelous mane of dark
brown hair streaked. then she had their conventional bedroom done
over in mirrors. smoky mirrors on the walls & ceiling. she packed away
the old pink chenille bedspread & replaced with a huge fake fur throw.
the new sheets had a leopard skin design & the lighting was a combination
of candlelight & those tiny high-intensity reading lamps.
the day that ted
was due back from pittsburgh, marge called him & said she realized that
he would be tired when he got home, but would he please, to humor her,
follow exactly the instructions on the notes he would find in the apartment.
ted, his curiosity aroused, agreed.
the first note (on the door) read: "the
fact that you're home makes me feel all warm & tingly. put your suitcase
down & go straight to the refrigerator."
the note on the refrigerator said:
"open the door & you will see a very dry martini in a pre-chilled glass. take
your drink to the guest bathroom."
in the guest bathroom ted had instruc-
tions to soak in the tub of steaming hot water which was awaiting him,
while he sipped his martini.

scotch-taped to the towel he dried himself with was a note that said: "you have the most exciting body i have ever seen. if you want to see for yourself why you are the most sensual man in the world, come to the bedroom."

ted, thoroughly intrigued (& pretty warm & tingly himself after the bath & the martini), walked into the mirrored bedroom, caught sight of marge stretched out on the fur throw in a black bikini, her body reflected, reflected, reflected everywhere, & *flipped out*! he never left that bedroom again, & he let marge up only long enough to get food & drink occasionally.

*(1973)*

## THE DISCOVERY OF LSD A TRUE STORY

the dose of a mere
fifty micrograms totally altered
the consciousness of professor albert hofman
motel soda works intersection
swerve hit geode albert
inadvertently
inhaled it
blast core city ominous rock
spiraling rates of light
inhaled his consciousness
& exhaled
"phew! wow! pow! *zat* voss somsink!"

# LEROI JONES / AMIRI BARAKA (1934)

## PREFACE TO A TWENTY VOLUME SUICIDE NOTE

*(For Kellie Jones, born 16 May 1959)*

Lately, I've become accustomed to the way
The ground opens up and envelopes me
Each time I go out to walk the dog.
Or the broad edged silly music the wind
Makes when I run for a bus . . .

Things have come to that.

And now, each night I count the stars,
And each night I get the same number.
And when they will not come to be counted,
I count the holes they leave.

Nobody sings anymore.

And then last night, I tiptoed up
To my daughter's room and heard her
Talking to someone, and when I opened
The door, there was no one there . . .
Only she on her knees, peeking into

Her own clasped hands.

*March 1957*

309

## IN MEMORY OF RADIO

Who has ever stopped to think of the divinity of Lamont Cranston?
(Only Jack Kerouac, that I know of: & me.
The rest of you probably had on WCBS and Kate Smith,
Or something equally unattractive.)

What can I say?
It is better to have loved and lost
Than to put linoleum in your living rooms?

Am I a sage or something?
Mandrake's hypnotic gesture of the week?
(Remember, I do not have the healing powers of Oral Roberts . . .
I cannot, like F. J. Sheen, tell you how to get saved & *rich!*
I cannot even order you to gaschamber satori like Hitler or Goody Knight

& Love is an evil word.
Turn it backwards/see, see what I mean?
An evol word. & besides
who understands it?
I certainly wouldn't like to go out on that kind of limb

Saturday mornings we listened to *Red Lantern* & his undersea folk.
At 11, *Let's Pretend*/& we did/& I, the poet, still do, Thank God!

What was it he used to say (after the transformation, when he was safe
& invisible & the unbelievers couldn't throw stones?) "Heh, heh, heh,
Who knows what evil lurks in the hearts of men? The Shadow knows."

O, yes he does
O, yes he does.
An evil word it is,
This Love.

# CROW JANE

**For Crow Jane**
                    (Mama Death.

For dawn, wind
off the river. Wind
and light, from
the lady's hand. Cold
stuff, placed against
strong man's lips. Young gigolo's
of the 3rd estate. Young ruffians
without no homes. The wealth
is translated, corrected, a
dark process, like thought, tho
it provide a landscape
with golden domes.
                    'Your people
without love.' And life
rots them. Makes a silence
blankness in every space
flesh thought to be. (First light,
is dawn. Cold stuff
to tempt a lover. Old lady
of flaking eyes. Moon lady
of useless thighs.

**Crow Jane's Manner.**

                    Is some pilgrimage
to thought. Where she goes, in fairness,
"nobody knows." And then, without love,
returns to those wrinkled stomachs
ragged bellies / of young ladies
gone with seed. Crow
will not have. Dead virgin
of the mind's echo. Dead lady
of thinking, back now, without
the creak of memory.
                    Field is yellow. Fils dead
(Me, the last . . . black lip hung

in dawn's grey wind.  The last,
for love, a taker, took my kin.

Crow.  Crow.  Where
you leave my
other boys?

## Crow Jane in High Society.

(Wipes
her nose
on the draperies.  Spills drinks
fondles another man's
life.  She is looking
for alternatives.  Openings
where she can lay all
this greasy talk
on somebody.  Me, once.  Now
I am her teller.
(And I tell
her symbols, as the grey movement
of clouds.  Leave
grey movements
of clouds.  Leave, always,
more.

Where is she?  That she
moves without light.  Even
in our halls.  Even with
our laughter, lies, dead drunk
in a slouch hat famous king.
Where?

To come on so.

## Crow Jane The Crook.

Of the night
of the rain, she
reigned, reined, her
fat whores and horse.

(A cloud burst,
and wet us. The mountain
split, and burned us. We thought
we were done.

        Jane.
Wet lady of no image. We
thought, you had left us. Dark
lady, of constant promise. We thought
you had gone.

2.

My heart is cast in bitter
metal. Condiments, spices
all the frustration of earth,
that has so much more desire

than resolution. Want than pleasure.
Oh, Jane. (Her boat bumps at the ragged
shore. Soul of the ocean, go out, return.
Oh, Jane, we thought you had gone.

**The dead lady canonized.**

           (A thread
of meaning. Meaning light. The quick
response. To breath, or the virgins
sick odor against the night.

           (A trail
of objects. Dead nouns, rotted faces
propose the night's image. Erect
for that lady, a grave of her own.

           (The stem
of the morning, sets itself, on
each window (of thought, where it
goes. The lady is dead, may the Gods,

           (those others
beg our forgiveness. And Damballah, kind father,
sew up
her bleeding hole.

# BLACK DADA NIHILISMUS

      . Against what light

is false what breath
sucked, for deadness.
      Murder, the cleansed

purpose, frail, against
God, if they bring him
      bleeding, I would not

forgive, or even call him
black dada nihilismus.


The protestant love, wide windows,
color blocked to Mondrian, and the
ugly silent deaths of jews under

the surgeon's knife. (To awake on
69th street with money and a hip
nose. Black dada nihilismus, for

the umbrella'd jesus. Trilby intrigue
movie house presidents sticky the floor.
B.D.N., for the secret men, Hermes, the

blacker art. Thievery (ahh, they return
those secret gold killers. Inquisitors
of the cocktail hour. Trismegistus, have

them, in their transmutation, from stone
to bleeding pearl, from lead to burning
looting, dead Moctezuma, find the West

a grey hideous space.

2.

From Sartre, a white man, it gave
the last breath.  And we beg him die,
before he is killed.  Plastique, we

do not have, only thin heroic blades.
The razor.  Our flail against them, why
you carry knives?  Or brutaled lumps of

heart?  Why you stay, where they can
reach?  Why you sit, or stand, or walk
in this place, a window on a dark

warehouse.  Where the minds packed in
straw.  New homes, these towers, for those
lacking money or art.  A cult of death,

need of the simple striking arm under
the streetlamp.  The cutters, from under
their rented earth.  Come up, black dada

nihilismus.  Rape the white girls.  Rape
their fathers.  Cut the mothers' throats.
Black dada nihilismus, choke my friends

in their bedrooms with their drinks spilling
and restless for tilting hips or dark liver
lips sucking splinters from the master's thigh.

Black scream
and chant, scream,
and dull, un
earthly

hollering.  Dada, bilious
what ugliness, learned
in the dome, colored holy
shit (i call them sinned

or lost
>burned masters
>>of the lost
>>>nihil German killers
>>>>all our learned

art,' member
what you said
money, God, power,
a moral code, so cruel
it destroyed Byzantium, Tenochtitlan, Commanch
>>>>(got it, *Baby!*

For tambo, willie best, dubois, patrice, mantan, the
bronze buckaroos.

>>For Jack Johnson, asbestos, tonto, buckwheat,
>>billie holiday.

>>For tom russ, l'overture, vesey, beau jack,

(may a lost god damballah, rest or save us
against the murders we intend
against his lost white children
black dada nihilismus


## A POEM FOR BLACK HEARTS


For Malcolm's eyes, when they broke
the face of some dumb white man, For
Malcolm's hands raised to bless us
all black and strong in his image
of ourselves, For Malcolm's words
fire darts, the victor's tireless
thrusts, words hung above the world
change as it may, he said it, and
for this he was killed, for saying,
and feeling, and being/ change, all

collected hot in his heart, For Malcolm's
heart, raising us above our filthy cities,
for his stride, and his beat, and his address
to the grey monsters of the world, For Malcolm's
pleas for your dignity, black men, for your life,
black man, for the filling of your minds
with righteousness. For all of him dead and
gone and vanished from us, and all of him which
clings to our speech black god of our time.
For all of him, and all of yourself, look up,
black man, quit stuttering and shuffling, look up,
black man, quit whining and stooping, for all of him,
For Great Malcolm a prince of the earth, let nothing in us rest
until we avenge ourselves for his death, stupid animals
that killed him, let us never breathe a pure breath if
we fail, and white men call us faggots till the end of
the earth.


## BEAUTIFUL BLACK WOMEN . . .


Beautiful black women, fail, they act. Stop them, raining.
They are so beautiful, we want them with us. Stop them, raining.
Beautiful, stop raining, they fail. We fail them and their lips
stick out perpetually, at our weakness. Raining. Stop them. Black
queens, Ruby Dee weeps at the window, raining, being lost in her
life, being what we all will be, sentimental bitter frustrated
deprived of her fullest light. Beautiful black women, it is
still raining in this terrible land. We need you. We flex our
muscles, turn to stare at our tormentor, we need you. Raining.
We need you, reigning, black queen. This/ terrible black ladies
wander, Ruby Dee weeps, the window, raining, she calls, and her voice
is left to hurt us slowly. It hangs against the same wet glass, her
sadness and age, and the trip, and the lost heat, and the gray cold
buildings of our entrapment. Ladies. Women. We need you. We are still
trapped and weak, but we build and grow heavy with our knowledge. Women.
Come to us. Help us get back what was always ours. Help us. women. Where
are you, women, where, and who, and where, and who, and will you help
us, will you open your bodysouls, will you lift me up mother, will you
let me help you, daughter, wife/lover, will you

## DAS KAPITAL

Strangling women in the suburban bush
they bodies laid around rotting while martinis are drunk
the commuters looking for their new yorkers feel a draft
& can get even drunker watching the teevee later on the Ford
replay. There will be streams of them coming, getting off
near where the girls got killed. Two of them strangled by the maniac.

There are maniacs hidden everywhere cant you see? By the dozens
and double dozens, maniacs by the carload (tho they *are*
a minority). But they terrorize us uniformly, all over the place
we look at the walls of our houses, the garbage cans parked full
strewn around our defaulting cities, and we cd get scared. A rat
eases past us on his way to a banquet, can you hear the cheers raised
through the walls, full of rat humor. Blasts of fire, some woman's son will
stumble and die with a pool of blood around his head. But it wont be the
maniac. These old houses crumble, the unemployed stumble by us straining,
ashy fingered, harassed. The air is cold winter heaps above us consolidating
itself in degrees. We need a aspirin or something, and pull our jackets close.
The baldhead man on the television set goes on in a wooden way his unappe-
tizing ignorance can not be stood, or understood. The people turn the channel
looking for Good Times and get a negro with a pulldown hat. Flashes of
maniac shadows before
bed, before you pull down the shade you can see the leaves being blown down
the street too dark now to see the writing on them, the dates, and amounts
we owe. The streets too will soon be empty, after the church goers go on
home having been saved again from the Maniac . . . except a closeup of the
chief mystic's face rolling down to his hands will send shivers through you,
looking for traces of the maniacs life. Even there among the mythophrenics.

What can you do? It's time finally to go to bed. The shadows close around
and the room is still
Most of us know there's a maniac loose. Our lives a jumble of frustrations
and unfilled capacities. The dead girls, the rats noise, the flashing somber
lights, the dead voice on television, was that blood and hair beneath the
preacher's fingernails? A few other clues

we mull them over as we go to sleep, the skeletons of dollarbills, traces of
dead used up labor, lead away from the death scene until we remember a
quiet fit that everywhere is the death scene. Tomorrow you got to hit it
sighs through us like the wind, we got to hit it, like an old song at radio
city, working for the yanqui dollarrrrr, when we were children, and then
we used to think it was not the wind, but the maniac scratching against
our windows. Who is the maniac, and why everywhere at the same time . . .

## JOANNE KYGER (1934)


## MY FATHER DIED THIS SPRING


My father died this spring
        Well, I had meant to write more often
To a kind of hell it must be, with all unresolved difficulties.
      I had greens with vinegar last night—that's something
in common
           And I would have told him that—adding it
    to a list of possible conversations.
With the pictures on his dressing table
      of all his daughters
but he wasn't flinging out his arms to keep a soul there.
          You can't say he wasn't strange
    and difficult.
          How far does one go
to help a parent like a child—when he waits
    at the employees entrance in old clothes
    and I don't want him.
           Well he'll be there waiting
for me.  Demands just, wanted, or not
    are there to be met.
And let me see, yes the demon large,
    impossible and yields without vanishing
    no power, no satisfaction
      sitting on the back porch drinking beer
      following me to the sick squirrels in the cellar
And the material things, calling cards
    engraved watches, trunks that married life brings
    full of stuff
he left behind 10 years ago.  The golf clubs.  The fact is
    there was a man, a married man
and an old man.  it's impossible to know
    but strange how blood brings curiosity.

## THE PIGS FOR CIRCE IN MAY

I almost ruined the stew and Where
is my peanut butter sandwich I tore through the back of the car
I could not believe
there was One slice of my favorite brown bread and my stomach and
I jammed the tin foil and bread wrappers into the stew
and no cheese and I simply could not believe
and you Never
TALK when my friends are over.

This is known as camping in Yosemite.

Already I wish there was something done.
Odysseus found a stag on his way to the ship
I think of people *sighing* over poetry, *using* it,          I
don't know what it's for. Well,

Hermes forewarned him.          Can you imagine
those lovely beasts all tame    prancing around him?

She made a lot of pigs too.

I like pigs.  Cute feet, cute nose,    and I think

some spiritual value investing them.  A man and his pig together,
rebalancing the pure in them, under each other's arms, bathing,
eating it.

And when the time came, she did right
Let them go
They couldn't see her when she came back
from the ship, seating themselves and wept, the wind
took them directly north, all day
into the dark.
at least they were moving again

Sometimes I just go hobbling up and say
Just a little *Food*, please.  Usually a piece of bacon or toast
the coffee curling up in the pine groves of Yosemite.  There is a rock wall
in the night.
animals and something hot and dank on the sand trail in the sun,
waste.

Odysseus went down and got his comrades

'Circe says its ok to stay.'  And they were freely bathed and wined.
She had a lot of maids and a staid housekeeper.
I mean I admire her.  The white robes
and keeping busy
She fed her animals

wild acorns, and men crying inside

with a voice like a woman
from the sun and the ocean
She is busy at the center, planning out great
stories to amuse herself, and a lot of pets,
a neat household, gracious
honey and wine
She offers.
Purple linen on the chairs
Odysseus mopes
'Oh I'll give you your bores back'   They weep to see each other
a black ram
and a young ewe and the ship to hell
where persephone has left only one man with reason
She doesn't hold them back
a young man dies
that is his fault.

And she asked him to stay
climbing all day
pushing
strewn with boulders
the great leap it makes
into space, giddy, he rushes at her
the roar he makes
on the wide shelf bed
they both watch over the edge

and the Great Pigs waddle off in the sky—

## AUGUST 18

They said the moon wasn't going to rise no no
where will it come up so we can see what's happening
in the night
the light sharply behind us.
I saw him like a shadow rise

far above us, in the night
where the stars were, and he said, wait.
I can't wait.

Like stickle burrs the moon attacks us. The old things
closing around us. Everyone alone, groaning,
and the ring of light around the moon,

was there, it was hanging

I never finished, I lied, and through me

it came bursting

I never finished, and all alone
close to the moon
on the top of a hill or a piece of land
burr-like he closes over us.

## I HAVE NO STRENGTH FOR MINE.

I stay clear.
I won't listen. They can be wise on their own for thousands
of years
It's new.
It's a bunch of poo. It's a shining silver disk. Their poor bellies
slit open
their pink eyes & bunny tails up by their heels.
I come from the moon and drowned in the water. If you wait

the teacup will fill
up by itself in time. That mossy old ear hears the rumbles way down.
I'm singing with my long ears
I sleep on my side, I rise with the moon
and right through the moon and to the moon
and draw back with
the great bow
Arrows in their stiff form laid in sleep
and the moons stacked up like shields


## "WHEN I WAS WELL INTO BEING SAVORED"


When I was well into being savored, I didn't want
to pick about the bits and pieces of sociality.
Friendly, but moving smoothly into other places, my
pen, my staff of life was gone. Nothing in the way,
I speedily took to new roads.

So where have I gone to and where have I come from.
We smoke a joint and share a can of beer. Primitive
man was the first man, but is not valued on a level
of progression. We're always in touch, you see.

And he leaned across the table and spoke to me. It
was a visitor that placed value on everything I have.

But then I let the
smaller more tender fantasies take along much of my breathing
daylight moments alone. The desire to reveal myself takes
me from one group to another, and with sad longings I
place it on the table to serve. I tell my complaints.
I intricately recite the details of the day and the
possibilities of what they mean. Yet I know though this
time passes pleasantly, it has ended all possibilities
of creation, for it has all been done. But then again
this news is affirming for it clusters richly, densely,
and how I want to be heard!

And will this plot of the house never be completed?
Earwig skitters across my desk! Oh Lord, the possible
bells ringing, to bring me out of here.


# DON'T HOPE TO GAIN BY WHAT HAS PRECEDED

*Lincoln's Birthday*

      Back to silent big soap flakes
      falling steadily at my back.
                 Shamelessly, this indulgence
    stinks.  Repair to all earthly ties
  she collapses in heart break and dies.
  Goodbye, little white American.  And these
are the youngsters of the American dream—
Feeling and sensitive eat cookie mix off
    paper plates.  I don't want
    to be tied down to the kitchen speed.
And don't pre judge me because I
    am the judger, I am the voice.
Put all your garbage together and get some one
    to pick it up, in a little truck, run
    by gasoline—Can you dig your little pit
    to lie in?  It's not Art
  I'll tell you that.  It's the way
the lost American, poorly, made his way
upon the treasure troves of our home.
O Haul them away from here.  The rising
Sun over Tamalpais
             Sets at our backs
  In Ocean's Pacific every day.  Poor Christian
poor little moral Christian, eat your humble
    paper plates and towels.  Do not get
      dish pan hands.  Don't eat
    from the clay of the earth.  Call the undertaker
and save your money ahead.
             You're full of Bullshit
  you won't put on your garden.  Crawl
on your sorrowful hands

and knees to find the little point of light
in hubby's eyes.  Back to the cradle
the warm black hole of happiness
      dreamed for, brain spinner,
      garbage maker.


# "OF ALL THINGS FOR YOU TO GO AWAY MAD"


Of all things for you to go away mad on a tender morning like this
although grey for the 8th day in sunny california
because I asked you to change your shirt after the third day
because the neckline won't come clean
and you said you preferred dirty necklines
and I hurled the pancake turner on the floor
shouting what about appearances
and you said it took a long time to see through appearances
      and what do we care
      and you got no breakfast, no pancake, forget it.  I hope
         you eat some lunch.
               And at 12:30 you still got no lunch which information
via the phone I find out because I want to tell you I am sorry
about the pancakes and appearances, grey day, the Pride of Madeira
fallen over in the garden.  Plucked and plummed, all show, no heart,
heavy headed, no answer, breathe deeply.
                      Enough of slumber land.  I've put
                      beans on for dinner
We'll sit at the table, and don't put me on, the room in my heart
gets nourished, by your friendly handsome looks.  You read
a lot of books.

# JOHN WIENERS (1934)

## A POEM FOR PAINTERS

        Our age bereft of nobility
How can our faces show it?
I look for love.
    My lips stand out
dry and cracked with want
                    of it.
            Oh it is well.


Again we go driven by forces
we have no control over.  Only
                    in the poem
comes an image—that we rule
        the line by the pen
in the painter's hand one foot
                    away from me.
Drawing the face
        and its torture.
That is why no one dares tackle it.
Held as they are in the hands
                of forces
they cannot understand.
                That despair
is on my face and shall show
in the fine lines of any man.


I held love once in the palm of my hand.
        See the lines there.
                How we played
its game, are playing now
in the bounds of white and heartless fields.
        Fall down on my head,
love, drench my flesh in the streams
                of fine sprays.  Like
                        French perfume
        so that I light up as
                    morning glorys and

I am showered by the scent
     of the finished line.


                No circles
but that two parallels do cross
     And carry our souls and
bodies together as the planets
     Showing light on the surface
          of our skin, knowing
     that so much flows through
          the veins underneath.
The cheeks puffed with it.
     Our pockets full.


   2

Pushed on by the incompletion
     of what goes before me
I hesitate before this paper
     scratching for the right words.
Paul Klee scratched for seven years
     on smoked glass to develop
     his line, Lavigne says:  Look
at his face! he who has spent
     all night drawing mine.


The sun
also rises on the rooftops
     beginning with violet.
I begin in blue knowing what's cool.


   3

My middle name is Joseph and I
walk beside an ass on the way to
what Bethlehem, where a new babe is born.
     Not the second hand of Yeats but
first prints on a cloudy windowpane.


   4

America, you boil over

The cauldron scalds.
Flesh is scarred.
Eyes shot.

The street aswarm with
vipers and heavy armed bandits.
There are bandages on the wounds
but blood flows unabated.
                              Oh stop
                        up the drains.
          We are run over.


          5

Let us stay with what we know.
That love is my strength, that
I am overpowered by it:
                    Desire
                         that too
is on the face:  gone stale.
When green was the bed my love
and I laid down upon.
Such it is, heart's complaint,
You hear upon a day in June.
And I see no end in view
when summer goes, as it will,
upon the roads, like singing
companions across the land.


South of Mission, Seattle,
over the Sierra Mountains,
the Middle West and Michigan,
moving east again, easy
coming into Chicago and
the cattle country, calling
to each other over canyons,
careful not to be caught
at night, they are still out,
the destroyers, and down
into the South, familiar land,
lush places, blue mountains
of Carolina, into Black Mountain
and you can sleep out, or
straight across into states


I cannot think of their names
this nation is so large, like
our hands, our love it lives

with no lover, looking only
for the beloved, back home
into the heart, New York,
New England, Vermont, green
mountains and Massachusetts
my city, Boston and the sea
again to smell what this calm
ocean cannot tell us. The seasons.
Only the heart remembers
and records in the words

     6
At last, I come to the last defense.

My poems contain no
wilde beestes, no
lady of the lake, music
of the spheres, or organ chants.

Only the score of a man's
struggle to stay with
what is his own, what
lies within him to do.

Without which is nothing.
And I come to this
knowing the waste,
leaving the rest up to love
and its twisted faces,
my hands claw out at
only to draw back from the
blood already running there.

                    *6.18.58*

## A POEM FOR THE INSANE

The 2nd afternoon I come
back to the women of Munch.
Models with god over

their shoulders, vampires,
the heads are down and
blood is the water—
color they use to turn on.
The story is not done.
There is one wall
left to walk.  Yeah

Afterwards—Nathan
gone, big Eric busted,
Swanson down.  It is
right, the Melancholy
on the Beach.  I do not
                              split

I hold on to the demon
tree, while shadows drift
around me.  Until at last
there is only left the
Death Chamber.  Family Reunion
in it.  Rocking chairs and

who is the young man
who sneaks out thru
the black curtain, away
from the bad bed.

Yeah stand now
on the new road, with the
huge mountain on your
right out of the mist

the bridge before me,
the woman waiting
with no mouth, waiting
for me to kiss it on.

I will. I will walk with
my eyes up on you for
ever. We step into
the Kiss, 1897.
The light streams.

Melancholy carries
a red sky and our dreams
are blue boats
no one can bust or
blow out to sea.
We ride them
and Tingel-Tangel
in the afternoon.

*1958*

## A POEM FOR TRAPPED THINGS

This morning with a blue flame burning
this thing wings its way in.
Wind shakes the edges of its yellow being.
Gasping for breath.
Living for the instant.
Climbing up the black border of the window.
Why do you want out.
I sit in pain
A red robe amid debris.
You bend and climb, extending antennae.

I know the butterfly is my soul
grown weak from battle.

A Giant fan on the back of
              a beetle.
A caterpillar chrysalis that seeks
a new home apart from this room.

And will disappear from sight
at the pulling of invisible strings.
Yet so tenuous, so fine
   this thing is, I am
   sitting on the hard bed, we could
        vanish from sight like the puff
          off an invisible cigarette.
Furred chest, ragged silk under
    wings beating against the glass

    no one will open.

The blue diamonds on your back
are too beautiful to do
      away with.
I watch you
   all morning
      long.
With my hand over my mouth.


## AN ANNIVERSARY OF DEATH


He too must with me wash his body, though
at far distant time and over endless space
take the cloth unto his loins and on his face
engage in the self same rising as I do now.

A cigarette lit upon his lips; would they were mine
and by this present moon swear his allegiance.
If he ever looks up, see the clouds and breeches
in the sky, and by the stars, lend his eyes shine.

What do I care for miles? or rows of friends lined
up in groups? blue songs, the light's bright glare.
Once he was there, now he is not; I search the empty air
the candle feeds upon, and my eyes, my heart's gone blind

to love and all he was capable of, the sweet patience
when he put his lips to places I cannot name
because they are not now the same
sun shines and larks break forth from winter branches.

## TWO YEARS LATER

The hollow eyes of shock remain
Electric sockets burnt out in the
        skull.

The beauty of men never disappears
But drives a blue car through the
              stars.

## WHAT HAPPENED?

    Better than a closet martinet.
        Better than a locket
        in a lozenge.
        At the market, try and top it
            in the Ritz.

    Better than a marmoset
        at the Grossets,
     better than a mussel
        in your pockets.
        Better than a faucet
        for your locker,
        better not
      clock it.
    Better than a sachet
      in your cloche,

                 better than a hatchet
                  in Massachusetts,
                   Ponkapog.
              Pudget
         Sound
      lost and found.


Better than an asprin—
             apertif does it.
Better not ask
        how you caught it
             what has happened to me?


Better not lack it—
        or packet in at the Rickenbackers.
          Better tack it back
       in a basket
       for Davy Crockett


Better not stack it.
   Better stash it
        on the moon.


        Oh Pomagranate
        ah Pawtucket.


        Oh Winsocki or
        Naragansett.


        Better not claque it.  Better cash it in
        at Hackensack.
        Better not lock it
          up again.

# ROBERT KELLY (1935)

## THE SOUND

First she heard a sound
like thunder,
bright sky

or heavy armchairs
moved
on the floor above her

when she was alone in the house
so she went out
when the sun

came through mist
& walked into the shadow
of a maple on the soft road

she heard far off
a hammer in the woods
she followed it

down along the stream
to the second waterfall
there was a man

"I am building" he said
& went on hammering,
she watched the pale

groaning wood, his arm
swung from the elbow
going down

"I am the human soul"
she said
"& I heard your hammer

in my only woods"
"I am building" he said
"a house or a table,

a horse or a child,
springtime & little
flies with golden wings,

you hear the sound
of thunder from an
empty sky"

"I am an actress
in this play" she said
& there was the

thunder again
though his hands were
still now, his eyes

fixed on her,
wondering.
"I suppose

you are no one
& this hour
betrays me

now I am near
the end of my work.
Go back home

& let me settle
this strife I have
with the old wood,

the seasoned wood"
she heard him
but the thunder

was all over her mind.

## *from* THE BOOK OF PERSEPHONE

9   [Second Ode to Persephone]

I had awakened early
              without thinking of you even once
in the dim time half out of sleep

I had to be moving
             out into your country
before the sun burnt off the fog

            did & the world is drier now
& smells less of you,
        *Königin, Göttin* says the song,
I had to find you along the damp road
in the already lushness of the overgrown
              world
unlike you consents to be seen,
           Lady
who has just now taken Heidegger
             to speculate beside Tannhäuser
the perfection of your abscondite
Being
    found in the dark,
           La
           Die
             we have come for you to give us this
permission
      to be plural
      in your democracy.
Ycarcomed. Ruoy ni larulp the one thing we cant be,
             there is no,
Lady hidden under the tree of life
           whose rot is our root.
Putrefy, she says, for me
who am Mistress of Going Beneath the Ground.
           Die
into this extraordinary
        life on
Earthlady found in the mines of the dark, this Gem.
             I went in

because it was afternoon & cool inside,
polaroid blue sky of Hawaii dark as your flower,
she moved before us, moved
    where we were fixed
                dark in the experience of the plush seats,
seeing.
      The war was over. Being seen.
Seeing is the root of our rot, mortal senses, seeing seen. Touch!
And the ampersand of fleshy mysteries couples you
                        too, Lady,
        into the silent mind.


10

Earth is a woman who imagines us. She sings
to us her different children, spider, sparrow, bear.
We are hers but she's no mother. More mint
than chamomile, more leek than affable. Free!

Syringa! I lift my glad palm to shade a name,
a new known in the jungle of vocabulary.
I call after it Come see Come be seen You
fragrant in the middle noon, heartless flower

all loveliness is civilized; I hear Bruckner
at the door; the gardener releases Merlin
from love's impetuous stone. Crush crack, noise
of rusty bedsprings being fucked on. Hark! he speaks:

"I chose my cantilenar prison, I chose my gloom.
Deep in the Forest of How-wise-I-am I let her
& she caught me as I wished; we felt each other
skin by skin, then I let her lose me down the steps.

Down in the copper-mesh Faraday chamber snug
all the mortal radio was scrambled out. Blocked,
it left me free to ultimate telepathy—
I hear the whole world thought by thought.

It is as if a tree. I have everything but distance.
And as for her, I know every synapse in her head—
the only thing I ever loved her for at all.
For I was an old man, in love with difference."


11


Persephone is the woman buried
in ordinary life
Persephone is the source of her difference
hidden
under the circumstances of being sane
Persephone
is the difference between left & right signals
projected before us
a voice from the cloud & the voice from the ground
that tells me year after year
Persephone is the ghost inside the woman
Persephone is candlelight on apples & pears.
Chiaroscuro
no fancy, meant only
what we see
as Her painters worked for centuries
to declare
the dark embedded in
just exactly that ordinary light
she carries with her wherever she goes.


12     [Versions]

Under the *ground?*

Under the Event Horizon
                    where Time
            to some our eyes
                            freezes
                    with all it carries?
Time *is* travel.

Persephóne / Persephóneia   Phersephóne
        Persêphassa    Phersêphassa   Phersêphatta

her temple is called the Pherrapháttion.


PᵃRSᵉᵢPHᵃᵢₒₙE


            songs their vowels are,
            consonants the shocks.
            her N is death, is there, down way
                          out of sight,
                caressively
            his L is goad, is phallophor,
                  he is phallophor

so my novel is my poem is the same work]

Parsifal a male bodiment
of the Persephone—
             the grieving mother comma the lost years
                the encounter with the god
                    the god SHINES

           it is danger, there, in the woods of
           herself picking michaelmas daisies,

       in both cases, cases, the Return
brings fertility to the Terre Gastée,
                the wasted]

Perse/
      pierce/phallos,
             the piercing phallos
             buried in the woman:

the cock lost in the woman
is the girl lost in the ground.

14    [Third Ode to Persephone]

To plant three roses for you each one only a dollar

deep in the rainday calm I love the gloom of your sheen,
that the day is your bliss, I hide in the hutch of your arms—

be clear as you are clear in your unseen, Lady,
I bull my thick body up between yours for a moment even

to be your tree, o console me always that I so seldom am,
with the joy of I am never not, never not, so somewhat can

& seldom is always enough. Thy tree. Thy compassion wrung
from the bloody obstacle the lingering stones the weather

so many men forgot you who now repent of their sunshine
you only can blood me to bone you again. You are power.

My flesh is under your hand. You witch. You control.
The singsong is your charm. I am of the amongst you forever

who hear what they are heard to sing back—dark oily praises
from which things they never knew about come up onto earth

flowers & wheatfields to eat from the indigo distance you are.


16    [Fourth Ode to Persephone]

The kind of rose she wants called John F Kennedy
I think of a green rose with bullet holes in its head
but she means shape, the shape the way it holds bud
taut contract against the ordinary splay "but
its color is all wrong" and what is a rose itself
but a muscle of color? lips of fragrant light?

342 / Robert Kelly

## 17    [The Dance]

breast
below ground

to the hard footstep
pressed
milk spurts up


## 18    [The Glade]

Buried in noontime traffic
she looked to the right & said "A glade!"
And right there off Foxhall
a cut through sumac back into
a lawn or meadow bound by little woods.
"How many lovers must sneak in there"
I said & she said   "sneak,"   drawing the vowel full
like the string of a little tiny bow whose arrow was
my hand, on her meantime thigh had found
a hole in denim for my ear-finger to probe
through onto her marvelous cool young flesh inside
& then I knew she is the glade, or glad
comfort in the steady sun, time beating down.

*May 1976-June 1977*

# JAMES KOLLER (1936)

## THE UNREAL SONG OF THE OLD

this night cast iron over flat land
a skillet of cold grease

NO LIGHT WORTH THE FIRE TO MAKE IT

stands dark in the rain
only her belly dry   dog belly

through the walls
the old man   sand on his tongue
licking his song

the dog dark in straw
down to sleep
in her straw

the ground unfroze & mud
the grass down
where I walked in frost

tracks
GO FROM HERE

TASTE THE BLOOD THE BEAR FLESH
bear flesh & dogs
& I
chewing bear meat
in robes of bear
we sleep

THE SKY WITH STARS & MOON

the choking sand tongue
a song
yet to come

## "I HAVE CUT AN EAGLE"

I have cut an eagle
from wood
& he is a man I am a man
a starved thin dog an eagle a coyote
in a corner

no one will cut off my ears

I nose leaves & grass
on ridges where I run rabbits & mice
I sniff the air

I see a bearded hunter
he follows after me
long arms long rifle

I sit where he cannot see

across the creek before him
my ears are my own

I cover his eyes beat at his eyes
with wings talons splinter-sharp teeth
in his shoulders rip his legs

I pull him down
pull him down
run away

YAK YAK YAK

I hide & watch
he will never find my wooden legs

## SOME MAGIC

*for Don Allen*


I AM ALL THINGS. The grizzlies if I ain't
loud enough. He was an old man. THEY COME
THEY COME. The gray the white. They come
along side of the herds. The crippled the young
& their wolves. LIFE IS VERY DANGEROUS.
Until over. The hungry know. The sick the
lame. The herds are thinned. Nothing eats
too lame to procreate. He came to me one of
the lined his beard white his life very dangerous.
Won't be the same after you go. IT'S ALL IN
THE TREES. THERE IN THE ROCK. IN THE
AIR BENEATH THE ICE. To breathe. I can
tell you stories. Understand. He had no teeth.

ALL WOULD TURN YOU TO YOUR OWN DARK WOODS.
I can go anywhere do anything. I am myself
but I am also all else. Order. Within me.
Keeps the wind. I am in the snow. I can grow
into anything. I am caribou the wolf is one
with me. WE ARE HUNGERED FOR. HUNGRY.
There is no well-being. EAT. ONE GRUNTS
FOR ALL ELSE. The caribou is the wolf's
paw. I MOVE TO CHANGE TO FILL MYSELF.
Old man.

His teeth worn away. White snow gray down
to the old. HAVE NO CONTROL. Be filled.
Sick & young. Food. His face dark as shale.
Old man. Before you take a look before you.

Rock where now there are dead. Order.
Within all things sharp cliffs. Because they are
hungry and hunger rules. The wind will blow
me snow cover me. I know only what I am as
I enter into it as it numbs my feet. Go if you
have never been. Burn neither hoof nor tongue.

You are kin. The same mountain. Come up.
The wolf is ever there. They are one before
me. The snow fresh on my feet. I can neither
lie nor stand. The shape I am. I can tell
you many. IF YOU ARE KIN.

I AM THE SUN COME I AM THE SUN & STAND
MY GROUND I AM HIGH. They come over shale
splinter cliffs caribou come wolves run thin
the herds bring down the slow runners. There
are those who live no barriers. Their stomachs
old inexperienced. Thin the herds that the
healthy may go on. Not too many young or old.
The old man long beard no teeth. It is all
here if you've never been here. If you don't
do anything. Where there are trees. In the
rivers. Under the ice between the river &
the ice. Find a hole to come up the old man
said. I counted teeth.

NEEDS THAT ARE NOT YOUR OWN. Go. When
the way becomes all things. There is no
blowing me away I find my way out into the storm.
I AM A TREE SHALE ONE WITH ALL THINGS.
THE SAME. ONE & THE SAME. I do not lay
flat. The shale cuts at my air. As I come
to it. Between the rivers look around. ALL
IS ONE & ALL IS PART. THE CARIBOU FLANK
& THE WOLF STOMACH. The same river runs
through all dark woods. THE HUNGRY AND
THE HUNGERED FOR. The ground is one with
those who stand & those who move. TO FILL
THE WORLD I AM IN THAT IS IN ME. Stories
he said. He was a wolf. I can't hear you.
Too much water. Kin. For the big breakup.
On high ground.

## O DIRTY BIRD YR GIZZARD'S TOO BIG
## & FULL OF SAND

> he knew what I wanted
> wouldn't leave his spring
> I told him I'd sleep there with him
> & when he was sleeping soundly
> I went outside found dog droppings
>
> Ganuk, Ganuk, wake up
> you've shit in yr blankets
>
> he went out & I drank the spring

this the fellow
made the world

> got the birds together
>
> who can fly into the bear's asshole?
>
> wren did it
>
> came out with the bear's intestines
>
> the bear's end
>               he ate it

this the fellow
made the world

>               in certain circles

Caw Caw Caw

when bears go inside
they take off their coats
look like everybody else

"Do you speak English?"

>               in circles

Caw Caw Caw

"I speak American."

      Samuel Colt patented his revolver in 1836

      Abraham Lincoln pushed its production
        twenty-some years later

        mass production
        mass reduction

"I knew there was something wrong with you."

  he came to a bunch of boys
  throwing fat at one another

  he jeered at them
  they threw fat at him
      he ate it

  & threw dog droppings at the boys
  they threw fat at him

      he ate it
    threw more dog droppings at them
    & they threw fat

        it's still the same game

this the fellow
made the world

        what it is

## RON LOEWINSOHN (1937)

## THE STILLNESS OF THE POEM

The stillness of the jungle
a clearing amid the vines
which distant bird sounds enter,
timidly.  The overpowering silence
of the jungle clearing
into which Rhinoceri &
other wild beasts are always
charging suddenly from the canebrake
to reveal themselves
one instant
in all their natural savagery
or fear,
their nature made known to us
out of the jungle's quiet.

The stillness of the poem
a moment full of silence &
portent, like
the sudden halt of great machines.
Silence that becomes a fabric
to clothe the consciousness
... the events & observations of
a walk up Market Street
are admitted, as if
from a great distance,
the White Rhinoceros
charging
suddenly, in the form of a sailor
with a shopping bag
whom nobody notices.

## AGAINST THE SILENCES TO COME

This morning I fight against the silence
    (you aren't here).
The newspapers scream, the radio (no Mozart):
    a parade, a murder in Reno,
a sub lost in the Atlantic—129 men,
    officers & crew, fathers & husbands
in a mile & a half of water; no radio
    contact, silent.

Across the street the kids
    in the schoolyard scream, dis-
membering each other.
    You've watched them, you know.
Do you remember what you were like,
    as a kid? How cruel?

& what cruelty beyond the cruelty
    of silence?

I can hear it, right now,
    this morning, issuing
from myself,
    an effluvium,
to join the greater silence that
    contains me today,
that contains the house,
    the sound of my typewriter,
the sound of the refrigerator,
              "making cold."

That cruel universe that doesn't speak to us,
    try as we might
to put words on it:

          in the wind,
    in the streams, the Truckee River,
the "voices" of the water
    —obeying gravity under the moon.
& the wind in the trees,
    & the birds in the trees calling
to each other.

We're forgotten.
    They've forgotten us.
They never even considered us,
    & we can't change that,
try as we might to con-
    sole each other, & ourselves.

Now the teacher across the street screams
    at the kids thru a bullhorn.

    She screams.

    The kids ignore her.

Her screams are taken up, a thread
    in the fabric of silence that
contains her, & the kids, & the school,
    & me, here in this room
"flooded" with light.

What could she tell them, for Christ's sake,
    Did you have a happy Easter?

On the mountain at the top of the road
    the grass is silent.
My typewriter is silent
    (you aren't here).

The kids look at the teacher there
    on the high stairs.
She raises the bullhorn to her lips
    as if to drink.

    Yes, what were you going to tell us?
        Yes, what did you want to say to us?
           Yes, what did you want us to hear?
    They look at her, wide-eyed, they
    want, they want something
    from her.

& she screams at them:

Close your lips!
          Hands at your sides!
Eyes straight ahead!
          & close your lips!


In Reno that girl's body is put back
    together in the coffin.
Her lips are closed.
    Her arms are (once again) at her sides.
Her eyes stare straight ahead
    under the lids.  Her lips
are closed.
    She's entered into the cruelty of the universe,
silent.


In Reno there are men, the "scores"
    of men the newspapers screamed at us
about:
        "Scores of men in Sonja's diary!"
    The men to whom she talked as they screwed,
or after, lighting a cigarette & waving out
    the match:
             Hand me the ashtray, will you;
no, over there, behind the lamp.


There in Reno those Nevadans
    will never penetrate her.
There across the Sierras, across those snowy
    passes, she's become impenetrable,
heartless.


    She won't listen to us, & she won't
speak, the small bones in the front of her neck
    broken by a taut twine cord,
plunging her into the silence,
    there by the Truckee River.


Butchery! the newspapers scream.
    This butcher must be found!
—Their descriptions:
             her nude torso,
    a hand & part of an arm

on the bathroom floor, her head
    in a drawer, her heart—

The butchery was done before he ever touched her,
climbing up the back stairs, under
the moon, silent, with that cord
    in his pocket
               —she
was meat to him then, meat
    for his cock to penetrate,
poor lunatic.


Here, in this room
    flooded with morning light,
waiting to hear on the radio news
    of the parading Giants,
waiting to hear the squall of the crowds
    lining the streets as they pass
in their open cars, arms waving
    awkwardly, eyes dancing
over the crowd, eyes meeting & holding
    for a moment, the lips opening
to speak—there, out of that radio
    in the kitchen.
               & here I am
pounding on the keys of this typewriter
    "to make a song for you to hear."

You're there in some classroom,
    listening to some anthropologist
discuss the blood brotherhood of the Comanches,
    their instruments both of
violence & of music.
    & I sit here trying
"to make a song for you to hear."

The piano is here, useless as it is
    to me, instrumental as it is to you.
When I play it,
    by myself,
If anyone had asked me,
    What're you doing?

here in the apartment alone
    with the steel wires of the piano
taut, "doing my bidding,"
    the rock maple of the piano
my sounding board
    —I'd say, Goofing a round.
like a dog chasing my tail.

The chords of the piano
    plunge into the silence.

The house is empty,
    tho the light of the sun, silent & filled
with vitamins, floods it.
    The room is "bathed in light"
& I can stand in the middle of it
    by myself.

But at night
    the silence begins to part—the piano
its keys white & black under the moon
    whose light
streams thru these same windows.
    The streets are black, the mountain
is a black absence of stars
    in the near southwest.

In the other room you're
    asleep.
          Standing at the door I can hear
your breathing, your own physical music,
    the sound of your stomach,
your heart beating,
    your life flowing
thru your veins. Your eyes are closed;
    Reno, Carson City & Mt Rose flow
thru your mind like the Truckee River.
    One arm folded under your head,
the other across the pillow, there where I
    should be,
the cat's asleep in the curl of your stomach & legs.

The place is filled with you:
    your hands
have flipped these light switches
    flooding these rooms with light,
your hands have moved these pots, kind-
    ling flames under them, to cook,
for me.
    Your hands have cleared this table,
your breath has steamed this mirror
    scores of times, out of which your image
regarded you, silently,
    as I do now your curled form.
Your mouth, your lips, thru which your breath
    now moves, have moved over my body,
& they will again.


    Your hands have moved over this piano,
touching the keys,
    unlocking the silence.
                   RD told us
one afternoon in the kitchen:
    The beauty of a pun is that it allows 2 voices
to speak in a single word.
    —As you touch the keys Mozart comes
to life again in our apart-
    ment:  you & Mozart speak in the sing-
le act of your playing—the chords
    that moved within his mind now move in mine,
the ore of ink on the page
    is gold in the afternoon air.


    —& last night the 2 of us,
2 human beings locked
    in a single act; not "making"
love, but coming
    as close as the world allows to making
a single music:  the music of your coming
    thrilling me, making me come
to you, the fluids of our 2 bodies
    pouring a famil-
iar libation.
    This is us,

I said, the skin of my hand meeting
    the skin of your abdomen.
Us:  where your nipple rose
    to meet my fingers as you breathed,
our muscles taut, our 2 voices coming
    together to make a single chord,
the physical music our love unlocks

—Against the silences to come further harmonies
    are implied in the harmonies we state

# DAVID MELTZER (1937)

## THE EYES, THE BLOOD

### 1

My mother of the blue
Anglo-saxon eyes,
my father of the brown
eyed Jews, they fused
to form my exile
here on earth,
this year turning into next year
while the turn of my songs
goes out to renew source,
ancient sorrows
tomorrow become
newly-cast. The sky
swept of grey clouds
turns into a blue dome
unmarked by birds
or the gold of Monarchs.
My mother's eyes
hold the Bolinas sky
as in my father's eyes
the mud of its roads.

◆

Her father stood 6 foot 5
& in the old photo stands between railroad ties
holding a sledge-hammer,
cap aslant, blue-eyed.
My father's father in a snapshot,
short & stocky, holds me to the Kodak,
his face shaded by the brim of a pearl-grey fedora.
I adored him more than all the rest
for what he brought of Russia & Jews.
Chainsmoking Old Golds,
bouncing me on his knees,
he saw in my eyes dark roads
3 sons came to America to travel.

He could never accept it.
Born in Moscow, an intellectual,
America he could care for less.
An exile, he knew the mark,
could read it instantly in the eyes of others.
A light like pain's spark sudden in Cain's eyes
driven deep into the dark brown.


My mother's mother ran off with a lover
& left her to her widowed mother
whose life came carved from Plymouth Rock.
Tough, orderly, a gritty Yankee,
clean & decent, everything in place.
Blue-eyed *shiksa*, my father's servant.
Aunts & uncles would whisper the curse
of Christ in her blood
mixed in the children's blood.
A contamination.
By Law we were neither here nor there.
Dispossessed, exiled at birth by blood.
They held her to blame for it all.
Dachau, Belsen, Buchenwald.
In secret rage she bleached her brown hair wheat-blonde
& ladled-out chicken soup into their bowls.

♦

My mother's blue-eyed brother,
6 foot 2, blond crewcut, Lieutenant, US Navy,
visited our Brooklyn flat,
battle-ribbons flashing on his dark blue chest.
Pink-cheeked, he walked into our twilight livingroom,
sat down on the piano bench
& often hit a key as he talked.
We passed around a snapshot of the submarine
he worked on in Florida's green tropic mystery
where old Jews go to spend the end of their money
in mock *Pardes* under the sun,
pseudo-Riviera where they're rocked in wicker chairs
pushed by young Puerto Ricans in white uniforms
up & down the boardwalk,
roast on sparkling beaches,
skin turning parchment-brown,
Torah scroll,

the brown my father's skin turned
sunning himself on the stoop.
Cars moving constantly over Linden Boulevard.


2

Each family to its mysteries
whispered thru the branches.
A cousin in Syracuse with dark brown eyes
died the day before her 18th birthday.
A rare blood disease.
She had a pale narrow face
framed in famous long black hair
reaching her knees.
Her mother's pride,
the hair grew as the girl grew,
braided into one huge braid the day she died,
carried into the grave, her triumph.
She looked like a Russian countess
in a photo passed around the table by
Grandmother Sarah.
It runs in the family,
in the blood, in the eyes
the diluted tribe of Judah.

♦

Dark-eyed cousins.
Lonnie from Minneapolis
came to 'Frisco after high school
with his buddy Ivar.
One night they climbed Golden Gate Bridge
& sat across from each other,
each to his own tower,
kings in iron castles
swaying high above a new domain.
Sparkling Oakland, shimmering 'Frisco,
Marin's dark forests.
He showed me thick suede workgloves torn thru the palms,
edges burnt away, pulled back
like a row cut into earth for seed,
where he slipped going down,
grabbing cables on both sides to brake the slide.

Ivar told me Lonnie would climb anything.  St. Paul radio tower, the
highest peak there.  Lonnie climbed it after sign-off time.  Later someone
told him the power was turned on every hour on the hour.  Lonnie didn't
care.
Climbed skyscrapers, telephone poles, church steeples.
Once climbed to the top of the biggest water tank in town & tipped over
the edge in triumph, nearly drowned.
Last heard of Lonnie was holed-up in a cave in the Minneosta hills.
Meditating, fasting, climbing.


    3
Her tall blond blue-eyed men all came to California,
straight & proud they stood & each one remembered by my
      great-grandmother,
a century old & still going strong.
Broke her hip at 87 painting the outside of her home.

A Freeway now benedicts her frontyard with shadows.
Mexicans like snipers fill the run-down neighborhood splendour
3 blocks from LA County Jail.
She took me to its steps when I disobeyed her.
Until I was 13 she'd send me a yearly subscription
to the National Geographic Kodachrome world,
world she saw, world of postcards
where well-fed pink Americans all over the world
stood straight & proud beneath glossy-blue skies.
Blue the light breaking thru her blue eyes.
Radiance of new shores.
History of plains & railroads.
Marks in the land.  Carved-out places
where secure & righteous her forefathers spawned
blue-eyed generations of upright men & women
forever heroic in bright postcard light.

            ♦

She keeps an orderly home.
In a glass-doored bookcase stand leather albums of officers & gentlemen
who fought & perished in the Civil War; scrapbooks of family history fat
with luncheon programs, photographs, Lodge meeting announcements,
callingcards, clippings of concerts meetings, social news metal-typed black
on dried-out newspaper turned gold, prservede upon black scrapbook
pages, photos held in place by black triangles.  She keeps all evidence
she can find of her blue-eyed men
who came here to make it new, renew it right,

to reduce the space extended from the shore by green
timber vistas of the New World,
hills whose verdure dipped into dark forests
edging into shapely female plains
turning into painted deserts
into primordial mesas transformed into bayous
feeding into wide rivers roaring into waterfalls
filling lakes that hold reflections of great mountain ranges
& all of it, before that moment,
unmarked or tracked by the blue-eyed presence.
No wonder Indians thought them divine.
How to deny ownership's sure white stride?
They broke the seal of America's shore
& where they wounded earth
they closed the wound with cities
that spread as root-systems thru the landscape.
White rightness wed with the pure goal of progress.
Linked by telegraph & steam engine & automatic rifles.
No questions asked.  There was work to do.
Bridges, doors, connections to make new.
Soon to cramp all of it into zoos & cells
men & animals spend lifetimes breaking out of.

◆

*Lovelace.*
I saw it as cotton doilies over stiff armchairs
in my great-grandmother's living room.
White lace *mantillas*, white choirboy collars.
Doily dress of mandallas
worn over the dark skin of a Toltec hooker.
16 years old, her skin webbed white,
cunt hairs, beard curls,
loop & spring thru the weave.
Mid-noon *fiesta.*
Her bare feet on carpets of time-darkened flowers
break the tomb-quiet of my great-grandmother's living room.
I throw silver dollars at her feet,
aluminum pennies.
She does a split & juice from her slot sparkles
a snail-trail on petals of the rug's shadowy blossoms.
Tequila guzzled straight from the bottle
while *tortillas* cook on the griddle.
The old blue-eyed lady's stomach

would turn against our smells.
*Love. Lace.*
I saw it a dress on the Mexican whore
who stood in a doorway whispering,
Love, love, love, I got it!
Love, love, love, I got it, *si!*
See, I got it. You want it?
Take it, have it, come
on my great-grandmother's bed.
Sheets brittle as newspaper.
Everything stinks of sachets.
Gutstring guitars outside our window,
*mariachi* trumpets, thump of
the *gitaron*, boogie-woogie
V-J Day thru a metal Arvin radio.
I push into her,
she milks me with a frenzy.
It is no matter she will not let go
& covets Limoge teacups on teakwood stands
in the antique cupboard.
No matter she's a dream I tangle with in sheets,
look out to see two orange trees in the backyard,
not a leaf misplaced.
Their boughs kept trim by the old lady.
*Lovelace.* A space
where stars burn thru black to create
a lace illusion not unlike the common household doily
covering every stiff stuffed chair
in my great-grandmother's LA livingroom.

4

Grandmother Sarah
re-married at 90 & went back to Europe on her honeymoon.
No more hotel rooms
with milk & sweet butter on the windowledge.
No more Workman's Circle
monthly ghost-quest socials
for Grandfather Benjamin,
who came to America to become a tailor
& died on my bed in Brooklyn,
cancer spreading terrible wings within his body.
Grandmother Sarah
always a good touch for music & money

playing mandolin with thick fingers
as sun set over Broadway parkbenches 13 floors below.
Minor-key schmaltz trembling Yiddish grief,
pain & pride of time & tribe
in a lacey white blouse clicking her tongue
making music for her grandson, a wolf
in the room's only chair
listening to Russia, hearing Jews in Paradise.

When the music left her hands
Grandmother Sarah told me stories
of the village she was born in,
a river ran thru
its green & golden fields.
Young men intrigued by her dark beauty
called her The Gypsy.
But now, she'd say,
the village is no more,
its young men all dead,
bombed off the map by Germans
during the last war.

◆

What do I know of journey, they
who came before me
no longer here to tell of it
except baggage of old papers
bound-up & found in library stacks.
The crying of history makes it all vague.
Was it myth we all came here to be?

What do I know of journey, I
who never crossed the seas into the alchemy of USA
no longer anyone's dream of home.
Their great great grandchildren jump state's ship,
drown in void *Torah* is too late to warn of.
Here *tohu* is *bohu* & form void & America
another pogrom, another concentration camp
more subtle & final
than all Hitler's chemists could imagine.
Home, *ha-makom*, no longer hope.  It holds
light reaching back from eyes
watching Asians & Blacks die on TV.

We restore the shore & our dream is gone.
It mixes into shadows growing tall behind us.

      What do I know of journey,
they who came before me
kept what they left but now they are gone.
Invisible shells cast off
& in flaming hair arise
orphans of collapsed Shekinah
caught between earth's end & heaven's end
& what do I know of journey,
I a child when children were murdered
waiting on lines with their mothers & fathers,
gone in gas or the flash of atomic *ain-sof*
squinted at in movie-theatres.
Ancients sit on stoops too tired to mourn,
turn inward to blood rivers mourning lost *shtetls*.
They can not take me with them
& I can not bring them back
& what do I know of journey, I
who never spoke their language.
The old ones are dead or dying
& what is left desires less & less
& what is less is what is left
& children run off screaming
*Elohim Elohim!*
into freeways filled with the starlight of cars.

# EDWARD SANDERS (1939)


## THE FUGS


Everything lives and nothing is dead.

Golden Lizards fly in the sun,
that's true somewhere.
But everything knows, there IS
a gnosis

παντα ρει ξ παντα breathes.
I feel enormous breathings.
Come feel. Come feel it pretty humans.

Blink open o rock
with wild daffodil life!

Slide down your slick black stockings o earth!
Slide away the thin meadow's skin from your belly!

Meadow larks fuck in your scented lace
& all of it lives. All the sucking systems, and all the
women overarch'd w/ a thousand breasts,
all beast-giggles & star pelts
above and below the
Plate of the Earth in the Ocean
breathe

thru a thousand Peace Eye tambourine caresses
in Ra's makepeace dactyls darting from afar.

I believe I believe.
Tear open th' brain valves.
Where you walk lives.

## PINDAR'S REVENGE

Αριστον μεν υδωρ
Pindar


I know that the sun rising
is a temporary thing,
that the sun obtuse on clouds
at 30 thousand feet from the
airline windows is an
equal particle, that
Ra is a shard, an
ostracon from a forbidden
cycle of the aeons.
Nor god nor pulsing phantom forever
but that I live at the mansion of earth
for eighty years in the warmth,
the children off to space,
the chickens still crowing
at sun up, but our
hearts beat lugubrium lugubrium lugubrium
at Ra's pink-fingered sinking

42 billion years
then zap
then 42
zap
we are caught

The meat chain
born of
the prostrate,
born of the
cusping egg—
caught, ended,
slashed. We are
led by the calf
to the thin
arroyo
to be slaughtered in droves
driven into the eyes and
slashings of the manglers,

that little drama,
no matter,

42
zap
"we are now
in the
electromagnetic
cycle"

IT lives.
Enormous breathings
& compressions
of IT

> July 24, 1965
> returning to N.Y. 30,000
> feet, from Berkeley Poetry
> Conference. The quote and
> the concept of the 42 billion
> year zap, are from Olson.

## HOLY WAS DEMETER WALKING TH' CORN FURROW

It was impossible for one to read
C. Kerényi's *Eleusis* and *Eleusis and the
Eleusinian Mysteries* by George Mylonas,
without falling in love with Demeter.
In 1967, this love was combined with a
long-visioned *idea* of making love w/the Earth!
That is, the visionary embodiment of the

Egyptian sem-ta ⚲ i.e. earth-fuck. Such a

possibility, as felt in early '67, triggered
off a hunger for instant Elysium. The vision
was of a plowed field—springtime—bright
sunlight—and Demeter, her arms full-laden
with corn sheaves, approaches the angst-eyed

earthling, Edward Sanders, in April 1967,
as a personal *Be-in* that raised the earthling's
mind for all his life to the Permanent Nodule.

The first version of this poem was prepared for
a reading w/ Ted Berrigan at Israel Young's
Folklore Center on Sept. 5, 1967.

---

Fucked the corn-meat
sprouted of the river
in the fetish of the lob.

Sucked off the corn-clits
curly and cute
in the earth squack

spurt strands swirling
the soil

> When Deo walked down
> the dusty spring road—
> I nearly fell afaint
>
> I tried to
> tell her "I am
> no Poseidon"
>
> but she smiled
> & said this: "O earthling
> even a poet
> as thou art,
> and a punkly one,
> can be a thrill
> to the λουσία
>
> for I have been
> washed in the River!
> And all are good!
> And oh how I shall love thee,
> little pale poet of earth!"

Not a word more mouthing
**Demeter,**
pale as husk fibres,
shy as new corn
        near to the
           husk tip

bent over the furrow
with blessings
by the fresh-plowed river bank

Total Beauty in the odors
of new sprouted dirt.

Bent over   Bent down
& I flipped it to the
buns, and knew at once
the god-rose in the
god-snatch, felt the marvelous
silky corn styles serving
as crotch hair

Knew her for hours &
spurted thru the
blessings, droplets
of spangled jissom
in the Red Halls of
Demeter, the Goddess.
Pumped in the berry bushes,
to know her, suck off
the wineberries
smeared on her buttocks,
ate Demeter, corngirl,
out of her salinity
ahhh  ❁  ahhh  ❀  ahhh

                  Demeter     pale as husk-fibres
                  shy as new corn
                      near to the
                        husk tip

                  Total Beauty in the odors
                  of new sprouted dirt.

A mocha milk shake
is not so sweet
as your buns
pouring out
  the godly

    bun sqush

And then Demeter
turned around
and sank to her
knees  knee caps sink
out of sight
in the plow-clods,
white goddess-palms
reach up
rub my knees,
& then to suck
my poor pale
earthling prong —

see her crouched there
(the vision, forever in mind, of)
husk fibres hanging out of ass,
white new corn
is as white as her
corn teeth padded by goddess lips,
sliding & sliding & sliding
till the subject of heaven
is brought up again
to a spurting earthling's mind.

   And later
   she lay down spread
   in loam dirt

   leg of the Deo to th' south east
   leg of the Deo crookt up
      to th' south southwest

   the back of her snug

in a pure 'n' perfect
north-south furrow

I shall kiss the fibres
shall buss th'
o'er laid soil with
wan lips & desirable

freckles of your
belly as Indian
corn in an
autumn bundle.

Torrid was th' goddess groin
tongue-moth frying
in the
candle of the earth-clit

And maybe you think
that when dark Deo came
that it was not
a different experience —

One wd have thought
that the gods were rerunning
the submergence of Atlantis

so much did
the plow-plot
quake around us
as my poet's tongue
flash-flitted my Deo
10,000 times

till grope-quake
seized her crotch's
pink lick-node

"ahh, sweet
poet of earth," she cried,

"o sing to me

sing to me."

& the pale beams of the
Cosmic Intrusion
enter
the brain —

glorious Da-Mater
walking away —

o watch her walk away!
dripping my come over
cornleaf, back
to her bower among the deathless,

burnished buttocks etching the Sky —
honed of a finer tool than ever
carved a grope grape — rose
leaves not as interesting as
the crinkles of her ass
ahh for another pinch
of skuz from thy
omphalic glory*
my lady of the corn.

ahh what a thrill
is a god grope

# ANNE WALDMAN (1945)

## LADY TACTICS

she
    not to be confused with she, a dog
                she, not to be confused with she, Liberty
      she a waif
          she a wastrel
               she, a little birdie
she, not to be confused with pliable
        she in plethora
             she in blue
she with the pliers, or behind the plough
       she
         not to be confused with a jonquil
she in the imperative
         she the liveliest of creatures
    she, not to be confused with Pandora or plaintiff
         or getting seasick or prim
she, a prima donna
           she a secret she a dreamer
she in full force, she rushing home
    she at a desk or in a book
      she, not to be confused with she, a secretary
she a goddess
        she, not to be confused with the Slovak
she, not a slug
         she in season, she in health, she recumbent
    she recuperating                        .
       she, not to be confused with mutton
       she a muse
she on a mission, not languishing
      she in the landscape, she in silk
  she, not to be confused with juniper
      with jodhpurs
     she with idiosyncrasies
   she in labor
        she, not to be confused with the conifer
she in consanguinity

she at long last
she, wind, sea, Pompeii, deliberation, home
she in middle C
she the sharpest
she, obliged
she in distinguished sentiments
not to be confused with sentimental
or sly


## PRESSURE

When I

see you

climb the walls

I climb them too

No way out of the cosmic mudhole!

no way out of the telephone booth

the classroom

the VW bus the igloo

no way out of the

Quonset hut

the tea for two

the greenhouse, the waterproof tent

the motel room, the

split-level ranch house

the hacienda, the chalet

the icy castle

the formidable mountain

the haunted house

the 747

the rickety porch

the lazy afternoon

my mother's house

Emily Dickinson's staircase

the hospital ward

no way out of Chicago

or Cleveland or Detroit

no way out of the 60-story office building

the church, the temple, the mosque

the Long Island Rail Road Station

the A train the D train the BMT

the 9th Street crosstown bus

the rain, the 10-inch snow piling up

outside my window

the refreshingly hot shower

no way out of the poolroom

the bowling alley

the noisy bar

the enormous bathtub

the Chinese restaurant

the delicatessen

the department store

the trolley

no way out of the desert

off the Alps

out of the tunnel

out of the river the lake the ocean the bay

off the skis

out of the arena

out of the spotlight

the movie theatre

the motion picture screen

no way out of the barn

the farm, the chicken coop

the stable the hay loft

no way out of the doctorate the MA the BA the PHD

the toolshed, the library

my sneakers

no way out of Africa

off Europe, out of Asia

no way off the jeep

the circus the rodeo

the Donizetti opera

*La Fille du Regiment*

no escape from Joan Sutherland's astounding voice

or the barking dogs chasing the deer weakened from

a long winter

no escape from the guitar or the cello or the

harpsichord

no escape from the mailman, the endless mail

no way out of the stationery store

the print shop

the newspaper office

the glossy IBM retail showroom on William Street

the poker game

the family dinner

the cocktail party

the birthday celebration

no way out of Christmas, off New Year's

out of Philadelphia, Texas, Independence, Mo.

no way out of the sleeping bag no way no way

no way out of the celery patch

the organic vegetable garden

the ancient forest

the deep ravine

the glistening valley

the starry night

the Louvre

the Met

the numerous art galleries of New York City & L.A.

the simple chat, no escape

the zoo no escape

the coat hangers no escape

the history of Russia no escape

China, Japan

the history of music, no escape

the voices of the Pygmies singing in the Ituri rain forest

gamelan no escape

Mozart's legacy

& Satie's

no way out of prison

no way off progress of collapse

no way out of the White House

or the Senate or the Capitol

no way no way

no way out of money

even when you're out of it

no way out of whippoorwills swallows gulls

the swimming pool, Bellows Falls

The Great Chain Of Being, no escape

The Magnetic Field, no escape

The Continental Shelf, no escape

The Great Barrier Reef

no escape no escape

the piper cub no return

the next acceptance speech no return

the last hurrah the middle age

no way out of TV, no way off Mars

the moon, the sun's radiant energy

no way no way

no way out of structural anthropology

or brain chemistry

or pain killers or pain

no way off pleasure

the rainbow, no escape

the cab ride, no escape

solar flares, no escape

The World Trade Center no escape

The Amazon no escape

amazing grace, no escape

autumn, no escape

my window, no escape

& midnight stubborn midnight no escape

no return no way off

no way out of midnight

black midnight deep midnight

now coaxing midnight gentle midnight no escape

# BIOGRAPHICAL NOTES AND BIBLIOGRAPHIES

JOHN ASHBERY was born on July 28, 1927, in Rochester, N.Y., and grew up on his father's farm in Sodus, 30 miles to the east, near Lake Ontario. He attended the Deerfield Academy, and, while still a student there, some of his poems were published pseudonymously (after being pirated by a classmate) in *Poetry* magazine. He studied at Harvard (B.A., 1949), where he was on the editorial board of the *Harvard Advocate*, and took an M.A. at Columbia in 1951, writing a thesis on novelist Henry Green. He worked as a copywriter with Oxford University Press and McGraw-Hill in New York from 1951 until gaining a Fulbright scholarship in 1955 to study in France, first at Montpellier, and then in Paris. He remained in France (except for a ten-month period in 1957-58, which included graduate courses in French literature at NYU) until 1965. He was art critic for the European edition of the *New York Herald Tribune* in Paris from 1960 to 1965, writing a weekly column, and also reviewed for *Art International*. He was an editor of the magazine *Locus Solus*, 1961-62, on the editorial board of *Art and Literature*, 1964-67, and, upon returning to the United States, an executive editor of *Art News* from 1965 to 1972. In 1956, W. H. Auden selected his manuscript of *Some Trees* for the Yale Younger Poets award, and he was awarded Guggenheim fellowships in 1967 and 1973, and National Endowment for the Arts grants in 1968 and 1969. He won a National Institute of Arts and Letters award in 1969 and the Shelley Memorial Award in 1973, and in the same year was guest of honor at Poetry Day sponsored by the Modern Poetry Association in New York. In 1976 he won the triple crown of poetry for *Self-Portrait in a Convex Mirror*: the National Book Award, the National Book Critics Award, and the Pulitzer Prize. He continues to live in New York and teaches in the graduate writing program at Brooklyn College.


*POETRY*

*Turandot and Other Poems.* New York: Tibor de Nagy, 1953.
*Some Trees.* New Haven: Yale, 1956. Reprinted New York: Corinth, 1970; New York: Ecco Press, 1978.
*The Poems.* New York: Tiber Press, 1960.
*The Tennis Court Oath.* Middletown, CT: Wesleyan, 1962.
*Rivers and Mountains.* New York: Holt, 1966. Reprinted New York: Ecco Press, 1977.
*Selected Poems.* London: Cape, 1967.
*Three Madrigals.* New York: Poet's Press, 1968.
*The Double Dream of Spring.* New York: Dutton, 1970. Reprinted New York: Ecco Press, 1976.
*The New Spirit.* New York: Adventures in Poetry, 1970.
*Three Poems.* New York: Viking, 1972.
*The Vermont Notebook.* Los Angeles: Black Sparrow, 1975.
*Self-Portrait in a Convex Mirror.* New York: Viking, 1975.
*Houseboat Days.* New York: Viking, 1977.
*As We Know.* New York: Viking, 1979.
*Shadow Train.* New York: Viking, 1981.

## OTHER

*A Nest of Ninnies* (novel), with James Schuyler. New York: Dutton, 1969; Calais, VT: Z Press, 1975.
*Three Plays.* Calais, VT: Z Press, 1978.

## BIBLIOGRAPHY

David K. Kermani, *John Ashbery: A Comprehensive Bibliography.* New York: Garland, 1976.

## SECONDARY

David Lehman, ed., *Beyond Amazement: New Essays on John Ashbery.* Ithaca: Cornell, 1980.
David Shapiro, *John Ashbery: An Introduction to the Poetry.* New York: Columbia, 1979.

PAUL BLACKBURN was born in St. Albans, Vermont, on November 24, 1926, son of poet Frances Frost. He spent his youth in Vermont, New Hamsphire, South Carolina, and New York City. He was educated at NYU and the University of Wisconsin, where he received his B.A. in 1950. He was a Fulbright scholar at the University of Toulouse in southern France, 1954-55, and *lecteur américain* in 1955-56. He studied the language of the troubadors at both Wisconsin and Toulouse and lived in Spain various periods from 1954 through 1957. When he returned to New York, he was an active presence in the poetry scene of the Village and Lower East Side, frequently organizing and taping readings, while earning a living as encyclopedia editor and translator, and later poet-in-residence at City College. In 1967, a Guggenheim Fellowship took him back to France and Spain. He married for the third time, and a son, Carlos, was born in 1969. That same year he moved to Cortland, N.Y., teaching at the state college until his death from cancer on September 9, 1971.

## POETRY

*The Dissolving Fabric.* Palma de Mallorca: Divers Press, 1955. Reprinted Toronto: Mother/Island, 1966.
*Brooklyn-Manhattan Transit.* New York: Totem Press, 1960.
*The Nets.* New York: Trobar, 1961.
*Sing-Song.* New York: Caterpillar, 1966.
*The Cities.* New York: Grove, 1967.
*In. On. Or About the Premises.* London: Cape Goliard, 1968.
*The Assassination of President McKinley.* Mt. Horeb, WI: Perishable Press, 1970.
*Three Dreams and an Old Poem.* Buffalo: Intrepid Press, 1970.
*Early Selected y Mas.* Los Angeles: Black Sparrow, 1972.
*The Journals*, ed. Robert Kelly. Los Angeles: Black Sparrow, 1975.
*Halfway Down the Coast.* Northampton, MA: Mulch Press, 1975.
*By Ear.* New York: # Magazine, 1978.
*Against the Silences.* London & New York: Permanent Press, 1980.

## TRANSLATIONS

*Proensa.* Palma de Mallorca: Divers Press, 1953.
*The Cid.* New York: American R. D. M. Corp., 1966.
*Peire Vidal.* New York: Mulch Press, 1972.
*Proensa: An Anthology of Troubador Poetry.* Berkeley: California, 1978.
*Poems of Federico García Lorca.* San Francisco: Momo's Press, 1979.

## OTHER

*Sixpack*, no. 7/8 (Spring-Summer 1974). Blackburn issue.

## BIBLIOGRAPHY

Kathleen Woodward. *Paul Blackburn: A Checklist.* La Jolla: University of
California Library, 1980.

ROBIN BLASER: "He was born in Denver, Colorado, May 18, 1925; grew up in
Twin Falls, Idaho; began university with a first trip outward from there with a
journalism fellowship at Northwestern, 1943; followed by a year at the College of
Idaho, Caldwell, Idaho, where a dean said he 'stuck out like a sore thumb'; and
then went to Berkeley in 1944, where he was bowled over by Jack Spicer and
Robert Duncan. Another poetry began. At Berkeley, he received a B.A. in 1952,
an M.A. in 1954, and an M.L.S. in 1955. The most startling teacher there was
Ernst Kantorowicz.

He worked as a librarian at Harvard from 1955 to 1959, when he met John
Wieners and Charles Olson, and at the California Historical Society and San Fran-
cisco State College Library from 1960 to 1965. Before leaving the U.S., he parti-
cipated in the Berkeley Poetry Conference of 1965. In 1966 he moved to Vancou-
ver, British Columbia, and began teaching at Simon Fraser University. He is now
a naturalized Canadian.

He edited the two issues of *Pacific Nation* in 1967-1969. He has edited *The
Collected Books of Jack Spicer* (1975). By his own description, a slow writer who
is never given more than a few poems a year, he has been building a single work
since 1960, which when completed will be called 'The Holy Forest.' In recent
years he has also been tape-recording conversations regularly with a few friends
and poets ('in order to have a prose which is direct language'), to make a book
on everything to be called 'Astonishments.' A second tape-recorded book remains
to be completed. This one is composed of dialogue with the filmmaker Dennis
Wheeler during the two years he battled leukemia. During the last year, Blaser has
written an essay on Mary Butts for the reissue of her *Imaginary Letters* and put
together a selected poems of George Bowering with an essay on his work. Whatever
it all comes to, Blaser sees it all as a map outward from Idaho, good until the time
he goes back."

POETRY

*The Moth Poem.* San Francisco: Open Space, 1964.
*Les Chimeres* (versions of Gérard de Nerval). San Francisco: Open Space, 1965.
*Cups.* San Francisco: Four Seasons, 1968.
*Image-Nations 1-12 & The Stadium of the Mirror.* London: Ferry Press, 1974.
*Image-Nations 13 & 14.* North Vancouver: Cobblestone Press, 1975.


OTHER

*Caterpillar,* no. 12 (July 1970). Blaser-Spicer issue.


GREGORY CORSO: "Born by young Italian parents, father 17 mother 16, born in New York City Greenwich Village 190 Bleecker, mother year after me left not-too-bright-father and went back to Italy, thus I entered life of orphanage and four foster parents and at 11 father remarried and took me back but all was wrong because two years later I ran away and caught sent away again and sent away to boys home for two years and let out and went back home and ran away again and sent to Bellevue for observation where I spent 3 frightening sad months with mad old men who peed in other sad old men's mouths, and left and went back home and knew more than father and stepmother did about woe and plight of man at age of 13 so ran away again and for good and did something really big and wrong and was sent to prison for three years at age of 17, from 13 to 17 I lived with Irish on 99th and Lex, with Italians on 105th and 3rd, with two runaway Texans on 43rd, etc. until 17th year when did steal and get three years in Clinton Prison where an old man handed me *Karamatsov, Les Misérables, Red and Black,* and thus I learned, and was free to think and feel and write, because when I wanted to write before, when I used to tell my father that I want very much to write, he used to say, a poet-writer ain't got no place in this world. . . .

Came out 20 well read and in love with Chatterton, Marlowe and Shelley, went home, stayed two days, left family forever, but returned at night to beg their forgiveness and retrieve my stamp collection. Got mad job in Garment District; lived in Village and one night 1950 in a dark empty bar sitting with my prison poems I was graced with a deep-eyed apparition: Allen Ginsberg. Through him I first learned about contemporary poesy, and how to handle myself in an uninstitutional society, as I was very much the institutional being. Beyond the great excited new joyous talks we had about poetry, he was first gentle person and dear friend to me. Quit job later and lived in Village with kind girl until 1952 when I went to Los Angeles and got, by fluke, good job on *Los Angeles Examiner,* cub reporting once a week, rest of week working in file-morgue. Left 7 months later to ship out on Norwegian line to South America and Africa and did. Went back to Village, did nothing but get drunk and sleep on rooftops till 1954 when beautiful now dead Violet Lang brought me to Harvard where I wrote and wrote and met lots of wild young brilliant people who were talking about Hegel and Kierkegaard. Had *Vestal Lady* published there by contributions from fifty or more students from Radcliffe and Harvard. *Harvard Advocate* first to publish me. Then in 1956 went to S.F.

and there rejoined Allen, and Ferlinghetti asked for book of mine, *Gasoline*, stayed in S. F. five months, gave poetry reading with Allen, then we took off to Mexico. Wrote most of *Gasoline* there, and now Paris."

Twenty-two years later, Corso adds: "The spark of poesy is yet with me even though my produce of the last 18 years has been scant. Let's see . . . if I can recall correctly, [my 1957] autobio was conglom'd with my childhood woes of incarceration. Well, no such woes have befallen me ever since, except maybe for the one and only time I wedded. It lasted only four months but I got a 15 year old daughter out of it, so no true woe that venture. For the last three years I have been rearing a blessed little boy . . . his mother, like mine, flew the coop when he was 10 months old. I cared for and nursed him like a true loving mother would, then when he became two years old I met an angel of a girl-woman, and she is like a mother to him; indeed she is the best, and my son and I are blessed for that. I expect my new book of poems, my first in 9 years, to be ready for my publisher this year (1979). It is said that were it not for poesy I'd either be dead or in jail . . . well, I don't know about that; and 'if' serves no remedy."

## POETRY

*The Vestal Lady on Brattle and Other Poems.* Cambridge, MA: Richard Brukenfeld, 1955. Reprinted San Francisco: City Lights, 1967.
*Gasoline.* San Francisco: City Lights, 1958.
*Bomb.* San Francisco: City Lights, 1958.
*The Happy Birthday of Death.* New York: New Directions, 1960.
*Long Live Man.* New York: New Directions, 1962.
*Selected Poems.* London: Eyre & Spottiswoode, 1962.
*10 Times a Poem.* New York: Poets Press, 1967.
*Elegiac Feelings American.* New York: New Directions, 1970.
*The Herald of the Autochthonic Spirit.* New York: New Directions, 1981.

## OTHER

*The American Express* (novel). Paris: Olympia Press, 1961.
*Unmuzzled Ox*, no. 22 (Winter 1981). Corso issue.

## BIBLIOGRAPHY

Robert A. Wilson. *A Bibliography of Works by Gregory Corso, 1954-1965.* New York: Phoenix Book Shop, 1966.

ROBERT CREELEY: "I was born in Massachusetts, May 21, 1926, and raised there mainly. I went to Holderness School, Plymouth, N.H., and after that to Harvard, which I left in 1944, to go in the American Field Service, where I served in India and Burma until 1945, when I returned to Harvard. I left college in 1947, a half-year short of a degree, having married, etc. I lived then in Littleton, N.H., for about three years, after which we went to France, where we lived near Aix-en-Provence. After about a year and a half there, we moved to Banalbufar, Mallorca, Spain, where I started the Divers Press. I previously was an associate editor for Rainer Gerhardt's *Fragmente* (Freiberg im Breisgau, Germany), and also had association with Katue Kitasono's *Vou* (Tokyo, Japan). In 1954 I went to Black Mountain College, Black Mountain, N.C. at the invitation of Charles Olson and the faculty to teach writing. I had just begun editing the *Black Mountain Review* for the same college. I taught there for the spring term, then left, returning again the summer of 1955 to teach until January 1956. After that I lived in Taos and then San Francisco for short periods, returning to New Mexico in the fall of 1956 to teach at a boys' school in Albuquerque. Having secured an M.A. from the University of New Mexico in 1959, I took a job teaching on a coffee *finca* in Guatemala, where I presently live. (1959)

"Now, some twenty years later, the pattern of the 'life' previously noted seems to have been, even then, very evident. The constant, restless moving continues: to Canada (Vancouver), back to the east (Buffalo), to California (Bolinas/ San Francisco), and back and back to New Mexico (I live there much of the year, elsewise teaching fall semesters at the State University of New York at Buffalo, where I'm presently Gray Professor of Poetry and Letters—thinking of time and time's effects . . .). The friends of one's life very surely remain, despite the sad fact that some are now dead (yet never forgotten). To that company have come Warren Tallman, Stan and Jane Brakhage, R. B. Kitaj, Marisol, Bill Katz and Willy Eisenhart, John Duff, among others. In a sequence of three prints which Kitaj did, using a poem of mine, 'A Slight,' this quotation from Pound occurs: 'One isn't necessarily reading. One is working on the life vouchsafed'—which words I have looked at ('read') daily for at least some ten years now. I think they say what I might like to here." September 7, 1979

*POETRY*

*Le Fou.* Columbus, OH: Golden Goose Press, 1952.
*The Kind Of Act Of.* Palma de Mallorca: Divers Press, 1953.
*The Immoral Proposition.* Karlsruhe-Durlach: Jonathan Williams, 1953.
*All That Is Lovely in Men.* Asheville, NC: Jonathan Williams, 1955.
*If You.* San Francisco: Porpoise Bookshop, 1956.
*The Whip.* Worcester, Eng.: Migrant Press, 1957.
*A Form of Women.* New York: Jargon/Corinth, 1959.
*For Love: Poems 1950-1960.* New York: Scribner, 1962.
*Poems 1950-1965.* London: Calder and Boyars, 1966.
*Words.* New York: Scribner, 1967.
*Pieces.* New York: Scribner, 1969.
*The Charm: Early and Uncollected Poems.* San Francisco: Four Seasons, 1969.
*The Finger: Poems 1966-1969.* London: Calder and Boyars, 1970.
*A Day Book* (includes prose). New York: Scribner, 1972.
*His Idea.* Toronto: Coach House, 1973.
*Thirty Things.* Los Angeles: Black Sparrow, 1976.
*Away.* Santa Barbara: Black Sparrow, 1976.
*Selected Poems.* New York: Scribner, 1976.
*Hello: A Journal, Feb. 29-May 3, 1976.* New York: New Directions, 1978.
*Later.* New York: New Directions, 1979.

OTHER

*The Gold Diggers* (stories). Palma de Mallorca: Divers Press, 1954.
*The Island* (novel). New York: Scribner, 1963; London: Calder, 1964.
*The Gold Diggers and Other Stories.* London: Calder; New York: Scribner, 1965.
*A Quick Graph: Collected Notes and Essays*, ed. Donald Allen. San Francisco:
    Four Seasons, 1970.
*Listen* (radio play). Los Angeles: Black Sparrow, 1972.
*Contexts of Poetry: Interviews 1961-1971*, ed. Donald Allen. Bolinas, CA: Four
    Seasons, 1973.
*Presences*, with Marisol (prose). New York: Scribner, 1976.
*Mabel: A Story, & Other Prose.* London: Marion Boyars, 1976.
*Was That a Real Poem & Other Essays*, (includes "A Creeley Chronology" by Mary
    Novik), ed. Donald Allen. Bolinas, CA: Four Seasons, 1979.


RECORDINGS

*Robert Creeley Reads.* London: Turret Books/Calder & Boyars, 1967.
*The Door.* Munich: S Press, 1975.
*For Love.* Munich: S Press, 1975.


SECONDARY

*Athanor*, no. 4 (Spring 1973). Creeley issue.
*Boundary 2*, 6:3/7:1 (Spring-Fall 1978). Creeley issue.
Cynthia Dubin Edelberg, *Robert Creeley's Poetry: A Critical Introduction.*
    Albuquerque: New Mexico, 1978.
Arthur L. Ford. *Robert Creeley.* Boston: Twayne, 1978.
Ann Mandel, *Measures: Robert Creeley's Poetry.* Toronto: Coach House, 1974.
Arthur Oberg, *Modern American Lyric.* New Brunswick, NJ: Rutgers, 1978.
Warren Tallman, *Three Essays on Creeley.* Toronto: Coach House, 1970.


BIBILOGRAPHY

Mary Novik, *Robert Creeley: An Inventory, 1945-1970.* Kent, OH: Kent State;
    Montreal: McGill-Queen's, 1973.




DIANE DI PRIMA was born August 6, 1934 in New York City. She attended
Swarthmore College 1951-53, then left to concentrate on her own writing. From
1961 to 1963 she was coeditor with LeRoi Jones of *The Floating Bear*, and con-
tinued as sole editor of that newsletter of new writing until 1970. She has worked
as associate or contributing editor of *Yugen* and the early Totem Press books, of
*Signal, Kulchur, Guerrilla,* and *Intrepid.* In 1961 with LeRoi Jones and others she
founded the New York Poets Theater, and in 1964 she established the Poets Press

in New York City. In 1968 she moved to San Francisco, where she studied Zen Buddhism for four years with Shenryu Suzuki Roshi. In addition to giving scores of poetry readings she has conducted many poetry workshops in Arizona, Wyoming, Montana, New Mexico, Minnesota, Washington, Colorado, and California.

## POETRY

*This Kind of Bird Flies Backward.* New York: Totem Press, 1958. Reprinted New York: Paperbook Gallery, 1963.
*The New Handbook of Heaven.* San Francisco: Auerhahn, 1963; New York: Poets Press, 1968.
*Poets Vaudeville.* New York: Feed Folly Press, 1964.
*Earthsong: Poems 1957-59*, ed. Alan S. Marlowe. New York: Poets Press, 1968.
*Hotel Albert: Poems.* New York: Poets Press, 1968.
*L. A. Odyssey.* San Francisco: Poets Press, 1969.
*Revolutionary Letters.* San Francisco: City Lights, 1971.
*Kerhonkson Journal, 1966.* Berkeley, Oyez, 1971.
*Loba, Part I.* Santa Barbara: Capra Press, 1973.
*Freddie Poems.* Point Reyes, CA: Eidolon Editions, 1974.
*Selected Poems 1956-1976.* Plainfield, VT: North Atlantic Books, 1977.
*Loba: Parts I-VII.* Berkeley: Wingbow Press, 1978.

## OTHER

*Dinners and Nightmares* (stories). New York: Corinth, 1961; rev. ed., 1974.
*Memoirs of a Beatnik.* New York: Olympia Press, 1969.
*The Calculus of Variation* (stories). San Francisco: Privately printed, 1972.

EDWARD DORN was born in the prairie town of Villa Grove, Illinois, on April 2, 1929. "I was reared more or less alternately between the factory towns of Michigan and the vicinity of my birthplace. My father I have never known. Mother of French parents—Ponton. Lived on the farm mostly, and attended one-room schoolhouse, but my grandfather was a railroader. I played billiards with the local undertaker for a dime a point when I was in high school, away from school weeks on end. I was educated at the University of Illinois, and somewhat corrected at Black Mountain College."

After Black Mountain, he lived in San Francisco, Washington state, and Albuquerque, before teaching at Idaho State University, Pocatello, 1961-65, where he helped edit the magazine *Wild Dog.* He taught with LeRoi Jones and Robert Kelly at the State University of New York at Buffalo the summer of 1964 and participated in the Berkeley Poetry Conference the following summer. He was a Fulbright lecturer in 1965-66 and again in 1966-67 at the University of Essex, England, returning as a visiting professor of American literature in 1974-75. He was visiting poet at the University of Kansas in the spring of 1969, followed by a stay at the D. H. Lawrence Ranch in San Cristobal, N.M., that summer. He supported his family throughout the 1970s by a series of teaching jobs: at Northern Illinois University, Kent State, the University of California at Riverside (where he was Regents

Lecturer), UC San Diego at La Jolla, the University of Colorado, and the Naropa Institute. He has translated, with Gordon Brotherston, from the historical and contemporary literature of Central and South America, including Toltec and Nahuatl texts, Mayan codices, and the poetry of César Vallejo.


## POETRY

*The Newly Fallen.* New York: Totem Press, 1961.
*Hands Up!* New York: Totem/Corinth, 1964.
*From Gloucester Out.* London: Matrix Press, 1964.
*Idaho Out.* London: Fulcrum Press, 1965.
*Geography.* London: Fulcrum Press, 1965.
*The North Atlantic Turbine.* London: Fulcrum Press, 1967.
*Gunslinger, Book I.* Los Angeles: Black Sparrow, 1968.
*Gunslinger, Book II.* Los Angeles: Black Sparrow, 1969.
*Twenty-four Love Songs.* West Newbury, MA: Frontier Press, 1969.
*Gunslinger 1 & 2.* London: Fulcrum Press, 1970.
*Songs, Set Two: A Short Count.* West Newbury, MA: Frontier Press, 1970.
*The Cycle.* West Newbury, MA: Frontier Press, 1971.
*Gunslinger, Book III: THE WINTERBOOK prologue to the great Book IIII Kornerstone.* West Newbury, MA: Frontier Press, 1972.
*Recollections of Gran Apacherîa.* San Francisco: Turtle Island, 1974.
*Manchester Square*, with Jennifer Dunbar. London and New York: Permanent Press, 1975.
*The Collected Poems 1956-1974.* Bolinas, CA: Four Seasons, 1975; rev. eds., 1977, 1982.
*Slinger.* Berkeley: Wingbow Press, 1975.
*Hello, La Jolla.* Berkeley: Wingbow Press, 1978.
*Selected Poems*, ed. Donald Allen. Bolinas, CA: Grey Fox, 1978.
*Yellow Lola.* Santa Barbara: Cadmus Editions, 1981.


## OTHER

*What I See in the Maximus Poems* (prose). Ventura, CA and Worcester, Eng.: Migrant Press, 1960.
*The Rites of Passage: A Brief History* (novel). Buffalo: Frontier Press, 1965; rev. ed., *By the Sound*, Mount Vernon, WA: Frontier Press, 1971.
*The Shoshoneans: The People of the Basin-Plateau* (text by Dorn). New York: Morrow, 1966.
*Some Business Recently Transacted in the White World* (stories). West Newbury, MA: Frontier Press, 1971.
*The Poet, The People, The Spirit.* Vancouver: Talonbooks, 1976.
*Interviews*, ed. Donald Allen. Bolinas, CA: Four Seasons, 1980.
*Views* (prose). ed. Donald Allen. San Francisco: Four Seasons, 1980.

RECORDINGS

*Edward Dorn reads from The North Atlantic Turbine.* London: Stream Records, 1967.
*Gunslinger 1 & 2.* Munich: S Press, 1975, 1977.


BIBLIOGRAPHY

David Streeter, *A Bibliography of Ed Dorn.* New York: Phoenix Book Shop, 1973.


ROBERT DUNCAN: "Born in Oakland, California, in January 1919. Early features still at work in his art are the doubling of his birth family by adoption at the age of six months, his adopted father's profession of architecture, and his adopted family's Hermetic and Rosicrucian studies. In the late 1930s, emerging on his own, his disposition toward the national State and the War—as it remains today—was anarchist and apocalyptic; the more troubled that, as today, he has no affirming political or religious base. It is his sense that we are to adventure without possible guarantee. In the period 1945 to 1950 the poet Kenneth Rexroth was a signal and invaluable mentor. In the same years with the poets Jack Spicer and Robin Blaser in Berkeley, he fomented a 'Renaissance': a reinterpretation of the work of Stein, Joyce, Pound, H.D., Williams, D. H. Lawrence, not as 'we moderns,' but as links in a spiritual tradition. From 1950 to the death of Charles Olson in 1970, he identified himself and allied himself with the 'Black Mountain' followers of Williams and Lawrence—Olson, Creeley, Denise Levertov—while defining himself as a 'derivative' poet and naming Pound and H.D. particularly as his adopted sources. As his body was derivative from the genetic tradition, his language from the genetic language as a whole, so his mind and spirit he saw as derivative from the nature of Man.

"In 1951 he moved to San Francisco to live with the painter Jess, whose development of assemblage and paste-ups is reflected in and reflects in turn the development of Duncan's 'Grand Assembly,' and whose researches in iconography parallel Duncan's extension of image and symbol. The book *Letters* published in 1958 presents the culmination of his early work and the working ground of his mature poetry as it appears in *The Opening of the Field* (1960), *Roots and Branches* (1964), and *Bending of the Bow* (1968). Important prose works in this period are *The H.D. Book*—some fifteen chapters of which have appeared in little magazines over the past decade— which is still unfinished, and *The Truth and Life of Myth: An Essay in Essential Autobiography* (1968). A volume of essays has been announced by New Directions to be called *Fictive Certainties*, but after almost two years, Duncan is still undecided about the complete contents.

"Since 1968, Duncan has proposed a book *Ground Works* in which the poetry of his old age would gestate; the first volume to appear in 1983; the second in 1988, his seventieth year. Parts of both volumes have appeared in monographs: *Achilles' Song* (1969), *Tribunals* (1970), *Poems from the Margins of Thom Gunn's Moly* (1972), *A Seventeenth Century Suite* (1973), *Dante Etudes* (1974), *Veil, Turbine, Cord & Bird* (1979), and in *New Directions in Prose and Poetry*, nos. 23, 26, 34, and 40."

POETRY

*Heavenly City, Earthly City.* Berkeley: Bern Porter, 1947.
*Poems 1948-1949.* Berkeley: Berkeley Miscellany Editions, 1949.
*Medieval Scenes.* San Francisco: Centaur Press, 1950. New ed., Kent, OH: Kent State, 1978.
*Fragments of a Disorderd Devotion.* San Francisco: Privately printed, 1952. Reprinted San Francisco: Gnomon Press; Toronto: Island Press, 1966.
*Caesar's Gate: Poems 1949-1950.* Palma de Mallorca: Divers Press, 1955. New ed., Berkeley: Sand Dollar, 1972.
*Letters: Poems MCMLIII-MCMLVI.* Highlands, NC: Jargon, 1958.
*Selected Poems.* San Francisco: City Lights, 1959.
*The Opening of the Field.* New York: Grove, 1960; London: Cape, 1969; rev. ed. New York: New Directions, 1973.
*Roots and Branches.* New York: Scribner, 1964; New York: New Directions, 1969; London: Cape, 1970.
*Writing Writing: A Composition Book: Stein Imitations.* Albuquerque: Sumbooks, 1964. Reprinted Portland, OR: Trask House, 1971.
*A Book of Resemblances: Poems 1950-1953.* New Haven: Henry Wenning, 1966.
*Of the War: Passages 22-27.* Berkeley: Oyez, 1966.
*The Years as Catches: First Poems (1939-1946).* Berkeley: Oyez, 1966.
*Bending the Bow.* New York: New Directions, 1968; London: Cape, 1971.
*The First Decade: Selected Poems 1940-1950.* London: Fulcrum Press, 1968.
*Derivations: Selected Poems 1950-1956.* London: Fulcrum Press, 1968.
*Names of People.* Los Angeles: Black Sparrow, 1968.
*Play Time Pseudo Stein.* New York: Poet's Press, 1969; San Francisco: Tenth Muse, 1969.
*Poetic Disturbances.* San Francisco: Maya, 1970.
*Tribunals: Passages 31-35.* Los Angeles: Black Sparrow, 1970.
*Poems from the Margins of Thom Gunn's Moly.* San Francisco: Privately printed, 1972.
*A Seventeenth Century Suite.* San Francisco: Privately printed, 1973.
*An Ode and Arcadia*, with Jack Spicer. Berkeley: Ark Press, 1974.
*Dante.* Canton, NY: Institute of Further Studies, 1974.


OTHER

*Faust Foutu: An Entertainment in Four Parts.* San Francisco: White Rabbit, 1958; Stinson Beach, CA: Enkidu Surrogate, 1959.
*As Testimony: The Poem & The Scene* (prose). San Francisco: White Rabbit, 1964.
*Medea at Kolchis: The Maiden Head* (play). Berkeley: Oyez, 1965.
*The Sweetness and Greatness of Dante's Divine Comedy* (essay). San Francisco: Open Space, 1965.
*The Cat and the Blackbird* (children's story). San Francisco: White Rabbit, 1967.
*The Truth & Life of Myth* (essay). New York: House of Books, 1968. Reprinted Fremont, MI: Sumac Press, 1972.
*65 Drawings, A Selection . . . from One Drawing-Book, 1952-1956.* Los Angeles: Black Sparrow, 1970.

*Robert Duncan: An Interview by George Bowering & Robert Hogg.* Toronto: Beaver Kosmos, 1971.
*Ground Work* (prose). San Francisco: Privately printed, 1971.

## SECONDARY

*Audit/Poetry*, 4:3 (1967). Duncan issue.
*Maps*, no. 6 (1974). Duncan issue.
*Robert Duncan: Scales of the Marvelous*, eds. Robert J. Bertholf and Ian W. Reid. New York: New Directions, 1979.

## RECORDING

*Letters.* London: Stream Records, 1967.

LARRY EIGNER: "Palsied from a 1927 birth injury, Larry Eigner is still going along, now in Berkeley (since August 1978) rather than 12 miles north of Boston (in Swampscott) where he'd been from the start, pretty often wondering how much of anything is for the best, optimally speaking, hardly if at all able to tell when/where to stop considering, short of the biosphere as a whole. At the same time, as every day or fraction thereof is new, and you find things and their mass, weights, meanings, assays, as you come to them, realize them and within limits of possibility give them value, appreciate them—their import, with interactive, immediate feedback, intonations of speech/thought in the mind, emphases indicated by typography on the page (line- and stanza-breaks, lacunae, indents, commas). Not that appreciation isn't brief enough, and maybe the more things there are the less the meaning of any one thing or group of things anyway lasts. All right though. Nothing ever quite eternal and you sometimes imagine some miles in a foot or two."

## POETRY

*From the Sustaining Air.* Palma de Mallorca: Divers Press, 1953; enlarged ed., Eugene, OR: Toad Press, 1967.
*Look at the Park.* Lynn, MA: Privately printed, 1958.
*On My Eyes.* Highlands, NC: Jargon, 1960.
*The Music, the Rooms.* Albuquerque: Desert Review, 1965.
*Another Time in Fragments.* London: Fulcrum Press, 1967.
*The- / Towards Autumn.* Los Angeles: Black Sparrow, 1967.
*Air; the Trees.* Los Angeles: Black Sparrow, 1967.
*A Line That May Be Cut.* London: Circle Press, 1968.
*Valleys, Branches.* London: Big Venus, 1969.
*Flat and Round.* New York: Pierrepont Press, 1969.
*What You Hear.* London: Edible Magazine, 1972.
*Selected Poems*, eds. Samuel Charters and Andrea Wyatt. Berkeley: Oyez, 1972.

*Shape, Shadow, Elements, Move.* Los Angeles: Black Sparrow, 1973.
*Earth Birds.* Guildford, Eng.: Circle Press, 1973.
*Things Stirring Together or Far Away.* Los Angeles: Black Sparrow, 1974.
*Anything on Its Side.* New Rochelle, NY: Elizabeth Press, 1974.
*The Music Variety.* Newton, MA: Roxbury Poetry Enterprises, 1976.
*Watching How or Why.* New Rochelle, NY: Elizabeth Press, 1977.
*The World and Its Streets, Places.* Santa Barbara: Black Sparrow, 1977.
*Flagpole Riding.* Alverstoke, Eng.: Stingy Artist, 1978.
*Cloud, Invisible Air.* Rhinebeck, NY: Station Hill, 1978.
*Time, details, of a tree.* New Rochelle, NY: Elizabeth Press, 1979.

*OTHER*

*Country Harbor Quiet Act Around: Selected Prose*, ed. Barrett Watten. [San
Francisco]: This Press, 1978.

*RECORDING*

*Around New/Sound Daily/Means: A Selection of Poems.* Munich: S Press, 1975.

*BIBLIOGRAPHY*

Andrea Wyatt, *A Bibliography of Works by Larry Eigner, 1937-1969.* Berkeley:
Oyez, 1970.

WILLIAM EVERSON was born in Sacramento, California in 1912 and grew up in
the San Joaquin Valley, where he began to write, married, and planted a vineyard.
In World War II he was drafted as a conscientious objector, serving for three and a
half years at Waldport on the Oregon coast, where he was instrumental in establish-
ing a fine arts program and founding the Untide Press. After the war he gravitated
to the San Francisco Bay Area, joining the group of poets around Kenneth Rexroth,
the nucleus of the San Francisco Renaissance. At this time he remarried, then
converted to Catholicism, and in 1951 entered the Dominican Order, taking the
name of Brother Antoninus. He served for eighteen years, then, in 1969, left
abruptly to marry again. The author of over thirty books of verse he has grouped
them into a life-span trilogy called *The Crooked Lines of God.* Volume One, *The
Residual Years: Poems 1934-1949,* establishes the thesis of natural sufficiency.
Volume Two, *The Veritable Years: Poems 1949-1966,* posits the antithesis of
supernatural transcendence. Volume Three, *The Integral Years,* as work in progress,
charts the synthesis of God-in-nature. His honors include a Guggenheim fellowship
in 1949, a Pulitzer nomination in 1959, the Commonwealth Club of California's
silver medal in 1967, cowinner of the Shelley Memorial Award in 1978, and the
Book of the Year Award of the Conference on Christianity and Literature, an
affiliate of the Modern Language Association, the same year. Since 1971 he has
been poet-in-residence at Kresge College, the University of California at Santa Cruz.

*POETRY*

*These Are the Ravens.* San Leandro, CA: Greater West Publishing, 1935.
*San Joaquin.* Los Angeles: Ward Ritchie, 1939.
*The Masculine Dead: Poems 1938-1940.* Prairie City, IL: James A. Decker, 1942.
*The Waldport Poems.* Waldport, OR: Untide Press, 1944.
*War Elegies.* Waldport, OR: Untide Press, 1944.
*The Residual Years: Poems 1940-1941.* Waldport, OR: Untide Press, 1944.
*The Residual Years: Poems 1934-1946.* New York: New Directions, 1948.
        Enlarged ed., 1968.
*The Crooked Lines of God: Poems 1949-1954* (as Brother Antoninus). Detroit:
        University of Detroit Press, 1959.
*The Hazards of Holiness: Poems 1957-1960* (as Brother Antoninus). New York:
        Doubleday, 1962.
*Single Source: The Early Poems of William Everson, 1934-1940.* Berkeley: Oyez,
        1966.
*The Rose of Solitude* (as Brother Antoninus). New York: Doubleday, 1967.
*The Last Crusade* (as Brother Antoninus). Berkeley: Oyez, 1969.
*Tendril in the Mesh.* Aromas, CA: Cayucos Books, 1973.
*Man-Fate: The Swan Song of Brother Antoninus.* New York: New Directions,
        1974.
*River Root: A Syzygy for the Bicentennial of These States.* Berkeley: Oyez, 1976.
*The Veritable Years: 1949-1966.* Santa Barbara: Black Sparrow, 1978.
*The Masks of Drought.* Santa Barbara: Black Sparrow, 1979.


*OTHER*

*Robinson Jeffers: Fragments of an Older Fury.* Berkeley: Oyez, 1968.
*If I Speak Truth: An Inter View-ing,* with Jerry Burns. San Francisco: Goliards
        Press, 1968.
*Archetype West: The Pacific Coast as a Literary Region* (prose). Berkeley: Oyez,
        1976.
*Earth Poetry: Selected Essays and Interviews,* ed. Lee Bartlett. Berkeley: Oyez,
        1980.


*SECONDARY*

William E. Stafford, *The Achievement of Brother Antoninus: A Comprehensive
        Selection of his Poems with a Critical Introduction.* Chicago: Scott
        Foresman, 1967.


*RECORDINGS*

*The Savagery of Love.* New York: Caedmon, 1968.
*Poetry of Earth.* [Monterey, CA]: Big Sur Recordings, 1970.

## BIBLIOGRAPHIES

Lee Bartlett and Allan Campo, *William Everson: A Descriptive Bibliography 1934-1976.* Metuchen, NJ and London: Scarecrow Press, 1977.
David Kherdian, *Six Poets of the San Francisco Renaissance: Portraits and Checklists.* Fresno, CA: Giligia Press, 1967.

LAWRENCE FERLINGHETTI: "Probably born 1919 or 20 in Yonkers, N.Y. Some tampering with the birth certificate has been uncovered, some of it by himself. His mother was Clemence Monsanto, and he was her fifth and last son. She was enclosed in an asylum shortly after his birth which was itself preceded by the sudden death of his father. His father was an Italian auctioneer in Brooklyn who must have arrived WOP (With Out Papers) from Lombardy about the turn of the century. The family name was shortened to Ferling but restored by L.F. when of age. There was a French 'aunt' who took L.F. to France in swaddling clothes where they remained for an uncertain number of years. Her name was Emily Monsanto, descended from that same Sephardic-Portuguese Mendes-Monsanto who emigrated to the Virgin Islands in a Danish Crown Colony expedition after the Spanish Inquisition and was there knighted by the King of Denmark. L.F.'s first memory of America is eating tapioca pudding ( undercooked and called Cat's Eyes by the inmates) in an orphanage in Chappaqua, New York. He then spent many years in a mansion of a branch of the Lawrence family which founded Sarah Lawrence College in Bronxville, N.Y., where much-beloved Emily left him after serving as a French governess in that family. She later died in an asylum at Central Islip, Long Island, unknown to L.F.... As a poet, Ferlinghetti describes himself as an Unblinking Eye. He is now engaged in a long prose Work-in-Progress, one part of which is tentatively called, 'Her Too.' "

## POETRY

*Pictures of the Gone World.* San Francisco: City Lights, 1955.
*A Coney Island of the Mind.* New York: New Directions, 1958.
*Tentative Description of a Dinner Given to Promote the Impeachment of President Eisenhower.* San Francisco: Golden Mountain, 1958.
*One Thousand Fearful Words for Fidel Castro.* San Francisco: City Lights, 1961.
*Starting from San Francisco.* New York: New Directions, 1961; rev. ed., 1967.
*Where Is Vietnam?* San Francisco: City Lights, 1965.
*An Eye on the World: Selected Poems.* London: MacGibbon & Kee, 1967.
*The Secret Meaning of Things.* New York: New Directions, 1969.
*Tyrannus Nix?* New York: New Directions, 1969.
*Back Roads to Far Places.* New York: New Directions, 1971.
*Open Eye, Open Heart.* New York: New Directions, 1973.
*Who Are We Now?* New York: New Directions, 1976.
*Northwest Ecolog.* San Francisco: City Lights, 1978.
*Landscapes of Living & Dying.* New York: New Directions, 1979.
*Endless Life: The Selected Poems.* New York: New Directions, 1981.

*The Populist Manifestos.* San Francisco: Grey Fox, 1981.
*A Trip to Italy & France.* New York: New Directions, 1981.

## OTHER

*Her* (novel). New York: New Directions, 1960; London: MacGibbon & Kee, 1966.
*The Howl of the Censor,* ed. J. W. Ehrlich. San Carlos, CA: Nourse, 1961.
    Reprinted Westport, CT: Greenwood Press, 1976.
*Unfair Arguments with Existence* (plays). New York: New Directions, 1963.
*Routines* (plays). New York: New Directions, 1964.
*The Mexican Night* (travel journal). New York: New Directions, 1970.
*The Illustrated Wilfred Funk.* San Francisco: City Lights, 1971.
*Literary San Francisco,* with Nancy J. Peters. San Francisco: City Lights/Harper &
    Row, 1980.

## RECORDINGS

*Poetry Readings in "The Cellar,"* with Kenneth Rexroth. Fantasy, LP 7002,. 1958.
*Tentative Description of a Dinner to Impeach President Eisenhower, and Other
    Poems.* Fantasy, LP 7004. 1959.
*America Today!* The World's Great Poets, vol. 1, with Allen Ginsberg and Gregory
    Corso. CMS Records, LP 617. 1971.
*Lawrence Ferlinghetti.* Deland, FL: Everett/Edwards, 1972.
*Selected Poems.* Munich: S Press, 1978.

## SECONDARY

Neeli Cherkovski. *Ferlinghetti: A Biography.* New York: Doubleday, 1979.

## BIBLIOGRAPHIES

David Kherdian, *Six Poets of the San Francisco Renaissance: Portraits and
    Checklists.* Fresno, CA: Giligia Press, 1967.
Bill Morgan, *Lawrence Ferlinghetti: A Comprehensive Bibliography.* New York:
    Garland, 1981.

ALLEN GINSBERG: "Born June 3, 1926, the son of Naomi Ginsberg, Russian
émigrée, and Louis Ginsberg, lyric poet and schoolteacher, in Paterson, New Jersey.
Grammar & high schools Paterson, B.A. Columbia College 1948; associations with
Jack Kerouac, Wm. S. Burroughs, Herbert H. Huncke & Neal Cassady begun 1945
NYC and next decade after with Gregory Corso, Peter Orlovsky companion 1954 &
poets Michael McClure, Philip Lamantia, Gary Snyder & Philip Whalen in San Fran-
cisco became known 1955 on as 'Beat Generation' and/or 'San Francisco Renais-
sance' literary phases; acquaintance with William Carlos Williams 1948 & study of
his relative-footed American speech prosody led to *Empty Mirror* early poems with
W.C.W. preface, as later Williams introduced *Howl.*
    Illuminative audition of William Blake's voice simultaneous with Eternity-vision

1948 and underground bust-culture Apocalypse-realization conduced to 8-month stay NY State Psychiatric Institute & later preoccupation with Gnostic-mystic poetics and politics, residence in India & Vietnam Japan visit 1962-3, mantra chanting beginning with Hare Krishna Mahamantra and Buddhist Prajnaparamita (Highest Perfect Wisdom) Sutra same years, & experiment with poetic effects of psychedelic drugs beginning 1952 and continuing with Dr. Timothy Leary through Cambridge experiments 1961; certain texts *Howl* part II (1955) and *Wales Visitation* (1967) were written during effects of peyote & LSD respectively.

Travel began early 1950s half year Mayan Mexico, several voyages years Tangiers-Europe late 50s on, earlier merchant marine sea trips to Africa & Arctic, half year Chile Bolivia & Peru Amazon 1960, half year Cuba Russia Poland Czechoslovakia culminating May Day 1965 election as King of May (Kral Majales) by 100,000 Prague citizens.

Literary awards: obscenity trial with *Howl* text declared legal by court SF 1957, Guggenheim Fellowship 1963-64, National Institute of Arts and Letters Grant for poetry 1969. Contributing editor: *Black Mountain Review* No. 7 edited by Robert Creeley; Advisory Guru: *The Marijuana Review*; writing published variously in *Yugen, Floating Bear, Kulchur, Big Table, City Lights Journal, C, Evergreen Review, Fuck You/A Magazine of the Arts, Atlantic Monthly, Life, New Yorker, Look, NY Times, Izvestia, Rolling Stone, Underground Press Syndicate,* etc.

Participated in college poetry readings & NY literary scene 1958-61 with LeRoi Jones & Frank O'Hara; *Pull My Daisy*, Robert Frank film 1959; early Trips Festivals with Ken Kesey, Neal Cassady & Merry Pranksters mid-60s; Vancouver '63 & Berkeley '65 Poetry Conventions with Olson, Duncan, Creeley, Snyder, Dorn & other poet friends; Albert Hall Poetry Incarnation, readings with Vosnesensky in London, and anti-Vietnam War early Flower Power marches in Berkeley 1965.

Attended mantra-chanting at first Human Be-In San Francisco 1967; conferred at Dialectics of Liberation in London & gave poetry readings with poet father Louis Ginsberg there & in NY; testified U.S. Senate hearings for legalization of psychedelics; arrested with Dr. Benjamin Spock blocking Whitehall Draft Board steps war protest NY same year. Teargassed chanting AUM at Lincoln Park Yippie Life-Festival Chicago 1968 Presidential convention, then accompanied Jean Genet & William Burroughs on front line Peace 'Conspiracy' march led by Dave Dellinger.

Mantric poetics & passing acquaintance with poet-singers Ezra Pound, Bob Dylan, Ed Sanders, & Mick Jagger led to music study for tunes to Wm. Blake's *Songs of Innocence and Experience*: this homage to visionary poet-guru Blake, occasioned by visit to West Coast to touch a satin bag of body-ashes of the late much-loved Neal Cassady, was composed one week on return from police-state shock in Chicago & recorded summer 1969. Chanted OM to Judge & Jury December 1969 Anti-War Conspiracy trial Chicago; thereafter interrupted by Miami Police on reading poetry exorcising police bureaucracy Prague & Pentagon, rapid Federal Court Mandatory Injunction declared texts Constitutionally protected from police censorship. Pallbore funerals late Kerouac & Olson, last few 60s winters spent outside cities learning music, milking cows & goats.

In 1971 began daily hour subvocal-mantra heart meditation, Swami Muktananda teacher; brief journey Bengal Jessore Road Calcutta to E. Pakistan refugee camps & revisited Benares. Jamming at home & recording studios w/Dylan & Happy Traum learned Blues forms. *Kaddish* play mounted NY Chelsea Theater. Researched & publicized CIA subsidization Indochinese opium traffic; assembled 16 phono albums *Collected Poems Vocalized 1946-71* from decades' tape archives, completed second album Blake songs.

Began study Kagu lineage Tibetan style Buddhist meditation in 1972, Chog-yam Trungpa, Rinpoche teacher; took Refuge and Boddhisattva vows; extended poetic practice to public improvisation on blues chords with politic Dharma themes. Adelaide and Central Australia meeting with Aboriginal song-men, Darwin Land travel with Russian poet Andrei Vosnesensky. Jailed with hundreds of peace pro-testors, Miami Presidential Convention; essays in defense of Tim Leary, Abbie Hoff-man, John Lennon etc. from Federal Narcotics Bureau entrapment, as member of P.E.N. Freedom to Read Committee.

1973—Poetry International London & Rotterdam; meetings with Basil Bunting & Hugh MacDiarmid, tour Scotland/Inner Hebrides. Taught poetics Naropa Seminary; all autumn retreat Buddhist study including month's 10 hour daily sitting practice.

1974—Inducted member American Institute of Arts and Letters. National Book Award for *Fall of America*; apprenticed rough carpentry wooden cottage neighboring Gary Snyder Sierra land; with Anne Waldman founded Jack Kerouac School of Disembodied Poetics, Naropa Institute, codirector teaching subsequent summers.

1975—Poet-percussionist on Bob Dylan's Rolling Thunder Review tour.

1976—Reading Akademie der Kunste, Berlin with Wm. Burroughs; *First Blues* recordings produced by John Hammond, Sr.; several months fall seminary retreat with Chogyam Trungpa.

1977—Read thru Blake's entire Works, wrote 'Contest of Bards,' narrated TVTV-N.E.T. film *Kaddish*, presented poetry/music Nightclub Troubadour L.A. under Buddhist auspice, thereafter NY Other End & Boston Passim folk clubs. Read with Robert Lowell St. Mark's NY; taught Blake's *Urizen* Naropa Institute spring, summer discoursed on 'Literary History Beat Generation 1940s.' Attended U. of Cal. Santa Cruz LSD Conference with Dr. Albert Hoffman; visited Kauai.

1978—Naropa summer discourse on 'Meditation & Poetics'; composed music for Blake's *Tyger* to trochaic heart-beat meters; acted 'the Father,' danced, sang Blake & visited Kerouac's grave with Dylan in *Renaldo & Clara* film. Composed 'Plutonian Ode' and arrested twice at Rocky Flats Colo. Nuclear Facility with Orlovsky & Daniel Ellsberg practicing sitting meditation on railroad tracks blocking train bearing Plutonium/'fissile materials': conviction appealed.

1979—Taught Blake's *Lambeth* Prophetic Books Naropa winter; National Arts Club Gold Medal for Distinction in Literature."

*POETRY*

*Howl and Other Poems.* San Francisco: City Lights, 1956.
*Empty Mirror: Early Poems.* New York: Totem/Corinth, 1961.
*Kaddish and Other Poems. 1958-1960.* San Francisco: City Lights, 1961.
*Reality Sandwiches, 1953-60.* San Francisco: City Lights, 1963.
*Planet News, 1961-1967.* San Francisco: City Lights, 1968.
*Airplane Dreams: Compositions from Journals.* Toronto: House of Anansi, 1968; San Francisco: City Lights, 1969.
*Iron Horse.* Toronto: Coach House, 1972; San Francisco: City Lights, 1974.
*The Fall of America: Poems of These States 1965-1971.* San Francisco: City Lights, 1972.
*The Gates of Wrath: Rhymed Poems 1948-1952.* Bolinas, CA: Grey Fox, 1972.

*First Blues: Rags, Ballads & Harmonium Songs, 1971-74.* New York: Full Court, 1975.
*Sad Dust Glories: Poems During Work Summer in Woods.* Berkeley: Workingman's Press, 1975.
*Mind Breaths: Poems 1972-1977.* San Francisco: City Lights, 1978.
*Poems All Over the Place, Mostly 'Seventies.* Cherry Valley, NY: Cherry Valley Editions, 1978.

OTHER

*The Yage Letters*, with William S. Burroughs. San Francisco: City Lights, 1963.
*Indian Journals: March 1962-May 1963.* San Francisco: Dave Haselwood, 1970.
*Improvised Poetics*, ed. Mark Robison. Buffalo, NY: Anonym Press, 1971.
*Gay Sunshine Interview.* Bolinas, CA: Grey Fox, 1974.
*Allen Verbatim: Lectures on Poetry, Politics, Consciousness*, ed. Gordon Ball. New York: McGraw-Hill, 1974.
*The Visions of the Great Rememberer* (prose). Amherst, MA: Mulch Press, 1974.
*Chicago Trial Testimony.* San Francisco: City Lights, 1975.
*To Eberhart from Ginsberg.* Lincoln, MA: Penmaen Press, 1976.
*Journals: Early Fifties—Early Sixties*, ed. Gordon Ball. New York: Grove, 1977.
*As Ever: The Collected Correspondence of Allen Ginsberg & Neal Cassady.* Berkeley: Creative Arts, 1977.
*Take Case of My Ghost, Ghost*, with Jack Kerouac. N.p.: Ghost Press, 1977.
*Composed on the Tongue.* Bolinas, CA: Grey Fox, 1980.

RECORDINGS

*Howl and Other Poems.* Fantasy, LP 7013. 1959.
*Kaddish.* Atlantic Verbum Series 4001. New York, 1966.
*William Blake's Songs of Innocence and Experience Tuned by Allen Ginsberg.* MGM Records, FTS 3083. New York, 1970.
*Live at St. Mark's, New York City.* Munich: S Press, 1977.

SECONDARY

Jane Kramer, *Allen Ginsberg in America.* New York: Random, 1968.
Thomas F. Merrill, *Allen Ginsberg.* New York: Twayne, 1969.
Eric Mottram, *Allen Ginsberg in the Sixties.* Brighton, Eng.: Unicorn Bookshop, 1972.
Paul Portuges, *The Visionary Poetics of Allen Ginsberg.* Santa Barbara: Ross-Erikson, 1978.

BIBLIOGRAPHY

George Dowden, *A Bibliography of the Works of Allen Ginsberg.* San Francisco: City Lights, 1970.

BARBARA GUEST was born in Wilmington, North Carolina, in 1920; she grew up in California, attending U.C.L.A. and graduating from the University of California at Berkeley, before moving to New York. "I continue to live in New York City, and although my interest in painting has not diminished, I have been less concerned with the work of the 70s. The past several years I have been engaged on a biography of the poet H. D., perhaps the most difficult task with which I have presented myself."

## POETRY

*The Location of Things.* New York: Tibor de Nagy, 1960.
*Poems: The Location of Things, Archaics, The Open Skies.* New York: Doubleday, 1962.
*The Blue Stairs.* New York: Corinth, 1968,
*I Ching: Poems and Lithographs,* with Sheila Isham. New York: Mourlot, 1969.
*Moscow Mansions.* New York: Viking, 1973.
*The Countess from Minneapolis.* Providence: Burning Deck, 1976.
*Biography.* Providence: Burning Deck, 1980.

## OTHER

*Goodnough,* with B. H. Friedman. Paris: G. Fall, 1962.
*Seeking Air* (novel). Santa Barbara: Black Sparrow, 1978.

ANSELM HOLLO: "I was born on April 12, 1934, in Helsinki, Finland, of Baltic (Finnish-German-Swedish-Polish-etc.) parentage. After travels & sojourns in Sweden, Germany, Austria, & Spain, I have lived & worked in England & the United States since 1958—the last thirteen years in different parts of the U.S. (Buffalo, Iowa City, Lansing, Baltimore, a.o.) as a teacher of writing, reading, hearing, & translation. The new American poetry has become a very real place to be: the company of masters & friends. It moved me here, & it's still moving, faster & more variously than ever."

## POETRY

*Sateiden Valilla [Rainpause].* Helsinki: Otava, 1956.
*St. Texts and Finnpoems.* Worcester, Eng., and Ventura, CA: Migrant Press, 1961.
*& It Is A Song.* Birmingham, Eng.: Migrant Press, 1965.
*Faces & Forms.* London: Ambit Books, 1965.
*Poems/Runoja* (bilingual ed.). Helsinki: Otava, 1967.
*The Man in the Treetop Hat.* London: Turret Books, 1968.
*The Coherences.* London: Trigram Press, 1968.
*Maya: Works, 1959-1969.* London: Cape Goliard; New York: Grossman, 1970.
*Sensation 27.* Canton, NY: Institute of Further Studies, 1972.
*Alembic.* London: Trigram Press, 1972.

*Some Worlds.* New Rochelle, NY: Elizabeth Press, 1974.
*Heavy Jars.* West Branch, IA: Toothpaste Press, 1977.
*Sojourner Microcosms: Poems New & Selected, 1959-1977.* Berkeley: Blue Wind, 1977.
*Phantom Pod*, with Joe Cardarelli and Kirby Malone. Baltimore: Pod Books, 1977.
*Curious Data.* Buffalo, NY: White Pine, 1978.
*Lunch in Fur.* St. Paul, MN: Truck Press, 1978.
*With Ruth in Mind.* Barrytown, N.Y.: Station Hill, 1979.
*Finite Continued.* Berkeley: Blue Wind, 1980.


*TRANLSATIONS*

*Red Cats: Selections from the Russian Poets.* San Francisco: City Lights, 1962.
*Selected Poems*, by Andrei Voznesensky. New York: Grove, 1964.
*Helsinki: Selected Poems*, by Pentii Saarikoski. London: Rapp and Whiting; Chicago: Swallow Press, 1967.
*Selected Poems*, by Paavo Haavikko. London: Cape Goliard; New York: Grossman, 1968.
*The Twelve and Other Poems*, by Aleksandr Blok. Lexington, KY: Gnomon Press, 1971.


*RECORDING*

*With Ruth in Mind.* Barrytown, NY: Widemouth Tapes, 1978.


LEROI JONES adopted the name Imamu (Swahili title for respected spiritual leader) AMIRI BARAKA in 1966, following his embracing of the Kawaida branch of the Muslim faith. He was born in Newark, New Jersey, on October 7, 1934, his father a postal worker (later supervisor), his mother a social worker. He graduated two years ahead of his age in high school and attended the Newark extension of Rutgers before transferring to Howard University, where he received a B.A. in 1954. He later took courses at the New School in New York and at Columbia University, mostly in philosophy and German literature. He joined the U.S. Air Force and served with the Strategic Air Command as a climatographer and aerial gunner, stationed most of the time in Puerto Rico. After his discharge in 1957, he settled in New York, married, and with his wife Hettie founded the magazine *Yugen* and the Totem Press, while earning a living as editor, jazz critic, and reviewer. He also coedited the poetry newsletter, *Floating Bear*, with Diane DiPrima. He taught courses in contemporary poetry at the New School in 1963, at the State University of New York at Buffalo in the summer of 1964, and, intermittently, at Columbia. His play, *Dutchman*, won an Obie for the best American play of 1964 (a film was also made of it), and he was awarded a Guggenheim fellowship in 1965. A visit to revolutionary Cuba in 1960, reported as the essay "Cuba Libre," heightened his political awareness, but even more decisive was the assassination of Malcolm X. Shortly after, he turned away from his white friends and moved uptown to Harlem, where he founded the Black Arts Repertory Theatre. In 1966 he moved back to Newark, setting up a black cultural center called Spirit House in a slum building. He married again, and became active in the political affairs of his city, determined to rebuild the black community, a New Ark. During the Newark riots of 1967, he was arrested for allegedly possessing illegal firearms, sentenced and fined, although an appeal led to a retrial and acquittal. He was a delegate to the Black Power Conference of 1968 and secretary-general of the short-lived National Black Political Assembly, and is presently chairman of the Congress of Afrikan Peoples. In recent years his politics (and poetics) have become increasingly Maoist-Leninist, with his poetry reflecting his growth from bohemian to black nationalist to international Marxist.

### POETRY

*Preface to a Twenty-Volume Suicide Note.* New York: Totem/Corinth, 1961.
*The Dead Lecturer.* New York: Grove, 1964.
*Black Art.* Newark: Jihad Publications, 1966.
*Black Magic: Poetry 1961-1967.* Indianapolis: Bobbs-Merrill; London: MacGibbon & Kee, 1969.
*It's Nation Time.* Chicago: Third World, 1970.
*Spirit Reach.* Newark: Jihad Publications, 1972.
*Afrikan Revolution.* Newark: Jihad Publications, 1973.
*Hard Facts.* Newark: Jihad Publications, 1976.
*AM/TRAK.* New York: Phoenix Bookshop, 1979.
*Selected Poems of Amiri Baraka-LeRoi Jones.* New York: Morrow, 1979.

### OTHER

*Blues People: Negro Music in White America.* New York: Morrow, 1963; London: MacGibbon & Kee, 1965.
*Dutchman and The Slave* (plays). New York: Morrow, 1964; London: Faber, 1965.
*The Moderns: New Fiction in America* (ed.). New York: Corinth, 1964; London: MacGibbon & Kee, 1965.
*The System of Dante's Hell* (novel). New York: Grove, 1965; London: MacGibbon & Kee, 1966.
*Home: Social Essays.* New York: Morrow, 1966; London: MacGibbon & Kee, 1968.
*The Baptism and The Toilet* (plays). New York: Grove, 1967.
*Tales.* New York: Grove, 1967; London: MacGibbon & Kee, 1969.
*Black Music.* New York: Morrow, 1967; London: MacGibbon & Kee, 1969.
*Arm Yrself or Harm Yrself* (play). Newark: Jihad Publications, 1967.
*Black Fire: An Anthology of Afro-American Writing* (editor, with Larry Neal). New York: Morrow, 1968.
*Slave Ship: A Historical Pageant.* Newark: Jihad Publications, 1969.
*Four Black Revolutionary Plays.* Indianapolis: Bobbs-Merrill, 1969; London: Calder and Boyars, 1971.
*In Our Terribleness: Some Elements and Meaning in Black Style*, with Fundi (Billy Abernathy). Indianapolis: Bobbs-Merrili, 1970.
*A Black Value System.* Newark: Jihad Publications, 1970.
*Jello* (play). Chicago: Third World, 1970.

*Raise Race Rays Raze: Essays Since 1965.* New York: Random, 1971.
*Kawaida Studies: The New Nationalism.* Chicago: Third World, 1972.
*Three Books by Imamu Amiri Baraka (LeRoi Jones) [The Dead Lecturer, System of Dante's Hell, Tales].* New York: Grove, 1975.
*The Motion of History, and Other Plays.* New York: Morrow, 1978.
*What Was the Relationship of the Lone Ranger to the Means of Production?* New York: Anti-Imperialist Cultural Union, 1978.
*The Sidney Poet Heroical* (play). Berkeley: Reed & Cannon, 1979.
*Selected Plays and Prose.* New York: Morrow, 1979.

### SECONDARY

Kimberly W. Benston, *Baraka: The Renegade and the Mask.* New Haven: Yale, 1976.
Theodore R. Hudson *From Leroi Jones to Amiri Baraka: The Literary Works.* Durham, NC: Duke, 1973.
Werner Sollors, *Amiri Baraka/LeRoi Jones: The Quest for a Populist Modernism.* New York: Columbia, 1978.
*Boundary 2*, 6: 2 (Winter 1978). Jones/Baraka supplement.

### BIBLIOGRAPHY

Letitia Dace. *LeRoi Jones (Imamu Amiri Baraka): A Checklist of Works by and About Him.* London: Nether Press, 1971.


ROBERT KELLY was born in Brooklyn, N.Y., on September 24, 1935. He was educated at the City College of New York (A.B. 1955), with graduate courses in medieval studies at Columbia University, 1955-58. Early friendships with David Antin, George Economou, Jerome Rothenberg, Diane Wakoski, Jackson Mac Low, Rochelle Owens, Clayton Eshleman, and Armand Schwerner were formative (see his richly autobiographical *Statement* from 1968). He was editor of the *Chelsea Review* in New York from 1958 to 1960; founding editor, with George Economou, of *Trobar* magazine and Trobar Books; editor of the newsletter *Matter* and Matter Books; and contributing editor of *Caterpillar* and *Sulfur.* He has taught at Bard College, Annandale-on-Hudson, N.Y., since 1961, where he is now a professor of English, living in a house on the edge of campus. He has also taught, more briefly, at Wagner College, Tufts University, and the State University of New York at Buffalo (summer 1964). He edited, with Paris Leary, the anthology *A Controversy of Poets* (1965), as well as Paul Blackburn's *Journals.*

### POETRY

*Armed Descent.* New York: Hawk's Well, 1961.
*Her Body Against Time.* Mexico City: El Corno Emplumado, 1963.

*Round Dances.* New York: Trobar Books, 1964
*Lunes.* New York: Hawk's Well, 1964.
*Lectiones.* Placitas, NM: Duende Press, 1965.
*Twenty Poems.* Annandale-on-Hudson, NY: Matter, 1967.
*Devotions.* Annandale-on-Hudson, NY: Salitter, 1967.
*Axon Dendron Tree.* Annandale-on-Hudson, NY: Matter, 1967.
*A Joining: A Sequence for H.D.* Los Angeles: Black Sparrow, 1967.
*Finding the Measure.* Los Angeles: Black Sparrow, 1968.
*Songs I-XXX.* Cambridge, MA: Pym Randall, 1968.
*Sonnets.* Los Angeles: Black Sparrow, 1968.
*The Common Shore, Books I-V: A Long Poem about America in Time.* Los
    Angeles: Black Sparrow, 1969.
*Kali Yuga.* London: Cape Goliard, 1970; New York: Grossman, 1971.
*Flesh: Dream: Book.* Los Angeles: Black Sparrow, 1971.
*The Pastorals.* Los Angeles: Black Sparrow, 1972.
*The Mill of Particulars.* Los Angeles: Black Sparrow, 1973.
*The Loom.* Los Angeles: Black Sparrow, 1975.
*The Convections.* Santa Barbara: Black Sparrow, 1978.
*The Book of Persephone.* New Paltz, NY: Treacle Press, 1978.
*The Cruise of the Pnyx.* Barrytown, NY: Station Hill, 1979.
*Kill the Messenger Who Brings Bad News.* Santa Barbara: Black Sparrow, 1979.
*The Alchemist to Mercury*, ed. Jed Rasula. Richmond, CA: North Atlantic, 1981.

*OTHER*

*The Scorpions* (novel). New York: Doubleday, 1967; London: Calder and
    Boyars, 1969.
*Statement.* Los Angeles: Black Sparrow, 1968.
*The Well Wherein a Deer's Head Bleeds* (play), in *A Play and Two Poems*, with
    Diane Wakoski and Ron Loewinsohn. Los Angeles: Black Sparrow, 1968.
*Cities.* West Newbury, MA: Frontier Press, 1971.
*In Time* (essays). West Newbury, MA: Frontier Press, 1971.
*A Line of Sight.* Los Angeles: Black Sparrow, 1974.

*SECONDARY*

*Vort*, no. 5 (Summer 1974). Kelly issue.

JACK KEROUAC was born March 12, 1922, in Lowell, Massachusetts, a descendant
of French-Canadian pioneers. Chronicler of the Beat Generation, the story of his
life is in his novels, which taken together make up "The Legend of Duluoz." He
considered his early education in the parochial schools of Lowell "what made it
possible for me to begin writing stories and even one novel at the age of eleven."
He attended Horace Mann School in the Bronx on a scholarship, and Columbia

College, 1940-41, dropping out to join the Merchant Marine and the Navy, and again in 1942, during which time he met Allen Ginsberg, William Burroughs, Neal Cassady and others who formed the nucleus of the Beats. Between 1943 and 1950 he hitchhiked throughout the United States and Mexico, working at odd jobs, until his first novel, *The Town and the City*, "written in tradition of long work and revision," was published. This was followed by the discovery of " 'spontaneous' prose" resulting in his classic *On the Road*, written in three weeks in 1951 on a continuous roll of teletype paper, but not published until 1957.

He summarized his development for the first edition of *The New American Poetry*: "At the age of 11 I wrote whole little novels in nickel notebooks, also magazines (in imitation of *Liberty Magazine*) and kept extensive horse racing newspapers going. The first 'serious' writing took place after I read about Jack London at the age of 17. Like Jack, I began to paste up 'long words' on my bedroom wall in order to memorize them perfectly. At 18 I read Hemingway and Saroyan and began writing little terse short stories in that general style. Then I read Tom Wolfe and began writing in the rolling style. Then I read Joyce and wrote a whole juvenile novel like *Ulysses* called 'Vanity of Duluoz.' Then came Dostoevsky. Finally I entered a romantic phase with Rimbaud and Blake which I called my 'self-ultimacy' period, burning what I wrote in order to be 'Self-Ultimate.' At the age of 24 I was groomed for the Western idealistic concept of letters from reading Goethe's *Dichtung und Wahrheit*. The discovery of a style of my own based on spontaneous get-with-it, came after reading the marvelous free narrative letters of Neal Cassady, a great writer who happens also to be the Dean Moriarty of *On the Road*. I also learned a lot about unrepressed wordslinging from young Allen Ginsberg and William Seward Burroughs."

Kerouac's "Belief & Technique for Modern Prose: List of Essentials" and "Essentials of Spontaneous Prose," which first appeared in the *Black Mountain Review*, may be read as statements on poetics, comparable to Pound's "Some Don'ts" and Olson's "Projective Verse" in usefulness and influence. About his own verse, Kerouac has said (*Paris Review* interview, 1968): ". . . I knocked it off fast like prose, using, get this, the size of the notebook page for the form and length of the poem, just as a musician has to get out, a jazz musician, his statement within a certain number of bars, within one chorus, which spills over into the next, but he has to stop where the chorus page *stops*." His series of poems, *San Francisco Blues* (a few of which were included in *Scattered Poems*), was written in April 1954, while *Mexico City Blues* was written in three weeks in August of 1955. His haiku, which Allen Ginsberg has said made him "a great poet . . . the best poet in the United States," as well as other poems written later in the 1950s and titled *Pomes All Sizes*, are as yet uncollected. He died of a stomach hemorrhage resulting from alcoholism, 21 October 1969, in St. Petersburg, Florida, and is buried in Lowell.

*POETRY*

*Mexico City Blues.* New York: Grove, 1959.
*Scattered Poems.* San Francisco: City Lights, 1971.
*Trip Trap: Haiku Along the Road*, with Albert Saijo and Lew Welch. Bolinas, CA: Grey Fox, 1973.
*Heaven & Other Poems.* Bolinas, CA: Grey Fox, 1977.

406 / Biographical Notes and Bibliographies

## OTHER

*The Town & the City* (novel). New York: Harcourt, 1950.
*On the Road* (novel). New York: Viking, 1957; critical ed., 1978.
*The Subterraneans* (novel). New York: Grove, 1958.
*The Dharma Bums* (novel). New York: Viking, 1958.
*Doctor Sax* (novel). New York: Grove, 1959.
*Maggie Cassidy* (novel). New York: Avon, 1959.
*The Scripture of the Golden Eternity.* New York: Totem/Corinth, 1960.
*Tristessa* (novel). New York: Avon, 1960.
*Lonesome Traveller* (prose sketches). New York: McGraw-Hill, 1960.
*Book of Dreams.* San Francisco: City Lights, 1961.
*Big Sur* (novel). New York: Farrar, Straus, 1962.
*Visions of Gerard* (novel). New York: Farrar, Straus, 1963.
*Desolation Angels* (novel). New York: Coward-McCann, 1965.
*Satori in Paris* (novel). New York: Grove, 1966.
*Vanity of Duluoz* (novel). New York: Coward-McCann, 1968.
*Pic* (novel). New York: Grove, 1971.
*Visions of Cody* (novel). New York: McGraw-Hill, 1973.
*Take Care of My Ghost, Ghost,* with Allen Ginsberg. N.p.: Ghost Press, 1977.

## RECORDINGS

*Readings by Jack Kerouac on the Beat Generation.* Verve Records, MG V-15005. 1959.
*Jack Kerouac, Steve Allen: Poetry for the Beat Generation.* Hanover Records, HML 5000. 1959.
*Jack Kerouac, Blues and Haikus.* Hanover Records, HM 5006. 1959.

## SECONDARY

Victor-Levy Beaulieu, *Jack Kerouac: A Chicken-Essay.* Toronto: Coach House, 1975.
Caroline Cassady, *Heart Beat: My Life with Jack & Neal.* Berkeley: Creative Arts, 1976.
Ann Charters, *Kerouac: A Biography.* San Francisco: Straight Arrow, 1973; rev. ed., New York: Warner American Library, 1974.
Barry Gifford, *Kerouac's Town.* Santa Barbara: Capra, 1973.
Barry Gifford and Lawrence Lee, *Jack's Book: An Oral Biography of Jack Kerouac.* New York: St. Martin's, 1978.
Allen Ginsberg, *The Visions of the Great Rememberer.* Amherst, MA: Mulch Press, 1974.
Robert A. Hipkiss, *Jack Kerouac, A Prophet of the New Romanticism.* Lawrence, KA: Regents Press of Kansas, 1976.
Charles E. Jarvis, *Visions of Kerouac.* Lowell, MA: Ithaca Press, 1974.
Dennis McNally, *Desolate Angel: Jack Kerouac, the Beat Generation and America.* New York: Random, 1979.
John Montgomery, *Jack Kerouac: A Memoir.* Fresno, CA: Giligia Press, 1970.
*Moody Street Irregulars: A Jack Kerouac Newsletter* (1977– ).

BIBLIOGRAPHY

Ann Charters, *A Bibliography of Works by Jack Kerouac, 1939-1975.* Rev. ed. New
York: Phoenix Bookshop, 1975.

KENNETH KOCH: "I was born in Cincinnati, Ohio, in 1925, and grew up there.
My formal education was at Harvard (A.B. 1948) and Columbia (Ph.D. 1959). I
have been married (to Janice Elwood) and have one daughter (Katherine). I teach
at Columbia and I live in New York. In addition to poetry, I write plays—most
recently produced in New York was *The Red Robins*, in 1978. I have also written
some books about teaching children to write poetry."

POETRY

*Poems.* New York: Tibor de Nagy, 1953.
*Ko; or, A Season on Earth.* New York: Grove, 1959.
*Permanently.* New York: Tiber Press, 1960.
*Thank You and Other Poems.* New York: Grove, 1962.
*Poems from 1952 and 1953.* Los Angeles: Black Sparrow, 1968.
*When the Sun Tries to Go On.* Los Angeles: Black Sparrow, 1969.
*Sleeping With Women.* Los Angeles: Black Sparrow, 1969.
*The Pleasures of Peace and Other Poems.* New York: Grove, 1969.
*The Art of Love.* New York: Random, 1975.
*The Red Robins.* New York: Vintage Books, 1975.
*The Duplications.* New York: Random, 1977.
*The Burning Mystery of Anna in 1951.* New York: Random, 1979.
*From the Air.* Wellingborough, Eng.: Skelton's Press, 1979.

OTHER

*Bertha and Other Plays.* New York: Grove, 1966.
*Wishes, Lies and Dreams: Teaching Children to Write Poetry.* New York: Chelsea
House, 1970.
*Interlocking Lives.* New York: Kulchur Press, 1970.
*A Change of Hearts: Plays, Films, and Other Dramatic Works 1951-1971.* New
York: Random, 1973.
*Rose, Where Did You Get That Red? Teaching Great Poetry to Children.* New
York: Random, 1973.
*I Never Told Anybody: Teaching Poetry Writing in a Nursing Home.* New York:
Random, 1977.
*The Red Robins, A Play.* New York: Performing Arts Journal Books, 1980.
*Sleeping on the Wing: An Anthology of Modern Poetry with Essays on Reading and
Writing*, with Kate Farrell. New York: Random, 1981.

RECORDINGS

*The Teaching and Writing of Poetry: An Interview with Kenneth Koch.* Cincinnati: Writer's Voice, 1974.
*Wishes, Lies, and Dreams: Teaching Children to Write Poetry.* Spoken Arts, SAC 6107-6108. 1974.

JAMES KOLLER was born in the Chicago suburb of Oak Park in 1936. Much of his childhood was spent on farms worked by his family in central Illinois. He graduated from North Central College in 1958, leaving the Midwest the following year to live in San Francisco and the Pacific Northwest. He edited *Coyote's Journal* and Coyote Books, and received NEA grants as editor (in 1968) and as poet (in 1973). He spent the winter of 1971-72 in a self-built cabin in the Illinois woods. Since 1972 he has lived near Brunswick, Maine.

POETRY

*Two Hands: Poems 1959-1961.* Seattle: James B. Smith, 1965.
*Brainard & Washington Street Poems.* Eugene, OR: Toad Press, 1965.
*Some Cows: Poems of Civilization and Domestic Life.* San Francisco: Coyote Books, 1966.
*The Dogs & Other Dark Woods.* San Francisco: Four Seasons, 1966.
*California Poems.* Los Angeles: Black Sparrow, 1971.
*Messages.* Canton, NY: Institute of Further Studies, 1972.
*Bureau Creek.* Brunswick, ME: Blackberry, 1975.
*Poems for the Blue Sky.* Santa Barbara: Black Sparrow, 1976.

OTHER

*If You Don't Like Me You Can Leave Me Alone* (novel). Brunswick, ME: Blackberry, 1976.

RECORDING

*Messages.* Munich: S Press, 1978.

SECONDARY

*The Savage*, no. 2 (Winter 1973). Koller issue.

JOANNE ELIZABETH KYGER: "I was born, November 19, 1934, in Vallejo, California, and within six weeks was in China, of which I have no recollection whatsoever. Memory starts in Florida with the birth of my first sister. By the birth of my second sister, when I was six, I was fairly educated. High school and college were spent in Santa Barbara. In 1957 I found poets in San Francisco, and poetry has been my involvement since then. From 1960 to 1964 I lived in Japan, but mostly California has been my home. The past ten years have been absorbedly lived north of San Francisco, in Bolinas." She participated in the University of California Poetry Conference in 1965, the University of British Columbia Winter Festival of 1970, and the Amsterdam Poetry Festival of 1978.

*POETRY*

*The Tapestry and the Web.* San Francisco: Four Seasons, 1965.
*The Fool in April.* San Francisco: Coyote Books, 1966.
*Places to Go.* Los Angeles: Black Sparrow, 1970.
*Joanne.* New York: Angel Hair Books, 1970.
*Desecheo Notebook.* Berkeley: Arif Press, 1971.
*Trip Out and Fall Back.* Berkeley: Arif Press, 1974.
*All This Every Day.* Bolinas, CA: Big Sky Books, 1975.
*The Wonderful Focus of You.* Calais, VT: Z Press, 1980.

*OTHER*

*The Japan and India Journals, 1960-64.* Bolinas, CA: Tombouctou, 1981.

DENISE LEVERTOV: "My mother was descended from the Welsh tailor and mystic Angel Jones of Mold, my father from the noted Hasid, Schneour Zalman (d. 1831), 'the Rav of Northern White Russia.' My father had experienced conversion to Christianity as a student at Königsberg in the 1890s. His lifelong hope was towards the unification of Judaism and Christianity. He was a priest of the Anglican Church (having settled in England not long before I was born), author of a Life of St. Paul in Hebrew, part translator of *The Zohar*, etc.

I was born in October 1923 at Ilford, Essex. I did lessons at home, and never attended any school or college, except for some years at a ballet school. However, we had a house full of books and everyone in the family engaged in some literary activity. Jewish booksellers, German theologians, Russian priests from Paris, and Viennese opera singers, visited the house; and perhaps my earliest memory is of being dandled by the ill-fated son of Theodor Herzl, the great Zionist.

During the war I received partial training and lots of experience as a (civilian) nurse. A different world! I was in London during all but a few of the air raids but it does not seem to have been such a memorable experience as one might expect.

In 1947 I met my husband in Geneva. We first lived in Paris, where I had been working earlier that year, and in Florence (on the G.I. Bill) but settled in New York at the end of 1948. Our son was born the next year. My husband had known Robert Creeley at Harvard, and through our friendship with him we later came to know a number of people connected with Black Mountain College, but never visited it. Cid Corman was the first U.S. editor to give a place to my poems (Charles Wrey Gardiner had first published my work in England). Marrying an American and coming to live here while still young was very stimulating to me as a writer for it necessitated the finding of new rhythms in which to write, in accordance with new rhythms of life and speech. My reading of William Carlos Williams and Wallace Stevens, which began in Paris in 1948; of Olson's essay, 'Projective Verse'; conversations and correspondence with Robert Duncan; a renewed interest through Buber in the Hasidic ideas with which I was dimly acquainted as a child; the thoughts and shared experiences of my husband; an introduction to some of the concepts of Jung; the friendship of certain painters such as Albert Kresch—have all been influential and continue to be so.

I feel the stylistic influence of William Carlos Williams, while perhaps too evident in my work of a few years ago, was a very necessary and healthful one, without which I could not have developed from a British Romantic with almost Victorian background to an American poet of any vitality."

"In recent years I've been developing the ideas written in 'Some Notes on Organic Form'—trying to refine and clarify the sense of the printed poem as a *score*, and to explicate (to students and in an essay, 'On the Linebreak,' *Chicago Review*, Winter 1979, and *Denise Levertov: In Her Own Province*, ed. Linda Wagner) the way in which not only rhythm but melody, pitch-pattern, can be indicated by attentive division of the lines."


## POETRY

*The Double Image.* London: Cresset Press, 1946.
*Here and Now.* San Francisco: City Lights, 1956.
*Overland to the Islands.* Highlands, NC: Jonathan Williams, 1958.
*With Eyes at the Back of Our Heads.* New York: New Directions, 1960.
*The Jacob's Ladder.* New York: New Directions, 1961; London: Cape, 1965.
*O Taste and See.* New York: New Directions, 1964.
*The Sorrow Dance.* New York: New Directions, 1967; London: Cape, 1968.
*Relearning the Alphabet.* New York: New Directions; London: Cape, 1970.
*To Stay Alive.* New York: New Directions, 1971.
*Footprints.* New York: New Directions, 1972.
*The Freeing of the Dust.* New York: New Directions, 1975.
*Life in the Forest.* New York: New Directions, 1978.
*Collected Earlier Poems 1940-1960.* New York: New Directions, 1979.
*Light Up the Cave.* New York: New Directions, 1981.


## OTHER

*In the Night: A Story.* New York: Albondocani Press, 1968.
*The Poet in the World* (essays). New York: New Directions, 1973.


## SECONDARY

Linda Wagner, *Denise Levertov.* New York: Twayne, 1967.
*Denise Levertov: In Her Own Province*, ed. Linda Wagner. New York: New Directions, 1979.

BIBLIOGRAPHY

Robert A. Wilson, *A Bibliography of Denise Levertov*. New York: Phoenix Book
Shop, 1972.

RON LOEWINSOHN: "Born 1937 in the Philippines. First came to U.S. with
parents in 1945, lived briefly in Los Angeles and the Bronx before settling in San
Francisco, a good place for a poet in his teens to be in the 1950s. Left in the mid-
60s to go to school at UC Berkeley, and then got phd'd at Harvard. Now back at
Berkeley, teaching American lit."

POETRY

*Watermelons.* New York: Totem Press, 1959.
*The World of the Lie.* San Francisco: Change Press, 1963.
*Against the Silences to Come.* San Francisco: Four Seasons, 1965.
*L'Autre.* Los Angeles: Black Sparrow, 1967.
*Lying Together, Turning the Head & Shifting the Weight* . . . Los Angeles: Black
    Sparrow, 1967.
*3 Backyard Dramas with Mamas.* Santa Barbara: Unicorn Presss, 1967.
*The Sea, Around Us.* Los Angeles: Black Sparrow, 1968.
*The Step.* Los Angeles: Black Sparrow, 1968.
*Meat Air: Poems 1957-1969.* New York: Harcourt, Brace, 1970.
*The Leaves.* Los Angeles: Black Sparrow, 1973.
*Eight Fairy Tales.* Los Angeles: Black Sparrow, 1975.
*Goat Dances.* Santa Barbara: Black Sparrow, 1976.

JACKSON MAC LOW: "(b. Chicago, 12 Sept. 1922) is an American poet, compo-
ser, playwright, and performance artist active since the 1940s and widely published
in anthologies, periodicals, and books.  Since 1954 he has used systematic chance and
related methods in composing poems, plays, music, and simultaneities (verbal/music-
al/visual works for groups or individuals, of which each performance is unique due
to spontaneous performers' choices and real-time chance systems).  Published and
performed in most countries of North America and Europe, as well as in Australia
and Japan, he has given readings and performances throughout the U.S. and Canada
and in England, Wales, Scotland, and the Netherlands, taking part in Sound Poetry
Festivals in London (1975, 1978), Glasgow (1978), and Toronto (1978).  His play
*The Marrying Maiden* (1958) was produced by The Living Theatre (New York, 1960-
61) with music by John Cage.  With its editor, La Monte Young, he copublished the
first edition of *An Anthology* (1963), which, under the impetus of the book's de-
signer, the late George Maciunas, gave rise to the Fluxus movement, of which he
was the first literary editor and which first presented his works in Europe in the

early 1960s. In summer 1969, as part of the Los Angeles County Museum of Art's Art and Technology Program, he produced computer-assisted poetry at Information International, Inc. New York State's Creative Artists Public Service Program (CAPS) awarded him a Fellowship in Multimedia in 1974 and one in Poetry in 1977, and he served on the CAPS Poetry Panel in 1975. In 1979 he served as Judge of the Literature Grants-in-Aid to Individual Artists for the Rhode Island State Council on the Arts."

### POETRY

*The Pronouns: A Collection of 40 Dances—for the Dancers—6 February-22 March 1964.* Bronx, NY: Privately printed, 1964; London: Tetrad Press, 1970; Barrytown, NY: Station Hill, 1979.
*Manifestos.* New York: Something Else, 1966.
*August Light Poems.* New York: Caterpillar, 1967.
*22 Light Poems.* Los Angeles: Black Sparrow, 1968.
*23rd Light Poem: For Larry Eigner.* London: Tetrad Press, 1969.
*Stanzas for Iris Lezak.* New York: Something Else, 1971.
*Four Trains . . . 4-5 December 1964.* Providence: Burning Deck, 1974.
*36th Light Poem in Memoriam Buster Keaton.* London and New York: Permanent Press, 1975.
*phone.* New York and Amsterdam: Printed Editions/Kontexts Publications, 1979.

### OTHER

*The Twin Plays: Port-au-Prince & Adams County Illinois.* New York: Something Else, 1966.

### SECONDARY

*Vort*, no. 8 (May 1975). Mac Low issue.
*Paper Air*, 2:3 (1980). Mac Low issue.

### RECORDING

*The Black Tarantula Crossword Gathas.* Munich: S Press, 1975.

MICHAEL MCCLURE: "I was born October 20, 1932 in Marysville, Kansas, and grew up in Seattle where I saw the cold ocean and gray-black beaches. I returned to Wichita for adolescence, the first year of college, and pursuit of jazz in nightclubs where I began to understand Parker and Monk and add them to what I knew of Blake, Yeats, Pound, the Surrealists and the anarchist philosophers. After a year in Tucson at the University I moved to San Francisco and met Robert Duncan, Rexroth, Ginsberg and Kerouac.

In 1955 I gave my first poetry reading at the Six Gallery with Snyder, Whalen, Lamantia, Rexroth and Ginsberg. In 1956 my book *Passage* was published—the year my daughter was born. My wife Joanne wrote her first poem that year. In 1959 I began writing essays on the biology of revolt, verbal censorship, drugs and Artaud. Then I wrote *The Blossom*—a play in projective verse. In the late fifties and early sixties my interests centered on biology, which then became a source for my perceptions.

In 1965 *The Beard*, my poem-play of a confrontation between Billy the Kid and Jean Harlow, was presented. It was arrested in San Francisco, Berkeley, and many times in Los Angeles. It received theatre awards in New York and was accepted in London as a dramatic poem. In the late sixties I wrote a second novel, *The Adept*, played esoteric pop music, and wrote songs and poetry. In the early seventies I traveled to the U.N. Environmental Conference at Stockholm, to East Africa, and to South America. Then I wrote a long poem, *Rare Angel*, and books of poems celebrating the Universe as the Messiah (*September Blackberries, Jaguar Skies, Antechamber*). My recent play, *The Red Snake*, is an adaptation of an Elizabethan revenge tragedy. *Josephine*, a play in projective verse, received the Obie for Best Play of 1978.

In *Antechamber* the title poem states:

> WE'RE
> INSTRUMENTS
> THAT
> PLAY
> ourselves."

## POETRY

*Passage.* Big Sur, CA: Jonathan Williams, 1956.
*Peyote Poem.* San Francisco: Semina, 1958.
*For Artaud.* New York: Totem Press, 1959.
*Hymns to St. Geryon and Other Poems.* San Francisco: Auerhahn, 1959.
*The New Book/A Book of Torture.* New York: Grove, 1961.
*Dark Brown.* San Francisco: Auerhahn Press, 1961; Dave Haselwood, 1967.
*Ghost Tantras.* San Francisco: Privately printed, 1964; Four Seasons, 1969.
*13 Mad Sonnets.* Milan: Fernanda Pivano, 1965.
*Poisoned Wheat.* San Francisco: Privately printed, 1965.
*Dream Table.* San Francisco: Dave Haselwood, 1965.
*Unto Caesar.* San Francisco: Dave Haselwood, 1965.
*Mandalas.* San Francisco: Dave Haselwood, 1965.
*Love Lion Book.* San Francisco: Four Seasons, 1966.
*Hail Thee Who Play.* Los Angeles: Black Sparrow, 1968; Berkeley: Sand Dollar, 1974.
*The Sermons of Jean Harlow and the Curses of Billy the Kid.* San Francisco: Four Seasons with Dave Haselwood, 1968.
*The Surge.* West Newbury, MA: Frontier Press, 1969.
*Hymns to St. Geryon/Dark Brown.* London: Cape Goliard, 1969; San Francisco, CA: Grey Fox, 1980.
*Little Odes & The Raptors* (play). Los Angeles: Black Sparrow, 1969.
*Star.* New York: Grove, 1970.
*The Book of Joanna.* Berkeley: Sand Dollar, 1973.

*Solstice Blossom.* Berkeley: Arif Press, 1973.
*Fleas 189-195.* New York: Aloe Editions, 1974.
*On Organism.* Canton, NY: Institute of Further Studies, 1974.
*Rare Angel (writ with raven's blood).* Los Angeles: Black Sparrow, 1974.
*September Blackberries.* New York: New Directions, 1974.
*A Fist Full (1956-1957).* Los Angeles: Black Sparrow, 1974.
*Jaguar Skies.* New York: New Directions, 1975.
*Man of Moderation.* New York: F. Hallman, 1975.
*Antechamber & Other Poems.* New York: New Directions, 1978.


## OTHER

*Meat Science Essays.* San Francisco: City Lights, 1963; enlarged ed., 1966.
*The Beard* (play). San Francisco: Privately printed, 1965; Coyote, 1967; New York: Grove, 1967.
*The Blossom; or, Billy the Kid* (play). Milwaukee: Great Lakes Books, 1967.
*Freewheelin' Frank, Secretary of the Angels, as Told to Michael McClure*, with Frank Reynolds. New York: Grove, 1967.
*The Shell* (play). London: Cape Goliard, 1968.
*The Cherub* (play). Los Angeles: Black Sparrow, 1970.
*The Mad Cub* (novel). New York: Bantam, 1970.
*The Adept* (novel). New York: Delacorte, 1971.
*Gargoyle Cartoons* (plays). New York: Delacorte, 1971.
*The Mammals* (plays). San Francisco: Cranium Press, 1972.
*Gorf* (play). New York: New Directions, 1976.
*The Grabbing of the Fairy* (play). St. Paul, MN: Truck Press, 1978.
*Josephine: The Mouse Singer* (play). New York: New Directions, 1980.


## RECORDING

*Ghost Tantras.* Munich: S Press, 1977.


## SECONDARY

*Margins*, no. 18 (1975). McClure symposium.


## BIBLIOGRAPHIES

Marshall Clements, *A Catalogue of Works by Michael McClure, 1956-1965.* New York: Phoenix Book Shop, 1965.
David Kherdian, *Six Poets of the San Francisco Renaissance: Portraits and Checklists.* Fresno, CA: Giligia Press, 1967.

DAVID MELTZER: "Born 1937, Rochester, New York. Lived in Brooklyn until I was 13. Moved to Long Island for an eventful year of family chaos. At 14 left for the West & stayed in L.A. for 6 formative years in which I met Wallace Berman & Robert Alexander, who were instrumental in turning me on to the fantastic possibilities of art & the self. Moved to San Francisco in 1957 and married in 1958. Spent many months reading at The Cellar with jazz. I no longer believe in the poet as a public target. I have decided to work my way thru poetry & find my voice & the stance I must take in order to continue my journey. Poetry is NOT my life. It is an essential PART of my life." (1959)

"To see through and towards. No difference. The moment to moment domestic event is also politics is also mystery. This desk, the garden, growing children, grey hairs, actual or imagined muses and demons, phonecalls in the middle of visions, Tina and I laughing and/or crying with new or old records— a natural and obvious progression. All the while letters leap off the tree.

*The Eyes, The Blood* was written in 1972 while we were living in Bolinas, California. It started out as a polemic but quickly moved beyond that intent to claim its own domain. My initial protest was directed against the Jewish law forbidding mixed marriages and yet, paradoxically, sanctioning the issue from a Jewish woman and non-Jewish male. In the process of writing the anger passed and I submitted, instead, to the sad beauty of my family's history." (1979)


*POETRY*

*Poems.* with Donald Schenker. San Francisco: Privately printed, 1957.
*Ragas.* San Francisco: Discovery Books, 1959.
*The Clown.* Larkspur, CA: Wallace Berman, 1960.
*The Process.* Berkeley: Oyez, 1965.
*The Dark Continent.* Berkeley: Oyez, 1967.
*Round the Poem Box: Rustic & Domestic Home Movies for Stan & Jane Brakhage.*
        Los Angeles: Black Sparrow, 1969.
*Yesod.* London: Trigram Press, 1969.
*From Eden Book.* San Francisco: Maya, 1969.
*Greenspeech.* Santa Barbara: Christopher Books, 1970.
*Luna.* Los Angeles: Black Sparrow, 1970.
*Knots.* Bolinas, CA: Tree Books, 1971.
*Bark: A Polemic.* Santa Barbara: Capra Press, 1973.
*Hero/Lil.* Los Angeles: Black Sparrow, 1973.
*Tens: Selected Poems 1961-1971.* New York: McGraw-Hill/Herder & Herder, 1973.
*The Eyes, the Blood.* San Francisco: Mudra, 1973.
*French Broom.* Berkeley: Oyez, 1973.
*Blue Rags.* Berkeley; Oyez, 1974.
*Harps.* Berkeley: Oyez, 1975.
*Six.* Santa Barbara: Black Sparrow, 1976.
*Two-Way Mirror.* Berkeley: Oyez, 1977.


*OTHER*

*We All Have Something to Say to Each Other* (essay). San Francisco: Auerhahn,
        1962.
*Journal of the Birth* (prose). Berkeley: Oyez, 1967.

*The Agency Trilogy: The Agency; The Agent; How Many Blocks in the Pile?*
(novels). North Hollywood, CA: Essex House, 1968.
*Orf* (novel). North Hollywood, CA: Essex House, 1969.
*The Martyr* (novel). North Hollywood, CA: Essex House, 1969.
*Isla Vista Notes: Fragmentary Apocalyptic Didactic Contradictions* (prose). Santa
Barbara: Christopher Books, 1970.
*The Brain-Plant Tetralogy: Lovely; Healer; Out; Glue Factory* (novels). North
Hollywood, CA: Essex House, 1970.
*Star.* North Hollywood, CA: Brandon House, 1970.
*The San Francisco Poets* (editor). New York: Ballantine Books, 1971. Revised as
*Golden Gate: Interviews with Five San Francisco Poets,* Berkeley: Wingbow
Press, 1975.
*Birth* (editor). New York: Ballantine Books, 1973.
*The Secret Garden: An Anthology in the Kabbalah* (editor). New York: Seabury
Press, 1976.
*Birth: An Anthology of Ancient Texts, Songs, Prayers and Stories* (editor). San
Francisco: North Point, 1981.

RECORDING

*Poet Song.* Vanguard, VSD 6519. 1969.

BIBLIOGRAPHIES

David Kherdian, *David Meltzer: A Sketch from Memory and Descriptive Checklist.*
Berkeley: Oyez, 1965.
David Kherdian, *Six Poets of the San Francisco Renaissance: Portraits and
Checklists.* Fresno, CA: Giligia Press, 1967.

FRANK O'HARA was born on June 27, 1926 in Baltimore, Maryland, and grew up
in Grafton, Massachusetts. Throughout his youth he studied music, first with private
teachers and then in 1941-44 as a special student at the New England Conservatory
of Music. In 1944, at the age of 17, he enlisted in the Navy and served for two years
as a sonarman third class on the destroyer USS *Nicholas,* sailing in the Pacific and to
Japan. Upon his return from the Navy, he attended Harvard College, where he
majored in music, then later English. While at Harvard, he roomed with Edward
Gorey and met John Ashbery and Violet (Bunny) Lang. Also at Harvard, he pub-
lished his first poems, in the *Harvard Advocate* (whose editorial board then included
Ashbery, Robert Bly, Kenneth Koch, Howard Moss, and Daniel Ellsberg). During
the summers he worked in a textile mill. He received his B.A. in 1950 and spent that
summer as a stage apprentice at the Brattle Theatre in Cambridge. In the autumn,
following the advice of his teacher John Ciardi, he went to the University of Michigan
at Ann Arbor, where he received an M.A. the following year and was awarded a major
Hopwood Award for Poetry. Meanwhile, his verse-plays *Try! Try!* (first version) and
*Change Your Bedding!* were produced by the Poets Theatre of Cambridge, along with
John Ashbery's masque *Everyman,* for which O'Hara had provided the music. In the
autumn of 1951, O'Hara moved to New York City, where he renewed his acquaint-

ance with the poets and painters he had known previously and where he met many others. He worked briefly as a private secretary for Cecil Beaton and began his long association with the Museum of Modern Art, working first at its front desk. Except for the period when he was an Editorial Associate for *Art News* (1953-55) and a leave of absence to accept a one-semester fellowship at the Poets Theatre in Cambridge, MA (in 1956), he worked for the museum for the rest of his life. At this time the museum was introducing Abstract Expressionism to a worldwide audience, and as part of his responsibilities, O'Hara selected important exhibitions of works by Robert Motherwell, Jackson Pollock, Franz Kline, David Smith, and Reuben Nakian, among others. At the time of his death, he had become an Associate Curator of Painting and Sculpture and had begun work on a major exhibition of paintings by Jackson Pollock, with exhibitions of Willem de Kooning and Barnett Newman planned to follow.

The late 1950s and early 1960s were a period of remarkable activity for O'Hara. He published several books of poems and monographs on Nakian, Motherwell, New Spanish Painting and Sculpture, and Pollock. At that time there was much interest in collaboration between poets and painters, and O'Hara created works with Larry Rivers *(Stones*, 1958-61), Norman Bluhm *(Poem-Paintings*, 1960), Franz Kline (1960), Jasper Johns (1963), Michael Goldberg (1963), Joe Brainard (1964), and Mario Schifano (1964). His plays *Loves Labor, The General Returns from One Place to Another*, and *Try! Try!* (II) were produced in New York and elsewhere; and he worked on or appeared in movies by Rudy Burckhardt (1953, 1964), John LaTouche (1953), Daisy Aldan (1955), Jonas Mekas (filmed 1959), Alfred Leslie (1963-66), and Charles Henri Ford (1965).

On July 24, 1966, at the age of 40, he was struck by a beach-buggy on Fire Island. He died the following evening. Although he had become an important presence in the art world by that time, it was not until his works were collected and published in the 1970s that the full extent of his accomplishment became known. On his tombstone is carved this quotation from his poem "In Memory of My Feelings": "Grace to be born and live as variously as possible."

## POETRY

*A City Winter and Other Poems.* New York: Tibor de Nagy, 1952.
*Oranges.* New York: Tibor de Nagy, 1953; New York: Angel Hair Books, 1969.
*Meditations in an Emergency.* New York: Grove, 1957; new ed., 1967.
*Second Avenue.* New York: Totem/Corinth, 1960.
*Odes.* New York: Tiber Press, 1960; Poet's Press, 1968.
*Lunch Poems.* San Francisco: City Lights, 1964.
*Love Poems (Tentative Title).* New York: Tibor de Nagy, 1965.
*In Memory of My Feelings: A Selection of Poems*, ed. Bill Berkson. New York: Museum of Modern Art, 1967.
*Two Pieces.* London: Long Hair Books, 1969.
*The Collected Poems of Frank O'Hara*, ed. Donald Allen. New York: Knopf, 1971.
*The Selected Poems of Frank O'Hara*, ed. Donald Allen. New York: Knopf, 1974.
*Hymns of St. Bridget*, with Bill Berkson. New York: Adventures in Poetry, 1974.
*Early Writing* (includes prose), ed. Donald Allen. Bolinas, CA: Grey Fox, 1977.
*Poems Retrieved*, ed. Donald Allen. Bolinas, CA: Grey Fox, 1977.

OTHER

*Jackson Pollock.* New York: Braziller, 1959.
*New Spanish Painting and Sculpture.* New York: Museum of Modern Art, 1960.
*Robert Motherwell.* New York: Museum of Modern Art, 1965.
*Nakian.* New York: Museum of Modern Art, 1966.
*Belgrade, November 19, 1963* (letter). New York: Adventures in Poetry, 1973.
*Art Chronicles 1954-1966.* New York: Braziller, 1975.
*Standing Still and Walking in New York*, ed. Donald Allen. Bolinas, CA: Grey Fox, 1975.
*Selected Plays.* New York: Full Court, 1978.


SECONDARY

*Audit/Poetry*, IV:1 (1964). O'Hara issue.
*Homage to Frank O'Hara*, ed. Bill Berkson and Joe LeSueur. Issued as *Big Sky*, no. 11-12 (1978); rev. ed., Berkeley: Creative Arts, 1980.
Alan Feldman. *Frank O'Hara.* Boston: Twayne, 1979.
*Panjandrum*, no. 2 & 3 (1973). O'Hara supplement.
Marjorie Perloff, *Frank O'Hara: Poet Among Painters.* New York: George Braziller, 1977; Austin: University of Texas Press, 1979.


BIBLIOGRAPHY

Alexander Smith, Jr., *Frank O'Hara: A Comprehensive Bibliography.* New York and London: Garland, 1979; rev. ed., 1980.


CHARLES OLSON was born in the central Massachusetts industrial city of Worcester on December 27, 1910, only son of an Irish mother and Swedish postman father. He was raised in Worcester, on the top floor of a "triple-decker" three-story wooden tenement on a dead-end street, though spending summers with his parents in Gloucester. He received an excellent education in the public schools, graduating from Classical High in 1928. Described as "a model student," he was class president and valedictorian, as well as regional champion orator, and won a tour of Europe as a prize. He chose Wesleyan over Harvard on the advice of his high-school debating coach, and was Phi Beta Kappa, editorial writer for the college newspaper, goalie on the soccer team, successful actor and orator. He continued at Wesleyan for an M.A., tracking down Melville's library as part of his research, and taking one of his courses at Yale. Each summer he returned to Gloucester, delivering mail like his father to help defray college expenses and acting in the local summer theater. The Depression reduced teaching opportunities, so he took a position at Clark University in his home town until deciding to continue advanced studies at Harvard, in a newly begun American studies program. He completed all course work for the Ph.D., but left without taking the degree after receiving a Guggenheim fellowship in 1938 for a study of Melville (the 400-page draft was abandoned but emerged after World War II in remarkably different form as *Call Me Ishmael*). During the war he served as assistant chief of the Foreign Language Division of the Office of War Information, drawing upon early experiences with his father's Swedish-American fraternal organizations and the Gloucester fishing community. After resigning from the OWI in protest against bureaucratic meddling and inefficiency, he served the Democratic Party as advisor and strategist, for which he was informally offered high governmental posts, but withdrew abruptly from partisan politics to become solely a writer.

He did not publish his first poem until age 35; he had twice turned his back on different careers of promise—that of a traditional scholar-academic and that of national politics (in both cases on the verge of success)—valuing more his independence. An early friendship with Edward Dahlberg and encounters with Ezra Pound proved decisive to his development, but not more so than his friendships with Robert Creeley and Robert Duncan. In 1948 he took a position teaching at Black Mountain College vacated by Edward Dahlberg, returning to teach regularly and to serve as rector of the school until its closing in 1956. Thereafter he returned to Gloucester and preoccupation with the *Maximus* series. At 6'7" he was an impressive physical presence, himself a "Maximus." He remained by choice in relative isolation and poverty, laboring at his work, until driven by the need to support his wife and son to accept a teaching post at the State University of New York at Buffalo—a most effective teacher there, as he had been at Black Mountain. He taught again, very briefly, at the University of Connecticut, until overtaken by cancer. He died on January 10, 1970, two weeks past his fifty-ninth birthday. Writing autobiographically, he described himself not so much as a poet or writer, but as "an archeologist of morning," and the phrase has stayed.

## POETRY

*Y & X.* Washington, DC: Black Sun, 1948.
*In Cold Hell, In Thicket.* Palma de Mallorca: Divers Press, 1953; San Francisco: Four Seasons, 1967.
*The Maximus Poems / 1-10.* Stuttgart: Jonathan Williams, 1953.
*The Maximus Poems / 11-22.* Stuttgart: Jonathan Williams, 1956.
*O'Ryan 2 4 6 8 10.* San Francisco: White Rabbit Press, 1958; expanded as *O'Ryan 12345678910*, 1965.
*Projective Verse.* New York: Totem Press, 1959.
*The Maximus Poems.* New York: Jargon/Corinth, 1960; London: Cape Goliard, 1970.
*The Distances.* New York: Grove, 1960.
*Maximus, From Dogtown—I.* San Francisco: Auerhahn, 1961.
*'West.'* London: Cape Goliard, 1966.
*Maximus Poems IV, V, VI.* London: Cape Goliard; New York: Grossman, 1968.
*Archaeologist of Morning.* London: Cape Goliard, 1970; New York: Grossman, 1973.
*The Maximus Poems, Volume Three*, eds. Charles Boer and George F. Butterick. New York: Grossman, 1975.
*Spearmint & Rosemary.* Berkeley: Turtle Island, 1975.
*The Horses of the Sea.* Santa Barbara: Black Sparrow, 1976.
*Some Early Poems.* Iowa City, IA: Windhover Press, 1978.

OTHER

*Call Me Ishmael* (prose). New York: Reynal & Hitchcock, 1947; New York: Grove, 1958; San Francisco: City Lights, 1967.
*Mayan Letters*, ed. Robert Creeley. Palma de Mallorca: Divers Press, 1953; London: Cape, New York: Grossman, 1968.
*A Bibliography on America for Ed Dorn.* San Francisco: Four Seasons, 1964.
*Human Universe and Other Essays*, ed. Donald Allen. San Francisco: Auerhahn, 1965; New York: Grove, 1967.
*Proprioception.* San Francisco: Four Seasons, 1965.
*Selected Writings*, ed. Robert Creeley. New York: New Directions, 1966.
*Pleistocene Man: Letters from Charles Olson to John Clarke during October, 1965.* Buffalo: Institute of Further Studies, 1968.
*Letters for Origin, 1950-1956*, ed. Albert Glover. London: Cape Goliard; New York: Grossman, 1970.
*The Special View of History*, ed. Ann Charters. Berkeley: Oyez, 1970.
*Additional Prose: A Bibliography on America, Proprioception, & Other Notes & Essays*, ed. George F. Butterick. Bolinas, CA: Four Seasons, 1974.
*The Post Office: A Memoir of His Father.* Bolinas, CA: Grey Fox, 1975.
*In Adullam's Lair.* Provincetown, MA: To the Lighthouse Press, 1975.
*Charles Olson & Ezra Pound: An Encounter at St. Elizabeths*, ed. Catherine Seelye. New York: Grossman, 1975.
*The Fiery Hunt and other plays.* Bolinas, CA: Four Seasons, 1977.
*Muthologos: The Collected Lectures and Interviews*, ed. George F. Butterick. Bolinas, CA: Four Seasons, 1978-79.
*Charles Olson & Robert Creeley: The Complete Correspondence*, ed. George F. Butterick. Vols. 1-  Santa Barbara: Black Sparrow, 1980- .

RECORDING

*Charles Olson Reads from Maximus IV, V, VI.* Folkways FL 9738. 1975.

SECONDARY

*OLSON: The Journal of the Charles Olson Archives*, no. 1-10 (1974-78).
Charles Boer, *Charles Olson in Connecticut.* Chicago: Swallow Press, 1975.
George F. Butterick, *A Guide to the Maximus Poems of Charles Olson.* Berkeley: California, 1978; rev. ed., 1980.
Don Byrd, *Charles Olson's* Maximus. Urbana: Illinois, 1980.
Ann Charters, *Olson/Melville: A Study in Affinity.* Berkeley: Oyez, 1968.
Paul Christensen, *Charles Olson: Call Him Ishmael.* Austin: Texas, 1978.
Robert von Hallberg, *Charles Olson: The Scholar's Art.* Cambridge, MA: Harvard, 1978.
Sherman Paul, *Olson's Push: Origin, Black Mountain, and Recent American Poetry.* Baton Rouge: Louisiana State, 1978.
Lynn Swigart. *Olson's Gloucester.* Baton Rouge: Louisiana State, 1980.
*Boundary 2*, 2: 1 & 2 (Fall 1973/Winter 1974). Olson issue.
*Maps*, no. 4 (1971). Olson issue.

*BIBLIOGRAPHY*

George F. Butterick and Albert Glover, *A Bibliography of Works by Charles Olson.*
New York: Phoenix Book Shop, 1967.

JOEL OPPENHEIMER: "i was born in yonkers, new york, in 1930, and educated in public schools there. abortive attempts at a career via engineering at cornell university, and liberal arts at the university of chicago, plus a stint trying to be an artist-type via the art students league in new york city. eventually ended up at black mountain college, studying with m.c. richards, paul goodman, and charles olson. three years there (no degree), then a year as peripatetic printer, finally settling in new york city. worked as typographic production man from 1953 to 1966, when i got into the teaching scam, followed by the journalism scam in 1969. i write a semiregular column for the *village voice*, covering sports, politics, kitsch, sex, etc, as well as occasionally reviewing restaurants, in what i see as an olsonian use of writing. was the first director (1966-68) of the poetry project at st. mark's church, and directed teachers and writers collaborative the next year; began teaching at city college as a writer in residence the following year. have been married twice (rena mary margaret julia ann furlong, 1952-60, nicholas patrick and daniel eben; helen joan bukberg, 1966-76, nathaniel ezra and lemuel shandy davin) and am raising my two youngest children by myself.

i see william carlos williams as my poetic grandfather, take occasional verse as 'the highest form of poetry,' believe a poem is an answer to a question you didn't know you'd asked yourself, and tend to write a discursive juxtapositional and highly personal body of work."

*POETRY*

*The Dancer.* Black Mountain, NC: Jonathan Williams, 1951.
*Four Poems to Spring.* Black Mountain, NC: Privately printed, 1951.
*The Dutiful Son.* Highlands, NC: Jonathan Williams, 1956.
*The Love Bit, and Other Poems.* New York: Totem/Corinth, 1962.
*In Time: Poems 1962-1968.* Indianapolis: Bobbs-Merrill, 1969.
*On Occasion: Some Births, Deaths, Weddings, Birthdays, Holidays, and Other Events.* Indianapolis: Bobbs-Merrill, 1973.
*The Woman Poems.* Indianapolis: Bobbs-Merrill, 1975.
*Acts.* Driftless, WI: Perishable Press, 1976.
*names, dates, & places.* Laurinburg, NC: Saint Andrews Press, 1978.
*Houses.* Buffalo, NY: White Pine, 1981.
*The Progression Begins.* New York: # Magazine, 1981.

OTHER

*The Great American Desert* (play). New York: Grove, 1966.
*The Wrong Season* (prose). Indianapolis: Bobbs-Merrill, 1973.
*Pan's Eyes* (stories). Amherst, MA: Mulch Press, 1974.
*Marilyn Lives!* New York: Delilah Books, 1981.

BIBLIOGRAPHY

George F. Butterick, *Joel Oppenheimer: A Checklist of His Writings.* Storrs, CT:
University of Connecticut Library, 1975.

JEROME ROTHENBERG: "Born 1931 in New York City, of Eastern European
Jewish parents whose discovery of America came only a decade before, I carry
that with me too—a little trouble-in-mind as well as for others with similar histories—
& it gives me a sense of multiple cultural worlds & of incongruities at the very
heart of thought. My process has been like what Samuel Makidemewabe (per
Howard Norman) said of the Cree Indian Trickster: 'to walk forward while looking
backward.' With past & future up for grabs, the possibility opened up—by the late
1950s—to make a near-total change in poetry, perception, language, etc., tied up
with earlier 20th-century 'revolutions of the word.' By mid-1960s it had become
'our own' & continues so today: a shared adventure with a generation, a century,
& with those in multiple times & places who have worked on those fundamentally
human acts of poesis—discoveries & witnessings—that define us as a species. My
own contributions (nomenclature & praxis) have included 'deep image,' ethno-
poetics, 'total translation,' poetics of performance, & assorted attempts 'to rein-
terpret the poetic past from the point of view of the present.' Residences: N.Y.C.
until 1972; thereafter on the Allegany Seneca Reservation (upstate New York) &
points west, having landed north of San Diego at the present writing. Clan affilia-
tion: Beaver. Current big project: a synthesizing anthology (assemblage) of the
20th-century avant-garde."

POETRY

*White Sun, Black Sun.* New York: Hawk's Well, 1960.
*The Seven Hells of the Jigoku Zoshi.* New York: Trobar Books, 1962.
*Sightings.* New York: Hawk's Well, 1964.
*The Gorky Poems.* Mexico City: El Corno Emplumado, 1966.
*Between: Poems 1960-63.* London: Fulcrum Press, 1967.
*Conversations.* Los Angeles: Black Sparrow, 1968.
*Poems, 1964-1967.* Los Angeles: Black Sparrow, 1968.
*Sightings I-IX, & Red Easy a Color.* London: Circle Press, 1968.
*Poems for the Game of Silence, 1960-1970.* New York: Dial, 1971; New Directions,
1975.
*A Book of Testimony.* Bolinas, CA: Tree Books, 1971.
*Esther K. Comes to America, 1931.* Greensboro, NC: Unicorn Press, 1974.

*The Cards.* Los Angeles: Black Sparrow, 1974.
*The Pirke & the Pearl.* San Francisco: Tree Books, 1974.
*Poland/1931.* New York: New Directions, 1974.
*The Notebooks.* Milwaukee: Membrane Press, 1976.
*A Seneca Journal.* New York: New Directions, 1978.
*Vienna Blood & Other Poems.* New York: New Directions, 1980.

## OTHER

*New Young German Poets* (ed. and trans.). San Francisco: City Lights, 1959.
*Ritual: A Book of Primitive Rites and Events* (editor). New York: Something Else, 1966.
*Technicians of the Sacred: A Range of Poetries from Africa, America, Asia, & Oceania* (editor). New York: Doubleday, 1968.
*Shaking the Pumpkin: Traditional Poetry of the Indian North Americas* (editor). New York: Doubleday, 1972.
*America a Prophecy: A New Reading of American Poetry from Pre-Columbian Times to the Present* (editor, with George Quasha). New York: Random, 1973.
*Revolution of the Word: A New Gathering of American Avant Garde Poetry, 1914-1945.* New York: Seabury, 1974.
*A Big Jewish Book: Poems & Other Visions of the Jews from Tribal Times to Present* (editor, with Harris Lenowitz and Charles Doria). New York: Anchor Press, 1978.
*Pre-Faces & Other Writings.* New York: New Directions, 1981.

## RECORDINGS

*Horse Songs & Other Soundings.* Munich: S Press, 1975.
*Jerome Rothenberg Reading from Poland/1931.* Milwaukee: New Fire/Membrane, 1979.

## SECONDARY

*Vort*, no. 7 (May 1975). Rothenberg issue.

ED SANDERS: "Born on the edge of the prairie in 1939. High school in Missouri, then to New York City in 1958, where spent the greater part of the next sixteen years. Met future wife, Miriam, in Greek class at New York University in the fall of 1958. Graduated with a B.A. in Greek, 1964.

Posters on walls, the Chessman case, the Fourth Avenue bookstores of the late 50s/early 60s, finding *Howl* by accident in a Missouri bookstore, *Yugen* and *Kulchur* magazines, finding an article about I. F. Stone in the gutter outside N.Y.U., beat poetry readings at the Living Theater and Gaslight Cafe in 1958-59, researching the Ezra Pound case, hearing Pete Seeger sing 'We Shall Overcome' on a peace walk in 1961, afternoons at Orientalia Bookstore, combined to add to the clutch of poetry brought to New York.

In 1961-62 participated in several lengthy peace walks through America. In the summer of '61 attempted, with others, to swim out in New London (CT) Harbor to board a Polaris atomic missile submarine in order to urge the crew to quit. A jail term resulted in which his first book, *Poem from Jail*, was written. Began formal study of Egyptian during the Polaris Action jail term, continuing in the fall of 1961 at the New School in New York.

From 1962-65 editor and publisher of *Fuck You/A Magazine of the Arts*. 1964 opened the Peace Eye Bookstore on the Lower East Side. Early 1965 formed a musical ensemble called The Fugs, whose practice sessions at the store became S.R.O. Fugs lived till early 1969, touring America and Europe, producing 6 albums. In 1970, solo album 'Sanders' Truckstop' was released. In 1970-71 researched the so-called Manson Family for a book published in 1971.

The 1970s thereupon became a decade of interwoven projects. In 1973 researched and wrote *Egyptian Hieroglyphics* as final assignment from Charles Olson. 1974-75 put together a ten-volume complete collected poetry. 1975 completed the first of a three-volume work, *Tales of Beatnik Glory*. 1974 began multi-volume poem on the life of Senator Robert Kennedy; during the next several years worked on a personal poetics to handle the poem, the result being *Investigative Poetry*, published by City Lights. 1974-79 wrote a novel, *Fame and Love in New York*; and in 1978 invented an electronic musical instrument, the Bardic Pulse-Lyre, with which to deliver his current poetry. In 1979 completed a two-hour musical/dramatic time-track, 'The Karen Silkwood Cantata,' tracing the life of the union martyr. Currently living in Woodstock, N.Y., working on improving the Bardic Pulse Lyre, on *Tales of Beatnik Glory* vols II and III, and on the Kennedy poem."

## POETRY

*Poem from Jail*, San Francisco: City Lights, 1963.
*King Lord / Queen Freak.* Cleveland: Renegade Press, 1964.
*The Toe Queen Poems.* New York: Fuck You Press, 1964.
*Peace Eye.* Buffalo: Frontier Press, 1965; enlarged ed., Cleveland, 1967.
*Fuck God in the Ass.* New York: Fuck You Press, 1967.
*Egyptian Hieroglyphs.* Canton, NY: Institute of Further Studies, 1973.
*20,000 A.D.* Plainfield, VT: North Atlantic Books, 1976.

## OTHER

*The Fugs' Song Book!* New York: Peace Eye Bookstore, 1965; Detroit: Artists' Workshop Press, 1966.
*Shards of God* (novel). New York: Grove, 1970.
*The Family: The Story of Charles Manson's Dune Buggy Attack Battalion.* New York: Dutton, 1971; Avon, 1972.
*Vote!*, with Abbie Hoffman and Jerry Rubin. New York: Warner Paperback Library, 1972.
*Tales of Beatnik Glory.* New York: Stonehill, 1975.
*Investigative Poetry* (prose). San Francisco: City Lights, 1976.

*Fame & Love in New York.* Berkeley: Turtle Island, 1980.
*The Party* (editor). Woodstock, NY: Poetry, Crime & Culture Press, 1980.
*The Z-D Generation.* Barrytown, NY: Station Hill, 1981.


JAMES SCHUYLER was born on November 9, 1923 in Chicago, and grew up in
Washington, D.C. and in Buffalo and East Aurora, N.Y. He attended Bethany
College in West Virginia—"an attractive group of buildings on a small, steep hill,"
he has described it—and served in the U.S. Navy during World War II. From 1947
to 1949 he lived in Italy, where he knew W. H. Auden well. In 1950 he returned
to New York City where he has lived for the most part until the present.
   In addition to his novels and books of poems, he has had several plays pro-
duced Off and Off-Off Broadway, including *Presenting Jane* (1953), *Shopping and
Waiting* (1953), *A Picnic Cantata* (with music by Paul Bowles, 1955), and *Unpack-
ing the Black Trunk* (written with Kenward Elmslie, 1965). He has also written
distinguished art criticism, principally for *Art News*, where he was an editorial
associate (1956-62). He has assembled art shows for the Museum of Modern Art
and has received grants from the Longview Foundation, Poets Foundation, National
Council on the Arts, and National Endowment for the Arts. He was awarded the
Pulitzer Prize for Poetry in 1980.


*POETRY*

*Salute.* New York: Tiber Press, 1960.
*May 24th or So.* New York: Tibor de Nagy, 1966.
*Freely Espousing.* New York: Doubleday, 1969.
*The Crystal Lithium.* New York: Random, 1972.
*A Sun Cab.* New York: Adventures in Poetry, 1972.
*Hymn to Life.* New York: Random, 1974.
*The Fireproof Floors of Witley Court.* Newark, VT: Janus Press, 1976.
*Song.* Syracuse, NY: Kermani Press, 1976.
*The Home Book: Prose and Poems, 1951-1970*, ed. Trevor Winkfield. Calais, VT:
   Z Press, 1977.
*The Morning of the Poem.* New York: Farrar, Straus, 1980.


*OTHER*

*Shopping and Waiting* (play). New York: American Theatre for Poets, 1953.
*A Picnic Cantata* (text by Schuyler, music by Paul Bowles). Columbia, ML 5068.
   1955.
*Alfred & Guinevere* (novel). New York: Harcourt, Brace, 1958.
*A Nest of Ninnies* (novel), with John Ashbery. New York: Dutton, 1969; Calais, VT:
   Z Press, 1975.
*What's for Dinner?* (novel). Santa Barbara: Black Sparrow, 1978.

GARY SNYDER was born in 1930 in San Francisco. "Grew up in Washington, Oregon, and California. He studied several years in Japan and traveled in India and throughout the Pacific. He now lives in rural northern California with his family. His work as a poet is closely tied to his studies of nature and human nature. He has been a Buddhist for many years."

## POETRY

*Riprap.* Ashland, MA: Origin Press, 1959.
*Myths & Texts.* New York: Totem/Corinth, 1960; New Directions, 1978.
*Riprap & Cold Mountain Poems.* San Francisco: Four Seasons, 1965.
*Six Sections from Mountains and Rivers Without End.* San Francisco: Four
    Seasons, 1965; expanded ed., 1970; London: Fulcrum Press, 1968.
*A Range of Poems.* London: Fulcrum Press, 1966.
*The Back Country.* London: Fulcrum Press, 1967; New York: New Directions,
    1968.
*The Blue Sky.* New York: Phoenix Book Shop, 1969.
*Regarding Wave.* New York: New Directions, 1970; London: Fulcrum Press, 1972.
*Manzanita.* Bolinas, CA: Four Seasons, 1972.
*The Fudo Trilogy.* Berkeley: Shaman Drum, 1973.
*Turtle Island.* New York: New Directions, 1974.

## OTHER

*Earth House Hold: Technical Notes & Queries to Fellow Dharma Revolutionaries.*
    New York: New Directions, 1969; London: Cape, 1970.
*The Old Ways: Six Essays.* San Francisco: City Lights, 1977.
*On Bread & Poetry*, with Lew Welch and Philip Whalen. Bolinas, CA: Grey Fox,
    1977.
*He Who Hunted Birds in His Father's Village: The Dimensions of a Haida Myth.*
    Bolinas, CA: Grey Fox, 1979.
*The Real Work: Interviews & Tales 1964-1979.* New York: New Directions, 1980.

## RECORDING

*There Is No Other Life: Selected Poems.* Munich: S Press, 1975.

## BIBLIOGRAPHIES

David Kherdian, *Six Poets of the San Francisco Renaissance: Portraits and*
    *Checklists.* Fresno, CA: Giligia Press, 1967.
David Norton, "Gary Snyder: A Checklist," *Schist*, no. 2 (Summer 1974), 58-66.

JACK SPICER was born on January 30, 1925 in Pasadena Hospital and grew up in Los Angeles, graduating from Fairfax High School in 1943. After two years at the University of Redlands, he traveled north and enrolled in the University of California at Berkeley in 1945, taking a B.A. and M.A. During these five years he was active in the "Berkeley Renaissance" with Robin Blaser and Robert Duncan. He was an instructor at the University of Minnesota for a year, and then returned to Berkeley in 1951. In the late summer of 1955 he traveled to New York City, and then in the fall to Boston where he worked in the Boston Public Library and came to know John Wieners and other young East Coast poets.

By 1957 he was back in San Francisco. In the spring he conducted a Magic Workshop for the S.F. State College Poetry Center, during the summer he wrote the poems of *After Lorca,* and in the fall edited a little magazine titled *J* and assisted Joe Dunn in planning the White Rabbit Press series of poets. By this time he had found himself as a poet, and as he became dedicated to what he conceived of as the "serial poem" he wrote his verse with specific books in mind. His mostly underground reputation as a West Coast Socratic teacher of poets spread among young writers from coast to coast. At his table in Gino & Carlo's bar (on Green Street in S.F.'s North Beach) he nightly held forth on his theories of poetry, castigating his young coterie and concocting ingenious embarrassments for his peers. By day he worked part-time on the Linguistic Atlas at the University of California and later at Stanford University.

He gave several lectures on poetry at the University of British Columbia 1965 Winter Festival, and participated in the July Berkeley Poetry Conference. A few weeks later he collapsed and on August 17 died from cirrhosis of the liver.

*POETRY*

*After Lorca.* San Francisco: White Rabbit, 1957; London: Aloes Books, 196-?; Toronto: Coach House, 1974.
*Homage to Creeley.* Annapolis, CA: Privately printed, 1959.
*Billy the Kid.* Stinson Beach, CA: Enkidu Surrogate, 1959.
*The Heads of the Town up to the Aether.* San Francisco: Auerhahn, 1962.
*Lament for the Makers.* San Francisco: White Rabbit, 1962; London: Aloes Books, 1971.
*The Holy Grail.* San Francisco: White Rabbit, 1964.
*Language.* San Francisco: White Rabbit, 1965.
*Book of Magazine Verse.* San Francisco: White Rabbit, 1966.
*A Book of Music.* San Francisco: White Rabbit, 1969.
*The Red Wheelbarrow.* Berkeley: Arif Press, 1971.
*The Ballad of the Dead Woodcutter.* Berkeley: Arif Press, 1972.
*Some Things from Jack.* Verona, Italy: Plain Wrapper Press, 1972.
*15 False Propositions About God.* South San Francisco, CA: ManRoot Books, 1974.
*Admonitions.* New York: Adventures in Poetry, 1974.
*An Ode and Arcadia,* with Robert Duncan. Berkeley: Ark Press, 1974.
*A Lost Poem.* Verona, Italy: Plain Wrapper Press, 1975.
*The Collected Books of Jack Spicer,* ed. Robin Blaser. Los Angeles: Black Sparrow, 1975.
*There Is an Inner Nervousness in Virgins.* Eureka, CA: Spotted Pig, 1975.
*One Night Stand & Other Poems,* ed. Donald Allen. San Francisco: Grey Fox, 1980.

OTHER

*Letters to Graham Mackintosh 1954.* Berkeley: privately printed, 1977.

SECONDARY

*Georgia Straight / Vancouver Free Press Writing Supplement*, no. 2 (Jan. 28-Feb. 4, 1970). Spicer issue.
*Caterpillar*, no. 12 (July 1970). Blaser-Spicer issue.
*Manroot*, no. 10 (Fall-Winter 1974-75). Spicer issue.
*Boundary 2*, 6: 1 (Fall 1977). Spicer issue.

BIBLIOGRAPHIES

Sanford Dorbin, "A Checklist of the Published Writings of Jack Spicer," *California Librarian*, 31: 4 (Oct. 1970), 251-61; "Spicer Bibliography: An Interim Report," *Schist*, no. 4-5 (1976-78), 180-87.

ANNE WALDMAN was born on April 2, 1945, and grew up on Macdougal Street in Greenwich Village. In 1964 she traveled to Greece, Egypt, Rome and Paris; and in 1965 attended the Berkeley Poetry Conference. She graduated from Bennington in 1966, and with Lewis Warsh founded *Angel Hair* magazine and books. Director of St. Mark's Poetry Center 1968-78; and edited *The World* magazine and several anthologies of contemporary American poetry. She writes: "Always loved hearing poetry out loud and had big vision about all the poets being shamans and making America well through poetry. Travels to South America led to composition of *Fast Speaking Woman* (started in my head on airplane—also indebted in part to Mazatec Indian Shaman Maria (Sabina), which was more or less completed in 1974 but expanded later and evolved through oral readings & still can be improvised upon. Spiritual leanings towards Tibet took me on pilgrimage with Michael Brownstein & John Giorno to India in 1973 to meet wise lamas who suggested a 'practice.' Founded the Jack Kerouac School of Disembodied Poetics at Tibetan Buddhist inspired Naropa Institute in the summer of 1974 with roommate Allen Ginsberg and have since then been both resident of rocky mountain spine teaching Gertrude Stein, Sappho, Emily Dickinson, as well as Lower East Side poetry community citizen when not traveling. Returned to India & Nepal with poet Reed Bye 1978. Have read & chanted poems in Berlin, Venice, Rome, Amsterdam, Rotterdam, Cambridge, Essex, London and many universities/poetry centers in USA. Inspired to write by sounds & love of words, also what comes into view as well as 'making' poems through cut-ups & other experiments. *Journals and Dreams* (1976) was breakthrough in terms of exploring decidedly female landscape. Kenneth Koch had told me early on he liked my 'vibrato like an opera singer's,' Allen Ginsberg said 'write long.' "

POETRY

*On the Wing.* New York: Boke Press, 1968.
*O My Life!* New York: Angel Hair Books, 1969.
*Baby Breakdown.* New York: Bobbs-Merrill, 1970.
*Giant Night.* New York: Corinth, 1970.
*No Hassles.* New York: Kulchur Foundation, 1971.
*Memorial Day*, with Ted Berrigan. New York: Poetry Project, 1971; London: Aloes
    Books, 1974.
*West Indies Poems.* New York: Adventures in Poetry, 1972.
*Spin Off.* Bolinas, CA: Big Sky, 1972.
*Self Portrait*, with Joe Brainard. New York: Siamese Banana, 1973.
*Life Notes.* Indianapolis: Bobbs-Merrill, 1973.
*Fast Speaking Woman & Other Chants.* San Francisco: City Lights, 1975;
    2nd enlarged ed. 1978.
*Sun the Blond Out.* Berkeley: Arif, 1975.
*Journals & Dreams.* New York: Stonehill, 1976.
*Shaman.* Waban, MA: Munich Editions from Shell, 1977.
*Countries.* West Branch, IA: Toothpaste Press, 1980.


OTHER

*The World Anthology: Poems from the St. Mark's Poetry Project* (editor).
    Indianapolis: Bobbs-Merrill, 1969.
*Another World: A Second Anthology of Works from the St. Mark's Poetry Project*
    (editor). Indianapolis: Bobbs-Merrill, 1971.
*Talking Poetics from Naropa Institute* (ed., with Marilyn Webb). Boulder & London:
    Shambala, 1978.


RECORDING

*Non Stop.* Munich: S Press, 1977.


SECONDARY

*Strange Faeces*, no. 5 (1971). Waldman issue.


LEW WELCH was born on 16 August 1926 in Phoenix, Arizona. He grew up in
California and attended high school in Palo Alto, where he was a track star. After
a year in the Air Force (1945), he attended Stockton Junior College for two years
and then transferred to Reed College in Portland, graduating in 1950. His B.A.
thesis was a study of the writing of Gertrude Stein, which William Carlos Williams
admired when he visited the college in the fall of that year and met Welch and his
classmates, poets Gary Snyder and Philip Whalen.

In the fall of 1951 he enrolled in the University of Chicago graduate school, but a nervous breakdown interrupted his studies; after psychoanalysis he became an ad copy writer with Montgomery Ward & Co. In late 1957 he moved to San Francisco, where he supported himself by driving taxicabs as he began to take an active part in the poetry scene.

Auerhahn published his long poem *Wobbly Rock* in 1960. He worked in salmon fishing, chiefly with Bill Yardas, in 1962 and 1963, until another breakdown sent him for refuge to the Trinity Alps country of northern California, where he batched in a shake cabin for more than a year and wrote his *Hermit Poems* and "The Way Back" series. He returned to San Francisco in late 1963 and lived there and in nearby Marin County, giving poetry readings in the Bay Area and along the coast from Vancouver, B.C. to San Diego and as far east as Utah and Colorado. In 1965 he participated in the University of California at Berkeley Poetry Conference, and his two books, *Hermit Poems* and *On Out* were published; *Courses* followed in 1968 and *The Song Mount Tamalpais Sings* in 1969. For some years he worked as a longshoreman checker on the docks of San Francisco, and conducted a poetry workshop for the University of California Extension.

In the spring of 1971 he moved to the Sierra foothills where he planned to build a cabin near Gary Snyder's home, but another depression overtook him and on May 23 he took his revolver and walked away into the forest, leaving a farewell note.

## POETRY

*Wobbly Rock.* San Francisco: Auerhahn, 1960.
*Hermit Poems.* San Francisco: Four Seasons, 1965.
*On Out.* Berkeley: Oyez, 1965.
*Courses.* San Francisco: Dave Haselwood, 1968; new ed., San Francisco: Cranium Press, 1968.
*The Song Mt. Tamalpais Sings.* San Francisco: Maya, 1969; expanded ed., Berkeley: Sand Dollar, 1970.
*Redwood Haiku & Other Poems.* San Francisco: Cranium Press, 1972.
*Ring of Bone: Collected Poems 1950-1971*, ed. Donald Allen. Bolinas, CA: Grey Fox, 1973.
*Trip Trap: Haiku Along the Road*, with Jack Kerouac and Albert Saijo. Bolinas, CA: Grey Fox, 1973.
*Selected Poems*, ed. Donald Allen. Bolinas, CA: Grey Fox, 1976.

## OTHER

*How I Work as a Poet & Other Essays, Plays, Stories*, ed. Donald Allen. Bolinas: CA: Grey Fox, 1973.
*I, Leo: An Unfinished Novel*, ed. Donald Allen. Bolinas, CA: Grey Fox, 1977.
*On Bread & Poetry*, with Gary Snyder and Philip Whalen. Bolinas, CA: Grey Fox, 1977.
*I Remain: The Letters of Lew Welch with the Correspondence of His Friends*, ed. Donald Allen. Bolinas, CA: Grey Fox, 1980.

SECONDARY

Aram Saroyan, *Genesis Angels: The Saga of Lew Welch & the Beat Generation.*
New York: Morrow, 1979.

PHILIP WHALEN: "I was born in Portland, Oregon, on 20 October 1923. 1927-41,
public school and high school in The Dalles, Oregon. 1941-42, residence in Portland;
various semiskilled jobs. 1943-46, U.S. Army Air Corps, Radio Operator & Mechan-
ics instructor. B.A. in Literature & Language, Reed College, 1951—first book of
poems, 'The Calendar,' written to fulfill thesis requirement. 1951-53, odd jobs &
starvations in San Francisco and Los Angeles. 1953-55, summers working as lookout
for the U.S. Forest Service. 1955, began giving poetry readings in San Francisco &
Berkeley, beginning at the Six Gallery and the San Francisco State College Poetry
Center in North Beach. 1957-58, Bailiff of the Circuit Court of Oregon for Lincoln
County. 1960, *Like I Say* and *Memoirs of an Interglacial Age* published. Reading
tour of New York & New England, 1959 and 1960. Contributed to *The New
American Poetry, 1945-1960* and to many other anthologies. Wrote more books
of poetry & two novels. Residence in Japan, 1966-67, 1969-71, teaching English
conversation. 1972, began residence at Zen Center, San Francisco; later the same
year, my first training period at Tassajara Zen Mountain Center. Ordained as Zen
priest, 1973; *shuso* (acting head monk) at Tassajara, 1975. My chief job for the
Zen Center has been that of an instructor in the Zen Center Studies Center.

'Sometimes I live in the country;
Sometimes I live in town, &c &c'

I've written very little poetry since 1974; I spend too much time reading and talking
with people and lecturing and probably not enough time doing the kind of listening
and watching & feeling that is the source of poetry. Naturally I think I should be
writing lots more and it makes me very sad to observe that I'm not writing anything—
a nonsensical place to be. But I am doing other work that I believe to be necessary.
I don't complain about the fact that I'm not watering the garden while I'm washing
my teeth, do I. The problem is figuring out how to hang up the toothbrush & get
out the door."

POETRY

*Self-Portrait, from Another Direction.* San Francisco: Auerhahn, 1959.
*Like I Say.* New York: Totem/Corinth, 1960.
*Memoirs of an Interglacial Age.* San Francisco: Auerhahn, 1960.
*Every Day.* Eugene, OR: Coyote, 1965.
*Highgrade: Doodles, Poems.* San Francisco: Coyote, 1966.
*T/O.* San Francisco: Dave Haselwood, 1967.
*On Bear's Head.* New York: Harcourt Brace, 1969.
*Severance Pay: Poems 1967-1969.* San Francisco: Four Seasons, 1970.
*Scenes of Life at the Capital.* Bolinas, CA: Grey Fox, 1971.
*The Kindness of Strangers: Poems, 1969-74.* Bolinas, CA: Four Seasons, 1976.

*Decompressions: Selected Poems.* Bolinas, CA: Grey Fox, 1977.
*Enough Said: Poems 1974-79.* San Francisco: Grey Fox, 1980.

OTHER

*You Didn't Even Try* (novel). San Francisco: Coyote, 1967.
*The Invention of the Letter: A Beastly Morality.* New York: Carp & Whitefish, 1967.
*Imaginary Speeches for a Brazen Head* (novel). Los Angeles: Black Sparrow, 1972.
*On Bread & Poetry*, with Gary Snyder and Lew Welch. Bolinas, CA: Grey Fox, 1977.
*Off the Wall: Interviews*, ed. Donald Allen. Bolinas, CA: Four Seasons, 1978.
*The Diamond Noodle.* Berkeley: Poltroon Press, 1980.

SECONDARY

*Intransit*, no. 5 (1967). Whalen issue.

BIBLIOGRAPHY

David Kherdian, *Six Poets of the San Francisco Renaissance: Portraits and Checklists.* Fresno, CA: Giligia Press, 1967.

JOHN WIENERS: "Born on January 6, 1934. I graduated from Boston College in June of 1954, and attended Black Mountain for the spring of 1955 and the summer of 1956. In between I worked in the Lamont Library at Harvard, until the day that *Measure* No. 1 arrived in Boston, and then they fired me. I first met Charles Olson on the night of Hurricane Hazel, September 11, 1954, when I 'accidentally' heard him read his verse at the Charles St. Meeting House. They passed out complimentary copies of the *Black Mountain Review* No. 1, and I aint been able to forget."

Another issue of *Measure* was edited in San Francisco at the height of the "Renaissance," and a third upon returning to Boston. After some years in New York City in the early sixties, Wieners attended the State University of New York at Buffalo, where he again studied with Charles Olson, receiving an M.A. degree in 1967. He was invited to participate in the Festival of the Two Worlds at Spoleto, Italy, in the summer of 1965, as well as the famous Berkeley Poetry Conference a few weeks later. He returned to Massachusetts from Buffalo, and after living for a while in Hanover, moved to Boston where he now lives, below Beacon Hill behind the state capitol building on a street named Joy.

POETRY

*The Hotel Wentley Poems.* San Francisco: Auerhahn, 1958; rev. ed., San Francisco: Dave Haselwood, 1965.
*Ace of Pentacles.* New York: James F. Carr & Robert A. Wilson, 1964.
*Chinoiserie.* San Francisco: Dave Haselwood, 1965.
*Pressed Wafer.* Buffalo: Gallery Upstairs, 1967.
*Asylum Poems.* New York: Angel Hair Books, 1969.
*Nerves.* London: Cape Goliard Press; New York: Grossman, 1970.
*Selected Poems.* London: Jonathan Cape; New York: Grossman, 1972.
*Playboy.* Boston: Good Gay Poets, 1972.
*Hotels.* New York: Angel Hair Books, 1974.
*Behind the State Capitol; or, Cincinnati Pike.* Boston: Good Gay Poets, 1975.

OTHER

*The Lanterns Along the Wall* (lecture). Cambridge, MA: Private printed, 1972.
*Woman.* Canton, NY: Institute of Further Studies, 1972.

RECORDING

*The Poetry of John Wieners.* McGraw-Hill Sound Seminars, 78152. 1970.

BIBLIOGRAPHY

George F. Butterick, "John Wieners: A Checklist," *Athanor*, no. 3 (Summer-Fall 1973), 53-63.

JONATHAN WILLIAMS: Three-Minute Autobiography. "Basil Bunting, who looks back over 80 years and a lifetime of making poems, and who believes that the facts are of no interest except, occasionally, to himself, has written a fine autobiography in five words: 'Minor poet, not conspicuously dishonest.' There is a mountain man's epitaph that runs:

> *he done*
> *what he could*
>
> *when he got round*
> *to it*

I am still learning how to condense, cranking out a host of gnomic oddments & inklings to appease the savage appetite of some fifty distinguished readers who find neither me nor the 500 sonatas of Domenico Scarlatti boring. The principal books of poems are *An Ear in Bartram's Tree* (1969), *Mahler* (1969), *Blues & Roots/Rue & Bluets* (1971), *The Loco Logodaedalist in Situ* (1972), and *Elite/Elate Poems* (1979).

They are all out of print except the last one. The next collection is finished and has the heaviest title of all: 'Glees . . . Swarthy Monotonies . . . Rince Cochon . . . & Chozzerai for Simon . . .' Who would buy such a thing in Franchise Land? It will be given to those fifty cosmic readers.

The gist is: born in Asheville, North Carolina in 1929. Educated at St. Albans School, Washington, D.C.; uneducated at Princeton. Studies with Karl Knaths in painting and with Stanley William Hayter in graphic arts. At Black Mountain College (1951-1956), I had the counsel of such men as Charles Olson, Aaron Siskind, Robert Duncan, and Lou Harrison. Having read in public some 950 times, and having published some 100 titles in the Jargon Society series, I've traveled almost constantly for 30 years and have known more people in the arts than anyone could deserve or could stand. The antidote was to take to my feet along rivers and mountains in the United States and in Europe, to listen to people with ground-sense and a knowledge of the local names of things. I now live with Tom Meyer, poet, in a remote valley of the Cumbrian Dales called Dentdale. I come back to North Carolina for at least one season of the year to try to encourage students, see friends, pay my respects to Mt. LeConte, galax leaves and the pileated woodpecker—and to find out if my cathexes are still working."

## POETRY

*Garbage Litters the Iron Face of the Sun's Child.* San Francisco: Jargon, 1951.
*Red/Gray.* Black Mountain, NC: Jargon, 1952.
*Four Stoppages.* Stuttgart: Jargon, 1953.
*The Empire Finals at Verona.* Highlands, NC: Jargon, 1959.
*Amen Huzza Selah.* Highlands, NC: Jargon, 1960.
*Elegies and Celebrations.* Highlands, NC: Jargon, 1962.
*In England's Green &.* San Francisco: Auerhahn, 1962.
*Paean to Dvorak, Deemer & McClure.* San Francisco: Dave Haselwood, 1966.
*Affilati Attrezzi per i Giardini di Catullo.* Milan: Lerici Editore, 1966.
*The Lucidities.* London: Turret Books, 1967.
*An Ear in Bartram's Tree: Selected Poems 1957-1967.* Chapel Hill: North
　　　Carolina, 1969; New York: New Directions, 1972.
*Mahler.* London: Cape Goliard; New York: Grossman, 1969.
*Blues & Roots/Rue & Bluets.* New York: Grossman, 1971.
*The Loco Logodaedalist in Situ: Selected Poems, 1968-70.* London: Cape Goliard;
　　　New York: Grossman, 1972.
*Untinears & Antennae for Maurice Ravel.* St. Paul, MN: Truck Press, 1977.
*Elite/Elate Poems: Selected Poems 1971-75.* Highlands, NC: Jargon, 1979.
*Shankum Naggum.* Rocky Mount, NC: North Carolina Wesleyan College, 1979.
*Homage, Umbrage, Quibble + Chicane.* Roswell, NM: DBA Editions, 1981.

## OTHER

*Lines About Hills Above Lakes* (prose). Fort Lauderdale, FL: Roman Books, 1964.
*Descant on Rawthey's Madrigal: Conversations with Basil Bunting.* Lexington,
　　　KY: Gnomon Press, 1968.
*Hot What?*, with Fielding Dawson and Lyle Bonge. Dublin, GA: Mole Press, 1975.

*I Shall Save One Land Unvisited: Eleven Southern Photographers* (editor). Frankfort, KY: Gnomon Press, 1978.
*Portrait Photographs.* Frankfort, KY: Gnomon Press, 1979.

*SECONDARY*

Guy Davenport, *Jonathan Williams, Poet.* Cleveland: Asphodel Book Shop, 1969.
*Vort*, no. 4 (Fall 1973). Williams issue.
*A 50th Birthday Celebration for Jonathan Williams,* ed. Jonathan Green. Frankfort, KY: Truck/Gnomon, 1979.

# GENERAL

Allen, Donald, and Creeley, Robert, eds. *The New Writing in the U.S.A.* Harmondsworth: Penguin, 1967.
\_\_\_\_\_, and Tallman, Warren, eds. *Poetics of the New American Poetry.* New York: Grove, 1973.
Altieri, Charles. *Enlarging the Temple: New Directions in American Poetry During the 1960s.* Lewisburg, Pa.: Bucknell University Press; London: Associated University Presses, 1979.
Bergé, Carol. *The Vancouver Report.* New York: Fuck You Press, 1964.
Berke, Roberta. *Bounds Out of Bounds: A Compass for Recent American and British Poetry.* New York: Oxford, 1981.
Carroll, Paul. *The Poem in Its Skin.* Chicago: Big Table, 1968.
\_\_\_\_\_, ed. *The Young American Poets.* Chicago: Follett, 1968.
Charters, Ann, ed. *Scenes Along the Road: Photographs of the Desolation Angels, 1944-1960.* New York: Portents/Gotham Book Mart, 1970.
Charters, Samuel. *Some Poems/Poets: Studies in American Underground Poetry Since 1945.* Berkeley: Oyez, 1971.
Clark, Tom. *The Great Naropa Poetry Wars.* Santa Barbara: Cadmus Editions, 1980.
*Contemporary Poets*, ed. James Vinson. 2d ed. London: St. James; New York: St. Martin's, 1975; 3d ed., 1980.
Cook, Bruce. *The Beat Generation.* New York: Scribner, 1971.
DeLoach, Allen, ed. *The East Side Scene: American Poetry, 1960-1965.* New York: Anchor Books, 1972.
Duberman, Martin. *Black Mountain: An Exploration in Community.* New York: Dutton, 1972.
Eshleman, Clayton, ed. *A Caterpillar Anthology.* New York: Anchor Books, 1971.
Faas, Ekbert, ed. *Towards a New American Poetics: Essays & Interviews.* Santa Barbara: Black Sparrow, 1978.
Feldman, Gene, and Max Gartenberg, eds. *The Beat Generation and the Angry Young Men.* New York: Citadel Press, 1958.
Greiner, Donald J., ed. *American Poets Since World War II.* Detroit: Gale, 1980.
Hassan, Ihab. *Contemporary American Literature, 1945-1972.* New York: Frederick Ungar, 1973.

Homberger, Eric. *The Art of the Real: Poetry in England and America Since 1939.* London and Toronto: Dent; Totowa, NJ: Rowman and Littlefield, 1977.

Howard, Richard. *Alone With America.* New York: Atheneum, 1969.

Krim, Seymour, ed. *The Beats.* Greenwich, CT: Fawcett, 1960.

Lally, Michael, ed. *None of the Above: New Poets of the U.S.A.* Trumansburg, NY: Crossing Press, 1976.

Lipton, Lawrence. *The Holy Barbarians.* New York: Julian Messner, 1959.

Malkoff, Karl. *Crowell's Handbook of Contemporary American Poetry.* New York: Crowell, 1973.

_____. *Escape from the Self: A Study in Contemporary American Poetry and Poetics.* New York: Columbia, 1977.

Mersmann, James F. *Out of the Vietnam Vortex: A Study of Poets and Poetry Against the War.* Lawrence, KS: Kansas, 1974.

Molesworth, Charles. *The Fierce Embrace: A Study of Contemporary American Poetry.* Columbia, MO: Missouri, 1979.

Myers, John Bernard, ed. *The Poets of the New York School.* Philadelphia: University of Pennsylvania School of Fine Arts, 1969.

Ossman, David. *The Sullen Art.* New York: Corinth, 1963.

Padgett, Ron, and Shapiro, David, eds. *An Anthology of New York Poets.* New York: Vintage, 1970.

Parkinson, Thomas F. *A Casebook on the Beat.* New York: Crowell, 1961.

Paul, Sherman. *The Lost America of Love: Rereading Robert Creeley, Edward Dorn, and Robert Duncan.* Baton Rouge: Louisiana State, 1981.

Perloff, Marjorie. *The Poetics of Indeterminacy: Rimbaud to Cage.* Princeton, NJ: Princeton, 1981.

Pinsky, Robert. *The Situation of Poetry: Contemporary Poetry and Its Traditions.* Princeton, NJ: Princeton, 1976.

*Poets of the Cities New York and San Francisco 1950-1965.* New York: Dutton, 1974.

Rexroth, Kenneth. *American Poetry in the Twentieth Century.* New York: Herder and Herder, 1971.

Rosenthal, M. L. *The Modern Poets: A Critical Introduction.* New York: Oxford, 1960.

_____. *The New Poets: American and British Poetry Since World War II.* New York: Oxford, 1967.

Stepanchev, Stephen. *American Poetry Since 1945.* New York: Harper, 1965.

Sutton, Walter. *American Free Verse: The Modern Revolution in Poetry.* New York: New Directions, 1973.

Thurley, Geoffrey. *The American Moment: American Poetry in the Mid-Century.* New York: St. Martin's, 1978.

Tytell, John. *Naked Angels: The Lives and Literature of the Beat Generation.* New York: McGraw-Hill, 1976.

Vendler, Helen. *Part of Nature, Part of Us: Modern American Poets.* Cambridge, MA: Harvard, 1980.

Wilentz, Elias, ed. *The Beat Scene.* New York: Corinth, 1960.